T0305409

Self-Employment as Precarious Work

Self-Employment as Precarious Work

A European Perspective

Edited by

Wieteke Conen

Assistant Professor, Amsterdam Institute for Advanced Labour Studies, University of Amsterdam, the Netherlands

Joop Schippers

Professor of Labour Economics, Universiteit Utrecht, Faculty of Law, Economics and Governance and Affiliated Researcher, Netherlands Interdisciplinary Demographic Institute, the Netherlands

 Edward Elgar
PUBLISHING

Cheltenham, UK • Northampton, MA, USA

Published by
Edward Elgar Publishing Limited
The Lypiatts
15 Lansdown Road
Cheltenham
Glos GL50 2JA
UK

Edward Elgar Publishing, Inc.
William Pratt House
9 Dewey Court
Northampton
Massachusetts 01060
USA

A catalogue record for this book
is available from the British Library

Library of Congress Control Number: 2019938736

This book is available electronically in the **Elgar**online
Social and Political Science subject collection
DOI 10.4337/9781788115032

ISBN 978 1 78811 502 5 (cased)
ISBN 978 1 78811 503 2 (eBook)

Typeset by Servis Filmsetting Ltd, Stockport, Cheshire

Printed and bound in Great Britain by TJ International Ltd, Padstow, Cornwall

Contents

List of contributors   vii
Preface   ix

1   Self-employment: between freedom and insecurity   1
    Wieteke Conen and Joop Schippers

PART I   DO WE HAVE TO WORRY ABOUT THE 'NEW
         SELF-EMPLOYED'? THEORY AND CONTEXT

2   Labour market flexibility, self-employment and precariousness   23
    Joop Schippers

3   Social protection for the self-employed: an EU legal
    perspective   40
    Hanneke Bennaars

4   Self-employment, pensions and the risk of poverty in old age   48
    Uwe Fachinger

PART II   SELF-EMPLOYMENT AND PRECARIOUS WORK
          IN EUROPE: EMPIRICAL RESULTS

5   Self-employment: independent 'enterprise', or precarious
    low-skilled work? The case of the UK   64
    Nigel Meager

6   Micro-entrepreneurship and changing contours of work:
    towards precarious work relations? Empirical findings
    from Austria   86
    *Dieter Bögenhold, Andrea Klinglmair, Zulaicha Parastuty and
    Florian Kandutsch*

7   Precariousness and social risks among solo self-employed in
    Germany and the Netherlands   108
    Wieteke Conen and Maarten Debets

8 Between precariousness and freedom: the ambivalent
   condition of independent professionals in Italy   132
   Paolo Borghi and Annalisa Murgia

9 Bogus self-employment in Sweden   153
   Dominique Anxo and Thomas Ericson

10 Precariousness among older self-employed workers in Europe   170
    Wieteke Conen

11 Migrant self-employment in Germany: on the risks,
    characteristics and determinants of precarious work   186
    Stefan Berwing, Andrew Isaak and René Leicht

PART III   IMPLICATIONS AND FUTURE RESEARCH
           AGENDA

12 The matter of representation: precarious self-employment and
    interest organizations   216
    Giedo Jansen and Roderick Sluiter

13 The 'new' self-employed and hybrid forms of employment:
    challenges for social policies in Europe   238
    Karin Schulze Buschoff

14 Between freedom and insecurity: future challenges   260
    Joop Schippers and Wieteke Conen

Index   271

Contributors

Dominique Anxo is a Professor of Labour Economics at Linnaeus University, Sweden.

Hanneke Bennaars is an Assistant Professor at the Social Law department of Leiden University, the Netherlands.

Stefan Berwing is a Researcher at the Institute for SME research, University of Mannheim, Germany.

Dieter Bögenhold is a Professor of Sociology at the Faculty of Economics and Management, University of Klagenfurt, Austria.

Paolo Borghi is a Postdoctoral Researcher at the Department of Social and Political Sciences, University of Milan, Italy.

Wieteke Conen is an Assistant Professor in the Amsterdam Institute for Advanced Labour Studies, University of Amsterdam, the Netherlands.

Maarten Debets is a PhD candidate at the research group Professional Performance and Compassionate Care, Amsterdam UMC, University of Amsterdam, the Netherlands.

Thomas Ericson is a Senior Lecturer and Researcher at Linnaeus University, Sweden.

Uwe Fachinger is a Professor of Economics and Demographic Change at the Institute of Gerontology, University of Vechta, Germany.

Andrew Isaak is Assistant Professor of Entrepreneurship at the SolBridge International School of Business, South Korea and affiliated with the Institute for SME Research, University of Mannheim, Germany.

Giedo Jansen is Assistant Professor at the Department of Public Administration at the University of Twente, the Netherlands.

Florian Kandutsch is a Researcher at the Department of Economics, University of Klagenfurt, Austria.

Andrea Klinglmair is a Project Manager at Diakonie de La Tour and Lecturer at the Department of Economics, University of Klagenfurt, Austria.

René Leicht is Head of the Research Area "Self-Employment" at the Institute for SME research, University of Mannheim, Germany.

Nigel Meager is a Principal Associate Fellow of the Institute for Employment Studies, United Kingdom.

Annalisa Murgia is Associate Professor at the Department of Social and Political Sciences, University of Milan, Italy.

Zulaicha Parastuty is a Researcher at Department of Innovation Management and Entrepreneurship, University of Klagenfurt, Austria.

Joop Schippers is a Professor of Labour Economics at Universiteit Utrecht, Faculty of Law, Economics and Governance and Affiliated Researcher, Netherlands Interdisciplinary Demographic Institute, the Netherlands.

Karin Schulze Buschoff is Head of the Research Unit 'Labour market policy' at the Institute of Economic and Social Research (WSI) and affiliated to the Free University Berlin, Germany.

Roderick Sluiter is a Postdoctoral Researcher at the Institute for Management Research at Radboud University, the Netherlands.

Preface

Since the 1970s, the long-term historical decline in self-employment as a proportion of total employment has slowed in most Western economies and in some countries even reversed. Traditionally, self-employment has been associated with independent entrepreneurship. Although there is still limited insight into the nature of new forms of self-employment, in recent times self-employment is increasingly interrelated with precarious forms of work. This book aims to provide evidence-based information to address current and future challenges related to the changing nature of self-employment and demonstrates where, when and why self-employment emerges as precarious work in Europe.

Being your own boss has not only been topical in private conversations and in the media, but the changing historical pattern also renewed interest in self-employment among economists and other social scientists. Since 2013, the editors of this book participated in a research project 'Self-employed without personnel: between freedom and insecurity', funded by the Hans-Böckler-Stiftung. The research was conducted by a research team from Utrecht University School of Economics (USE) in the Netherlands in collaboration with the Institute of Economic and Social Research (WSI) in Germany. The research project studied dynamics and consequences of making the transition into solo self-employment and examined attitudes and behaviour towards pensions and other social security provisions among self-employed.

In order to discuss the outcomes of the research project, an international meeting was organised at Utrecht University in 2016. Experts from various European countries presented their research and developments in self-employment were discussed intensely from different perspectives, providing us with new insights which we believe are valuable also to a broader group of scientists, students, policy makers and others interested in the subject. During this meeting, the idea was borne to bundle this knowledge in an edited volume; this book is the result of this endeavour.

In this preface we would like to thank all the authors of the single chapters in this book for their valuable contribution. We are also indebted to many other researchers who gave us helpful feedback and suggestions on various parts of the book and during presentations at seminars and conferences, a special mention deserves: Enrico Reuter, Silvia Rossetti, Sabina Stiller and Emanuela Carta. We also thank Utrecht University School of Economics (USE), which facilitated the research project and the Amsterdam Institute for Advanced Labour Studies for the stimulating work environment and freedom to work on the book. We are extremely grateful to the Hans-Böckler-Stiftung for its financial support. Finally, we wish to thank Emily Mew and Harry Fabian from Edward Elgar for providing continuous support and giving editorial guidance in preparing the manuscript for publication.

Wieteke Conen and Joop Schippers

1. Self-employment: between freedom and insecurity

Wieteke Conen and Joop Schippers

INTRODUCTION

At the turn of the nineteenth century, self-employment was much more common than today and could especially be found among farmers, tradesmen, craftspeople and freelance professionals. Throughout the twentieth century, self-employment continuously declined in most advanced economies while dependent work increased significantly; developments that went hand in hand with technical change favouring capital-intensive, large-scale production, the rise of the 'Fordist model' and a change in industrial organisation in most countries (OECD, 2000; Supiot, 2001). Self-employed workers were increasingly regarded as individuals who voluntarily sought to gain higher utility from income, autonomy, flexibility and other working conditions attributed to a job in self-employment. In case of low-ability, entrepreneurs would eventually drop out of self-employment (Rees and Shah, 1986; Hamilton, 2000; Hundley, 2001). Grounded in the entrepreneurship literature, self-employment was predominantly looked upon as a well-suited way of work for independent entrepreneurs and the self-employed were considered clear 'insiders' on the labour market.

Although the previous view towards self-employment has been dominant in various advanced economies for a long time, recent times seem to show a shifting trend and image. In contrast with the long-term historical decline in self-employment, the number and share of self-employed workers has been increasing in several European countries, and there has been a particular rise in own-account workers. Yet, the timing and occurrence of a 'renaissance' in self-employment differs considerably between countries (OECD, 2000; Broughton et al., 2016; Eurofound, 2017a; Eurofound, 2017b; Eurostat, 2018; Chapter 2 of this volume). Increases in self-employment have been attributed to a mixture of underlying mechanisms, including the growing importance of new business models and changes in the organisation of work, organisational decentralisation with increasing outsourcing activities by companies, changes in the institutional environment, and socio-cultural trends (Meager, 1992; Arum and Müller, 2004; Torrini, 2005; European Commission, 2010; Van Es and Van Vuuren, 2011; Kremer et al., 2017). A growing share of the 'new' self-employed are active in sectors like services and construction and largely tend to be own-account workers without personnel acting in occupations with low capital requirements. To date, there is only limited insight into the nature and returns of especially these new forms of self-employment. However, the group of new self-employed is increasingly associated with what has been called 'involuntary', 'dependent' and 'precarious' self-employment (Stone, 2006; Schulze Buschoff and Schmidt, 2009; Kautonen et al., 2010; Westerveld, 2012). Contrary to the view of the independent entrepreneur, this branch of literature emphasises the increasing heterogeneity among the self-employed and focuses on the group of rather vulnerable self-employed, regularly operating at the blurring boundaries between being an employee and employee-like self-employment.

This book aims to investigate the scale, nature and implications of self-employment as precarious work in Europe. We address several research questions that have received limited attention in the scientific literature to date and add to the existing knowledge in two marked ways. A first void in the literature concerns the limited insight into recent developments in the nature and quality of work among the self-employed in Europe. To what extent are the self-employed self-sufficient entrepreneurs and where and why have more precarious forms of self-employment emerged? Considering 'precariousness' to be more than only income from self-employment but also including social risk coverage, a second void this study aims to fill is where and how precarious self-employment relates to systems of social security and institutional surroundings.

Besides for scientific reasons, it is important to study self-employment as precarious work for societal reasons. Policy debates tend to be dominated by a strong emphasis on the promotion of entrepreneurship and SMEs and the encouragement of self-employment as a valid alternative for the unemployed, with little recognition of potential problems such as low and insecure incomes, poor social security and pension coverage, low levels of training/human capital development and deterioration in self-employed job quality. Presenting a wide variety of up-to-date information on the self-employed in a changing labour market, this book aims to support the policy debate and provide information for policy makers and other stake-holders who take an interest in or are involved in tackling the manifold challenges related to these changing working patterns. From a macro-level perspective, the combination of increasing shares of self-employed work-ers and their coverage in terms of social security provisions may have substantial consequences for the welfare of citizens as well as welfare state expenditures. Knowledge about self-employment as precarious work and insight into behaviour and attitudes towards social security helps to anticipate the requirements and feasibility of various policy measures in this field. Also at the meso-level, organisations (such as trade unions, specific organisations for the self-employed and actors in the financial sector) may benefit from this type of knowledge when developing and introducing relevant support.

This chapter initiates the conversation between theory, methods, evidence and consequences of self-employment as precarious work which is the focus of this book. It conceptualises precarious employment in the context of self-employment, examines developments in Europe and identifies avenues for fostering our understanding in this area of research.

PRECARIOUS WORK

Precarious employment is of all time, though varying in scale and taking expression in different ways in different periods and places. Employment through intermediaries, live-in domestic work and seasonal agriculture work bore a high risk of precarious employment in advanced economies already in the early twentieth century, prevailing in new and continuous ways to date (Vosko, 2006). Certain precarious forms of employment seem to persist, while others (largely) disappear and new forms disperse. Within the framework of this book, the question arises whether some forms of contemporary self-employment are to be considered a new expression of precarious employment.

After a century of massive changes in the organisation of work and legislative adaptations, nowadays a majority of workers in advanced economies earns a living through a standard employment relationship, which in the European context typically includes, for instance, protection against dangerous working conditions, exploitation, unfair treatment, unemployment and poverty in old age, insurance in case of sickness and disability, and parental leave. Non-standard or a-typical work is then any alternative employment relation, including day labour, on-call work, temporary help agency employment, independent contracting and other self-employment. Although non-standard work has been increasing in Europe in recent decades, still a minority of workers earn a living through alternative employment relations. Alternative employment relations may involve 'contingent work', referring to the notion that these relationships are on average less secure and more contingent on short-term changes in employer demand than is regular employment. An underlying concern with non-standard work arrangements thus are claims that these jobs are worse for workers than regular full-time jobs. However, whether the growth of non-standard employment is problematic depends ultimately on the quality of these non-standard jobs, which may largely vary within and between the various groups lumped together under the heading of 'non-standard employment' or 'contingent work' (Belous, 1989; Kalleberg et al., 2000; Cappelli and Keller, 2013). Whereas some alternative arrangements may in fact be quite regular and stable, some full-time regular jobs can be quite insecure. Within-group diversity is indeed substantial among the self-employed: for some the quality of work may be good and the continuity of work be quite secure, while for others self-employment is synonymous with insecure and low quality work (e.g. Eurofound, 2017a). In that light, it is increasingly acknowledged that the question needs to be directed away from the prevalence of non-standard work and towards the link between various arrangements and the actual and perceived quality of jobs (Vosko, 2006), which in essence implies a move away from the individual contracts approach towards the quality of work approach (Broughton et al., 2016).

Precarious work has been defined, conceptualised and examined in several ways. In recent work, Kalleberg (2018, p. 3) defines precarious work as "work that is *uncertain, unstable* and *insecure* and in which *employees bear the risks* of work (as opposed to businesses or the government) and *receive limited social benefits and statutory entitlements*". Several authors (e.g. Vosko, 2006; Porthé et al., 2010; Kalleberg, 2018) consider precarious employment a multidimensional construct composed of various dimensions and stress that analysing these dimensions – mostly related to the quality of work – is critical to establishing whether work is precarious. Rodgers (1989) was among the first to systematically examine the nature of precarious work by identifying several dimensions of precariousness: (1) income adequacy (or sufficient earnings for the worker and any dependants to maintain a decent standard of living); (2) welfare and legal protections (or protection through union representation or law); (3) degree of certainty of continuing employment; and (4) control over the labour process. Later typologies of precarious work sometimes solely rely on economic rewards such as earnings and fringe benefits, others also include aspects like autonomy and control over the labour process, degree of work uncertainty and employability factors (cf. D'Amours and Crespo, 2004; Kalleberg, 2011; Scott-Marshal and Tompa, 2011; Stone, 2006; Vosko, 2006; OECD, 2014; Eurofound, 2015; Broughton et al., 2016).

Whereas definitions and dimensions of precarious work in general are not tied to a specific form of employment, some seem more applicable to the situation of employees than of self-employed workers. For instance, in various countries statutory benefits and entitlements available to wage workers (in terms of, for instance, employment standards and insurance) are not or to a lesser extent available to the self-employed, and the self-employed often cannot form or join trade unions. On a related note the question arises what exactly 'precariousness' is in the context of self-employment. For instance, the self-employed almost by the very nature of their employment form have a relatively high degree of work uncertainty and naturally bear certain risks. This uncertainty in self-employment is considered 'part of the game' though, and may in addition have less of a detrimental effect if adequately anticipated by individuals and financial reserves are present to provide the self-employed with financial security in times of (temporary) absence of continuing work.

Analysing precarious work preferably includes various levels: job, person, household and community levels (Vosko, 2006). As a substantial share of individuals who have a job in self-employment are – probably more often than is the case with wage and salary workers in low income jobs – not or not completely dependent on this income, analysis at the household level may be of particular relevance when studying the self-employed. Think of someone who likes to make sculptures and decides to sell his/her products through a web store. This person may have a registered income that we would consider 'low' and this person could be labelled 'economically dependent'. However, if this person is not in it for the money and pieces together a living from other sources beyond this 'main job', it would be peculiar to call this person 'precariously self-employed'. This implicates that instead of trying to establish whether the self-employed have low incomes, are in low-paid jobs or whether they are economically (in)dependent, we may want to capture precariousness through other measurements and approaches than is common in research among wage workers. The measurement of dimensions of precarious work through statistical vehicles often is more complicated in the case of the self-employed than among wage workers (we will return to this issue in the next paragraph).

All in all, self-employment in relation to precarious work seldom has been at the centre of attention and research on precarious work typically assumes the situation of a wage worker. Building on before-mentioned and other earlier studies (including Schulze Buschoff and Schmidt, 2009; Choi, 2009; Conen et al., 2016; Conen, 2018; Kalleberg, 2018), we consider precarious work as an employment situation in which individuals or households are unable to fulfil fundamental physiological and security needs while working (within our framework: as self-employed). Throughout the book we emphasise three dimensions of precariousness which seem particularly relevant in the context of self-employment:

1. Income inadequacy while working (related to concepts such as in-work poverty, low-income households and financial resilience);
2. A lack of adequate social benefits and regulatory protection (related to concepts such as false or bogus self-employment and social security provisions);
3. Work with a high uncertainty of continuing work (related to concepts such as work insecurity, lack of employability and financial unrest).

We will further elaborate on these three dimensions, and the relation with various relevant concepts in this area, in the following section.

RESEARCH ON SELF-EMPLOYMENT AS PRECARIOUS WORK

Studies in the field of social policy and industrial relations tend to underline that self-employed, and own-account workers in particular, may be among the groups that are prone to bad jobs and in-work poverty (Kalleberg et al., 2000; Kalleberg, 2018). Unfortunately, the self-employed are left out of empirical analyses in a large majority of studies in this area (e.g. Parker, 2004; Crettaz, 2013). One of the main reasons probably is that particular problems arise with income from self-employment; income which is notoriously hard to measure and compare. As a result, to date little is known about how the group of self-employed is actually faring; this book aims to advance research in this area.

Income Adequacy

Despite individual and subjective differences, there are certain objective characteristics that most people would agree are necessary for a job to be considered 'a good job' (Kalleberg, 2011). "A basic requirement is that the job should pay a wage that is high enough to satisfy a person's basic needs. Another requirement is fringe benefits to also accommodate those needs" (Kalleberg, 2011, p. 9). Previous research that has examined the relationship between self-employment and payoff predominantly has used national labour force micro datasets or panel data, linking earnings profiles or job satisfaction to worker's characteristics. Other studies have been based on the spending patterns of the self-employed, which are typically easier to measure on a comparable basis with other groups. Research using these types of method shows that the self-employed tend to have lower (initial) average and median earnings than employees with the same observed characteristics, although their earnings also are more polarised (e.g. Hamilton,

2000; Lin et al., 2000; Åstebro and Chen, 2014; Conen et al., 2016; Sorgner et al., 2017). Research finds a consistently high level of job satisfaction and well-being among the self-employed (e.g. Blanchflower, 2000; Hundley, 2001; Taylor, 2004; Benz and Frey, 2008).

Previous research thus predominantly gives an idea about the relative earning profiles between self-employed and other groups in the labour market and some of its determinants. One of the main problems with earnings probably is that it relies on job-level income data for the self-employed, but there are various reasons why relying on this type of data may lead to an inaccurate picture. Difficulties stem, for instance, from the lack of clear distinction between the (incorporated) business income and the personal or household income and consumption; because the self-employed have incentives to define their income in a way that minimises taxation; because the self-employed are – probably more often than paid employees – not 'in it for the money'; and because the self-employed have large variation in their income flows (in year t they may earn a negative income, whereas in year t+x they earn high profits). Moreover, "because more and more individuals hold multiple jobs, and because people reproduce themselves in households, a focus on a main job does not capture fully the ways in which people piece together a living" (Vosko, 2006, p. 48). It thus seems important to take not only the job level, but also the individual and household level into account. Over time, several approaches have examined payoff from self-employment, taking into account additional sources of income (including in-work poverty, low-income households, material deprivation); all with their own merits and disadvantages.

Earnings at the job level do not capture whether one's job in self-employment is related to an overall precarious or self-sufficient household situation. In that light, the concept of in-work poverty has evolved rapidly and various approaches have been introduced; according to the Eurostat indicator individuals are considered to be at-risk of poverty when their annual equivalised household disposable income is below 60 per cent of the national median, and individuals are considered to be 'in-work' when they declare to have been 'employed' for more than half the income reference period of one year (Horemans and Marx, 2017). Studies find that self-employed, and own-account workers in particular, generally face significantly higher in-work poverty risks than contracted workers in Europe (Horemans and Marx, 2017; Eurofound, 2017c). The risk of in-work poverty among own-account workers went up from 23 per cent in 2007 to 25 per cent in 2014 (Eurofound, 2017c).

However, given that self-employment includes the opportunity of success as well as the risk of misfortune with your business and the potential large variation in income flows also between years, the question arises whether it is not only natural to see more polarised *annual* earnings and *annual* in-work poverty among these entrepreneurs. To take such considerations into account, the indicator of individuals in long-term low-income households may be relevant. Using this measure, a relatively high share of self-employed workers – as compared to employees – has been found to be in long-term low-income households (Statistics Netherlands, 2018).

Still, all of the previous measures take income data from self-employment as point of departure. Given the manifold difficulties arising from analysing income data for the self-employed, sometimes the concept of material deprivation is adopted as a complementary measurement (Parker, 2004; Nolan and Whelan, 2010; Crettaz, 2013; Horemans and Marx, 2017). Material deprivation refers to the inability for individuals or households to afford those consumption goods and activities that are typical in a society at a given point in time. Horemans and Marx (2017) find that the picture comparing poverty among employees and the self-employed changes drastically when this concept is taken as a starting point; in various countries employees and the self-employed do not significantly differ in their level of material deprivation. However, one problem with the concept of material deprivation is that little consensus exists as to which items should be included and why (Guio et al., 2016; Nolan and Whelan, 2010). Furthermore, in case of the self-employed, the concept is sometimes considered to underestimate poverty as business income may increase spending power and hence limits material deprivation (Eurofound, 2017c).

Yet another way of addressing income adequacy and poverty among self-employed workers while avoiding the use of income data is to ask for self-assessed evaluations of the financial situation. Information on the financial situation of the household was collected in the 2003, 2007, 2011 and 2016 European Quality of Life Survey (Eurofound, 2018). Figure 1.1 shows the percentages of respondents in the EU-28 who report facing 'difficulty' or 'great difficulty' in making ends meet with the household's total monthly income (as compared to 'some difficulty', 'fairly easily', 'easily' and 'very easily'). We used the recommended weight for analysis at the EU-28 level, which is available for second, third and fourth waves; that is, data for 2003 could not be included in a comparable way. We excluded individuals older than 60 years, because they may in some countries already receive particular pension benefits. The results show that 11 per cent of self-employed workers report facing 'difficulty' or 'great difficulty' in making ends meet with the household's total monthly income in the EU-28. This share has increased from 8 per cent in 2007 to 10 per cent in 2011 and 11 per cent in 2016.

European Member States largely differ in their self-employment developments and institutional conditions (e.g. Eurofound, 2017c). While

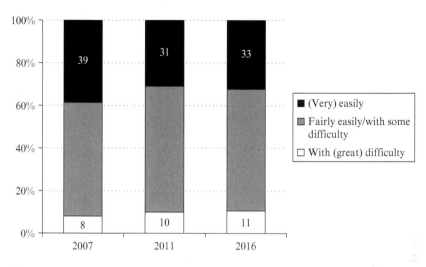

Figure 1.1   *Self-assessed financial situation of the household* among self-employed workers (aged 18 to 59 years) in the EU-28, 2007–2016, percentage*

income adequacy among self-employed workers may appear stable or only moderately changing at the aggregated European level, substantial contrastive developments may be taking place at the country level. Unfortunately, internationally-comparable data on changes in income adequacy seems scarce and sample sizes of self-employed at the country level seem particularly small. Nevertheless, Table 1.1 aims to provide some information on changes at the country level, that is, changes in the percentages of respondents who report facing 'difficulty' or 'great difficulty' in making ends meet with the household's total monthly income. Countries are clustered by welfare state type (Esping-Andersen, 1990). We used the recommended weights for analysis at the country level, which are available for all four waves.

The results indeed show considerable between-country variation. In Germany and some Eastern European Member States the share of self-employed with inadequate incomes at the household level seems to have

Table 1.1   Change in self-assessed financial situation of the household*
at the country level, percentage 'with great difficulty' and 'with
difficulty', period 2003–2007 compared to period 2011–2016**

	Decline	No significant change	Increase
Nordic		DK, FI, SE	
Continental	DE	AT	BE, NL, FR
Anglo-Saxon		IE	UK
Southern		IT, PT	GR, ES
Eastern	BU, PO	HU, RO	

Notes:
*   Survey question: "A household may have different sources of income and more than one household member may contribute to it. Thinking of your household's total monthly income: is your household able to make ends meet. . .?"
** Given the limited number of observations per country per wave of self-employed, we pooled together data for two subsequent waves.

Source: European Quality of Life Survey, 2003, 2007, 2011 and 2016 [own calculations].

been decreasing between the early 2000s and 2010s. However, in other countries – in particular the UK, several Continental and Southern European countries – the share of self-employed reporting facing difficulties seems to have increased over time. The question whether these increasing shares of self-employed with inadequate household incomes would be the consequence of a deteriorating position of existing self-employed or is due to a changing composition of the self-employment population (for instance due to an influx of individuals who otherwise would become unemployed or inactive, perhaps as a consequence of the financial crisis) cannot be answered using these data.

Future research may want to combine objective and subjective measures on income adequacy among the self-employed and examine the practicability and applicability of composite measures. For instance, Conen et al. (2016) suggest the concept of 'financial resilience', which is operationalised as a composite measure of self-reported annual household income (seven-point scale), financial means to bridge a period without work (six-point scale) and evaluation of the financial situation of the household (five-point-scale).

Social Benefits and Regulatory Protection

Self-employed workers have to deal with various social risks, including the risk of poverty in old age, the risk of disability and the risk of unemployment. From the angle adopted in the entrepreneurship literature it is often claimed that *self*-employed are (and are supposed to be) predominantly self-supporting, while from the point of view of adequacy of social protection it is often emphasised that they – or at least a part of them – should rather be considered self-*employed*, with a stronger focus on the dependent status (Westerveld, 2012). Lacking social security is another important dimension of precariousness, and may include, for instance, the absence of life and disability insurance, pensions and health and dental coverage. In Europe, there is a large divide between self-employed who do and do not participate in, for instance, disability insurance as well as pension savings (Schulze Buschoff, 2007; Schulze Buschoff and Schmidt, 2009; Choi, 2009; Conen et al., 2016; Spasova et al., 2017).

Welfare states as they have grown in Europe during the second half of the twentieth century typically took citizens in their role of employees as the focus of law and regulation. Employment status tends to determine the applicability of labour legislation as well as access to and coverage of insurance against social risks within the framework of statutory insurance systems. Self-employed workers in Europe have typically been excluded from access to certain insurance-based social protection schemes, although some categories of self-employed workers have received disparate treatment in some countries. Here you can think of certain historical categories of the self-employed – such as farmers and the liberal professions – who sometimes benefited from specific social protection schemes. Those in other types of self-employment, and especially new forms of self-employment, have in many countries had little or no access to public social protection (Conen et al., 2016; Spasova et al., 2017). Spasova et al. (2017) studied both statutory and effective access to social protection for self-employed in Europe; Figure 1.2 shows there is a great variety in access to insurance-based schemes.

One type of risk that is prominently addressed in relation to self-employment, also in the media, is the risk of poverty in old age. Earlier research on self-employed workers in relation to pension build-up concerns research in the area of *who* of the self-employed save for their retirement (in terms of socio-economic background), *how* they save (for instance, through retirement accounts, life insurances or annuity-like products) and how the coverage, contributions and benefits of solo self-employed, often in comparison with employees, *differ between countries* (e.g. Schulze Buschoff, 2007; Choi, 2009; Schulze Buschoff and Schmidt, 2009; Mastrogiacomo and Alessie, 2015). These studies typically make use of legal statutes and descriptive measures on pension savings. In addition, several studies seeking to explain pension savings and retirement planning *control* for self-employment status (e.g. Bottazzi et al., 2006; Almenberg and Säve-Söderbergh, 2011; Lusardi and Mitchell, 2011).

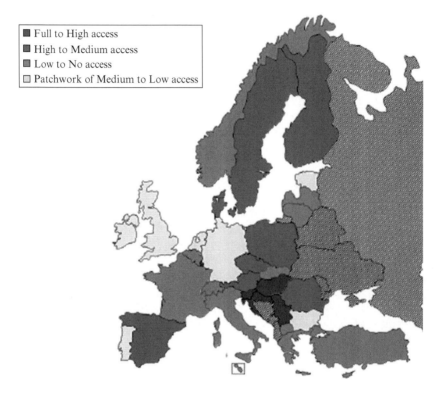

Source: Spasova et al., 2017, p. 47.

Figure 1.2   Statutory access to insurance-based schemes for self-employed in Europe, 2017

As with income data, little is known though about *how much* self-employed workers save and whether this is sufficient to live comfortably in old age. In that light it is often mentioned that 'unconventional ways' of retirement savings play an important, yet under-researched, role in the retirement build-up and planning of the self-employed (Mastrogiacomo and Alessie 2015). 'Unconventional' in this context refers to the fact that certain types of pension savings of the self-employed do not go via traditional second or third pillar schemes and therefore are more difficult to link to their pension destination. Examples of such savings include (but are not limited to): saving for retirement on a savings account, the anticipated selling of a store or other real estate, the anticipated selling of professional equipment, or saving accounts that are financially managed conjointly (for instance in family businesses). Hershey et al. (2017) find that the *involuntary* solo self-employed are less likely to save for retirement than their voluntary self-employed counterparts, and they envisioned a less optimistic future pension scenario for themselves.

From a legal perspective, the notion of false (or bogus) self-employment is often brought forward in relation to precarious work. False self-employment refers to the situation when workers register as self-employed but de facto qualify as employees, carrying out work under authority or subordination; for instance because employers 'convince' their (former) employees to make the transition into self-employment and return in their services as own-account workers. This form of self-employment is not seldom a way to circumvent, for instance, employment legislation, income tax contributions and/or employers' social security contributions. False self-employment not only has negative effects for the position of relatively vulnerable workers, it is also considered to contribute to the crumbling of the welfare state, as employers underplay their tax and contribution liabilities. Recent research lines in the area of law include, for instance, the potential role of EU competition law in regulating the 'new' self-employed (Daskalova, 2018) and social security outside the realm of the employment contract, that is, social security for the self-employed but also, for instance, platform workers and workers in the informal economy (Westerveld and Olivier, 2019).

Uncertainty of Continuing Work

Uncertainty may take form in various ways (e.g. employment insecurity, (lack of) employability, financial unrest) and may have consequences not only in terms of income, but also for individual well-being and family relations. Many of the current discussions on precarious work have a strong focus on the insecurity aspect (Kalleberg, 2018), but insecurity and attitudes towards risk have a different connotation in the context of the self-employed than in the context of wage workers. Various forms of insecurity seem more accepted among the self-employed, as they consider this to be the 'price' of being self-employed. Measurements of this dimension also typically assume the situation of wage workers and are seldom useful for providing information with respect to the self-employed. What exactly is being measured when self-employed workers are asked if they may lose their job in the next six months? Or whether their job is secure? A useful distinction may be between *job* insecurity and *employment* insecurity. Whether job insecurity is perhaps not particularly applicable to the self-employed (that is, the degree to which a person is likely to lose the current job), employment insecurity and the uncertainty of continuing work (i.e. how easy or hard it will be to find new, generally comparable, work) is. Furthermore, often the distinction between *objective* and *subjective* insecurity is made. Objective insecurity can be measured through indicators like tenure or the amount or costs of unemployment, whereas perceived cognitive insecurity ("My current job is secure") or affective insecurity ("Do you worry about the possibility of losing your job?") are subjective measures. Applied to the context of the self-employed, it would be useful to develop measures that capture objective and subjective *employment* insecurity rather than *job* insecurity. Insecurity in the labour market may lead to individuals becoming more fearful of long-term plans and commitments in other life domains; couples, for instance, often find economic stability a crucial condition for taking a long-term decision such as having children. Especially the involuntary solo self-employed often seem to experience their uncertainty as troublesome (Scherer, 2009; Conen et al., 2016; Kremer et al., 2017).

A lack of maintenance or improvement of employability among the self-employed is also sometimes considered a concern in the prospects of continuing work and career enhancement. The self-employed typically lack access to organisational policies – including formal training opportunities inside corporations – and must procure human capital accumulation by themselves (Smith, 2010). Earlier research of training of workers usually focuses on employees and rarely on self-employed workers. The limited number of studies in this area seem to indicate that the amount of training or the percentage of self-employed who receive training is lower than that of employees (e.g. Broughton et al., 2016; Conen and De Beer, 2019). On the one hand, these findings may signal that the self-employed lack sufficient training investment (due to constraints in funds, time, or access) to pursue sustainable careers. On the other hand, it may also mean that relatively highly skilled individuals select into self-employment or that the self-employed are more effective or rational in choosing the training they really need.

OUTLINE OF THE BOOK

This book is divided into three parts. The first part, consisting of Chapters 2 to 4, sketches the theoretical foundations and context that can be used to study self-employment as precarious work. The second part, consisting of Chapters 5 to 11, reports empirical studies on self-employment and precarious work in Europe. The third part, consisting of Chapters 12 to 14, addresses the implications of findings and puts forward suggestions for future research.

Chapter 2 presents Joop Schippers' exploration of labour market flexibility, self-employment and precariousness in Europe. The chapter examines the origins of new forms of self-employment, the implications in terms of economic and labour market position at the level of the individual, and relates the development of new forms of self-employment to the discussion on labour market flexibility that came up during the last quarter of the twentieth century.

Self-employment dynamics are highly shaped by institutional conditions. The institutional context is not only likely to affect the choice to become self-employed (Torrini, 2005), but also affects the extent to which the self-employed are able to gain sufficient income from a job in self-employment and have to deal with various types of social risk, including the risk of poverty in old age, the risk of disability and the risk of unemployment. In the short *intermezzo* Chapter 3, Hanneke Bennaars addresses the contours of the EU legal perspective to the social protection of self-employed.

In Chapter 4, Uwe Fachinger discusses, from a theoretical point of view, the relation between self-employment, pensions and the risk of poverty in old age. Some of the risks are determined by factors which may be influenced by individuals, and which have to be seen in the context of the ability and willingness of self-employed people to save part of their earnings. The other group of factors, which determine the risk of old age poverty, cannot be influenced by individual action or behaviour. These factors include the institutional and legal framework and developments in capital markets, which are often assumed to be constant over time, but in most cases this is not true. The stability and security of entitlements, the replacement rate, and the adjustment of pensions during retirement to maintain one's living standards are relevant to avoid poverty in old age.

The second part, reporting empirical studies, starts with country studies from various welfare state regimes, including the United Kingdom representing the liberal welfare state, Austria, the Netherlands and Germany representing continental welfare states, Italy the Mediterranean type of welfare state and Sweden the social-democratic welfare state. As private initiative was suppressed under communist rule for a substantial period of time, emerging post-socialist countries went through a fundamentally different process in the past decades than outlined in this introductory chapter; we did not include country studies from these regimes in this volume. The second part with empirical studies contains two studies related to labour force demographics: the position of the older and migrant self-employed.

In Chapter 5, Nigel Meager provides an analysis of the expansion of self-employment in the United Kingdom in recent decades, which encompass two periods (the 1980s and post-2000 period) of remarkable growth in self-employment. The chapter reviews both the literature and recent evidence and addresses the question to what extent developments can be interpreted as a positive development, reinforcing entrepreneurship and economic growth, or whether they are reinforcing labour market inequalities and generating new forms of disadvantage for the 'new self-employed'.

In Chapter 6, Dieter Bögenhold, Andrea Klinglmair, Zulaicha Parastuty and Florian Kandutsch observe an emerging trend towards one-person enterprises in Austria, nowadays representing more than 50 per cent of all Austrian companies. Using unique survey data collected among 626 Carinthian one-person enterprises, this chapter analyses rationalities of these microenterprises and their relation to precariousness among the solo self-employed in Austria. The authors find that one-person entrepreneurs who have been crowded out from the (dependent) labour market and are therefore driven by economic reasons (e.g. self-employment as an alternative to unemployment) are comparatively dissatisfied with their professional situation, are less optimistic regarding their entrepreneurial future, and generate lower incomes.

The Netherlands is among the European countries with the largest increase in the number of solo self-employed in recent years, whereas Germany has witnessed a much more moderate growth and recently even a decline. In Chapter 7, Wieteke Conen and Maarten Debets examine precariousness among the solo self-employed in Germany and the Netherlands and study behaviour and attitudes towards social risk. To that end, they analyse comparative survey data and qualitative interviews. The self-employed in both countries have to deal with various types of social risks (including the risk of poverty in old age, the risk of disability and the risk of unemployment) within different institutional contexts; this chapter addresses the question how the solo self-employed in the two countries deal with their insecure position.

In Chapter 8, Paolo Borghi and Annalisa Murgia outline a changing landscape of self-employment in Italy and zoom in on the situation of independent professionals. Based on a qualitative secondary analysis, four relevant characteristics of independent professionals are highlighted: the growing difficulty in defining successful professional careers; the ambivalence of autonomy that can lead to self-exploitation; the social protection gap in comparison with employees; and the new interest of traditional and emerging organisations dealing with their collective representation. In Italy, the risks connected to the ambivalent condition of being 'precariously free' seem to pose a challenge both for the new generation of independent professionals and for the organisational and institutional actors aimed at regulating and protecting this category of workers.

Dominique Anxo and Thomas Ericson analyse in Chapter 9 the extent to which bogus self-employment is prevalent in the Nordic countries and EU-28. Drawing on the 2015 wave of the European Working Condition

Survey and using standard econometric techniques, the authors find that Sweden displays a lower incidence of bogus self-employed compared to other EU Member States. The specificity of the industrial relations system in Sweden, with strong social partners, high union density and coverage rate of collective agreements in all sectors of the economy, may explain the limited development of bogus self-employment and its lower incidence compared to other Member States.

Self-employment among older workers is diverse. Some older workers have been self-employed much or all of their working lives, while others make the transition into self-employment after age 50 and, for some, as part of a transition to retirement. Wieteke Conen examines in Chapter 10 motives for older workers to work as self-employed and studies precariousness among self-employed men and women between 50 and 80 years of age. The question addressed is who works beyond the state pension age and why?

There has been a long-standing debate among scholars about the nature of migrant self-employment. A popular assumption of the narrative is that migrants are forced into low-wage sectors with poor working conditions due to a lack of resources and opportunities. In Chapter 11, Stefan Berwing, Andrew Isaak and René Leicht study the extent and determinants of precarious self-employment in Germany as well as which types of fields and occupations are most affected by precarious working conditions. An indicator is developed to operationalise precarious self-employment using the 2011 German Microcensus. The results from their quantitative analyses seem to debunk the assumption that equates migrant self-employment to precarious work.

On the macro-level, especially solo self-employed often remain invisible in discussions on socio-economic issues, because – almost by nature – they operate independently and have difficulties organising collective action. This raises the question of how their interests can be adequately included in socio-economic policy making. Chapter 12 investigates membership of interest organisations through the lens of precarious self-employment. Giedo Jansen and Roderick Sluiter construct a four-category typology of solo self-employment (i.e. secure traditional/precarity-prone traditional/ secure professional/precarity-prone professional) and study whether these different types of self-employed workers have diverging expectations of interest organisations, and/or diverging membership patterns. The authors conclude that the most notable group of self-employed are the precarity-prone professionals, who are not only most likely to deviate from traditional patterns of interest representations, but are also most willing to join a trade union.

In Chapter 13, Karin Schulze Buschoff puts forward that the emergence of the category of 'new self-employment' and the increasing hybridisation of employment presents a challenge for political actors in European countries. How do social security systems, and old-age pensions systems in particular, adapt to these developments? And to what extent do regulations at the EU level contribute to the social protection of the workers concerned? Although social inclusion initiatives for self-employment and hybrid employment at the EU-level thus far seems contradictory, various Member States seem to be developing viable systems to cope with the risks posed by increasingly flexible labour markets.

In Chapter 14, Joop Schippers and Wieteke Conen draw some general conclusions from the previous chapters on self-employment as precarious work in Europe, point to future policy challenges and present suggestions for future research.

REFERENCES

Almenberg, J. and Säve-Söderbergh, J. (2011). Financial literacy and retirement planning in Sweden. *Journal of Pension Economics and Finance*, 10(4), 585–98.

Arum, R. and Müller, W. (eds) (2004). *The Reemergence of Self-Employment: A Comparative Study of Self-Employment Dynamics and Social Inequality*. Princeton: Princeton University Press.

Åstebro, T. and Chen, J. (2014). The entrepreneurial earnings puzzle: mismeasurement or real? *Journal of Business Venturing,* 29(1), 88–105.

Belous, R.S. (1989). *The Contingent Economy: The Growth of the Temporary, Part-Time and Subcontracted Workforce*. Washington, DC: National Planning Association.

Benz, M. and Frey, B.S. (2008). Being independent is a great thing: subjective evaluations of self-employment and hierarchy. *Economica*, 75, 362–83.

Blanchflower, D.G. (2000). Self-employment in OECD countries. *Labour Economics*, 7, 471–505.

Bottazzi, R., Jappelli, T. and Padula, M. (2006). Retirement expectations, pension reforms, and their impact on private wealth accumulation. *Journal of Public Economics*, 90(12), 2187–212.

Broughton, A., Green, M., Rickard, C., Swift, S., Eichhorst, W., Tobsch, V. and Tros, F. (2016). *Precarious Employment in Europe: Patterns, Trends and Policy Strategies*. Brussels: European Parliament Directorate General for Internal Policies.

Cappelli, P. and Keller, J.R. (2013). Classifying work in the new economy. *Academy of Management Review*, 38(4), 575–96.

Choi, J. (2009). Pension schemes for the self-employed in OECD countries, *OECD Social, Employment and Migration Working Papers*, No. 84. Paris: OECD Publishing.

Conen, W.S. (2018). Do we have to worry about the 'new' solo self-employed? Self-sufficiency and precariousness among workers with different types of contract. *Host Country Discussion Paper – the Netherlands*. Brussels: European Commission.

Conen, W.S. and De Beer, P.T. (2019). Human capital investments and the value of work: comparing employees and solo self-employed. In: Van der Lippe, T. and

Lippényi, Z. (eds), *Investments in a Sustainable Workforce in Europe*. London: Routledge, forthcoming.

Conen, W.S., Schippers, J.J. and Schulze Buschoff, K. (2016). *Self-Employed without Personnel – Between Freedom and Insecurity*. Düsseldorf: Hans Böckler Foundation.

Crettaz, E. (2013). A state-of-the-art review of working poverty in advanced economies: theoretical models, measurement issues and risk groups. *Journal of European Social Policy*, 23(4), 347–62.

D'Amours, M. and Crespo, S. (2004). Les dimensions de l'hétérogénéité de la catégorie de travailleur indépendant sans employé: Éléments pour une typologie. *Relations Industrielles*, 59(3), 459–89.

Daskalova, V. (2018). Regulating the new self-employed in the Uber economy: what role for EU competition law? *German Law Journal*, 19(3), 461–508.

Esping-Andersen, G. (1990). *The Three Worlds of Welfare Capitalism*. Oxford: Polity Press.

Eurofound (2015). *New Forms of Employment*. Luxembourg: Publications Office of the European Union.

Eurofound (2017a). *Exploring Self-employment in the European Union*. Luxembourg: Publications Office of the European Union.

Eurofound (2017b). *Non-standard Forms of Employment: Recent Trends and Future Prospects*. Luxembourg: Publications Office of the European Union.

Eurofound (2017c). *In-work Poverty in the EU*. Luxembourg: Publications Office of the European Union.

European Commission (2010). *Self-employment in Europe 2010*. Luxembourg: Publications Office of the European Union.

European Foundation for the Improvement of Living and Working Conditions (2018). *European Quality of Life Survey Integrated Data File, 2003–2016* [data collection], *3rd edition*. UK Data Service. SN: 7348, http://doi.org/10.5255/UKDA-SN-7348-3.

Eurostat (2018). *Labour Force Survey*. Luxembourg: Eurostat Database.

Guio, A.C., Marlier, E., Gordon, D., Fahmy, E., Nandy, S. and Pomati, M. (2016). Improving the measurement of material deprivation at the European Union level. *Journal of European Social Policy*, 26(3), 219–33.

Hamilton, B.H. (2000). Does entrepreneurship pay? An empirical analysis of the returns to self-employment. *Journal of Political Economy*, 108, 604–31.

Hershey, D.A., Van Dalen, H.P., Conen, W.S. and Henkens, K. (2017). Are 'voluntary' self-employed better prepared for retirement than 'forced' self-employed? *Work, Aging and Retirement*, 3(3), 243–56.

Horemans, J., and Marx, I. (2017). Poverty and material deprivation among the self-employed in Europe: an exploration of a relatively uncharted landscape. *IZA Discussion Paper* No. 11007.

Hundley, G. (2001). Why and when are the self-employed more satisfied with their work? *Industrial Relations: A Journal of Economy and Society*, 40, 293–316.

Kalleberg, A.L. (2011). *Good Jobs, Bad Jobs. The Rise of Polarised and Precarious Employment Systems in the United States, 1970s to 2000s*. New York: Russell Sage Foundation.

Kalleberg, A.L. (2018). *Precarious Lives. Job Insecurity and Well-being in Rich Democracies*. Cambridge: Polity Press.

Kalleberg, A.L., Reskin, B.F. and Hudson, K. (2000). Bad jobs in America: standard and nonstandard employment relations and job quality in the United States. *American Sociological Review*, 65, 256–78.

Kautonen, T., Down, S., Welter, F., Vainio, P., Palmroos, J., Althoff, K. and Kolb, S. (2010). 'Involuntary self-employment' as a public policy issue: a cross-country European review. *International Journal of Entrepreneurial Behaviour and Research*, 16(2), 112–29.

Kremer, M., Went, R. and Knottnerus, A. (2017). *Voor de zekerheid: De toekomst van flexibel werkenden en de moderne organisatie van arbeid* [*For the Sake of Security. The Future of Flexible Workers and the Modern Organisation of Labour*]. The Hague: The Netherlands Scientific Council for Government Policy.

Lin, Z., Picot, G. and Compton, J. (2000). The entry and exit dynamics of self-employment in Canada. *Small Business Economics*, 15, 105–25.

Lusardi, A. and Mitchell, O.S. (2011). Financial literacy and retirement planning in the United States. *Journal of Pension Economics and Finance*, 10(4), 509–25.

Mastrogiacomo, M. and Alessie, R.J. (2015). Where are the retirement savings of self-employed? An analysis of 'unconventional' retirement accounts. *DNB Working Papers 454*. Amsterdam: Netherlands Central Bank.

Meager, N. (1992). Does unemployment lead to self-employment? *Small Business Economics*, 4(2), 87–103.

Nolan, B. and Whelan, C.T. (2010). Using non-monetary deprivation indicators to analyze poverty and social exclusion: lessons from Europe? *Journal of Policy Analysis and Management*, 29(2), 305–25.

OECD (2000). The partial renaissance of self-employment. In: *OECD Employment Outlook 2000 June*. Paris: Organisation for Economic Co-operation and Development

OECD (2014). *Employment Outlook*. Paris: OECD Publishing.

Parker, S.C. (2004). *The Economics of Self-Employment and Entrepreneurship*. Cambridge: Cambridge University Press.

Porthé, V., Ahonen, E., Vázquez, M., Pope, C., Agudelo, A., Garcia, A., Amable, M., Benavides, F.G. and Benach, J.(2010). Extending a model of precarious employment: a qualitative study of migrant workers in Spain. *American Journal of Industrial Medicine*, 53, 417–24.

Rees, H. and Shah, A. (1986). An empirical analysis of self-employment in the UK. *Journal of Applied Econometrics*, 1(1), 95–108.

Rodgers, G. (1989). Precarious work in Western Europe: the state of the debate. In: Rodgers, G. and Rodgers, J. (eds), *Precarious Jobs in Labour Market Regulation: The Growth of Atypical Employment in Western Europe*. Geneva: International Institute for Labour Studies, pp. 1–16.

Scherer, S. (2009). The social consequences of insecure jobs. *Social Indicators Research*, 93(3), 469–88.

Schulze Buschoff, K. (2007). *Neue Selbständige im europäischen Vergleich. Struktur, Dynamik und soziale Sicherheit*. Düsseldorf: Hans-Böckler-Stiftung.

Schulze Buschoff, K. and Schmidt, C. (2009). Adapting labour law and social security to the needs of the 'new self-employed' – comparing the UK, Germany and the Netherlands. *Journal of European Social Policy*, 19(2), 147–59.

Scott-Marshall, H. and Tompa, E. (2011). The health consequences of precarious employment experiences. *Work: A Journal of Prevention Assessment and Rehabilitation*, 38(4), 369–82.

Smith, V. (2010). Enhancing employability: human, cultural, and social capital in an era of turbulent unpredictability. *Human Relations*, 63(2), 279–300.

Sorgner, A., Fritsch, M. and Kritikos, A. (2017). Do entrepreneurs really earn less? *Small Business Economics,* 49(2), 251–72.

Spasova S., Bouget D., Ghailani D. and Vanhercke B. (2017). *Access to Social Protection for People Working on Non-Standard Contracts and as Self-Employed in Europe. A Study of National Policies*. European Social Policy Network (ESPN), Brussels: European Commission.

Statistics Netherlands (2018). *Armoede en sociale uitsluiting 2018* [Poverty and social exclusion 2018]. The Hague/Heerlen: Statistics Netherlands.

Stone, K.V. (2006). Legal protections for atypical employees: employment law for workers without workplaces and employees without employers. *Berkeley Journal of Employment and Labour Law*, 27(2), 251–86.

Supiot, A. (2001). *Beyond Employment. Changes in Work and the Future of Labour Law in Europe*. Oxford: Oxford University Press.

Taylor, M. (2004). Self-employment in Britain: when, who and why. *Swedish Economic Policy Review*, 11(2), 139–73.

Torrini, R. (2005). Cross-country differences in self-employment rates: the role of institutions. *Labour Economics*, 12(5), 661–83.

Van Es, F. and Van Vuuren, D.J. (2011). A decomposition of the growth in self-employment. *Applied Economics Letters*, 18(17), 1665–9.

Vosko, L.F. (ed.) (2006). *Precarious Employment: Understanding Labour Market Insecurity in Canada*. Montreal: McGill-Queen's University Press.

Westerveld, M. (2012). The 'new' self-employed: an issue for social policy? *European Journal of Social Security*, 14(3), 156–73.

Westerveld, M. and Olivier, M. (eds) (2019). *Social Security Outside the Realm of the Employment Contract*. Cheltenham, UK and Northampton, MA, USA: Edward Elgar Publishing.

PART I

Do we have to worry about the 'new self-employed'? Theory and context

2. Labour market flexibility, self-employment and precariousness

Joop Schippers

INTRODUCTION

For decades the idea of self-employment has been associated with images of a small shop keeper selling groceries to a well-known circle of clients, who could knock at the (back)door even after opening hours, or a farmer in one of the rural parts of Europe, working in his vineyard and bringing his home made goat's cheese to the local market every Saturday. During the first decades of the twenty-first century several European countries witnessed the emergence of new images of self-employed workers. For instance the image of a well, though casually dressed, young man or woman, sitting on a pavement with a latte macchiato and a laptop, waiting for the next business meeting – to discuss the proposal for an advertising campaign or a photo-reportage for a magazine. Or the image of a district nurse making her round along a series of older people in need of health care.

Even though these images cannot replace detailed European statistics, they do illustrate the world of self-employment – and especially of solo self-employment – is changing. Apart from a series of economic activities that has traditionally been within the domain of self-employment, Europe has witnessed a shift in self-employment towards other economic activities, especially in the service sector, but in some countries also in construction, care or transportation and logistics.

This chapter examines the origins of new forms of (solo) self-employment and deals with the question of what these new forms imply in terms of economic and labour market position at the individual level. We will relate the development of new forms of self-employment to the discussion on labour market flexibility that came up during the last quarter of the twentieth century. As the issue is in the centre of current policy debates, we will focus on the risk of precariousness for those in self-employment in terms of their economic and labour market position. This overview chapter is not about one specific country. Nonetheless, because some countries show a faster and stronger shift towards new forms of self-employment, the focus may sometimes be geared towards these countries.

SUPPLY-SIDE ECONOMICS AND GROWING LABOUR MARKET FLEXIBILITY

The continuous expansion of the welfare state and its inability to prevent and combat unemployment during times of economic crises – like the crises we have seen in the seventies and eighties of the previous century – gave rise to the development of new economic ideas opposing the Keynesian discourse that had been dominant in economic policy making since the end of the Second World War. Whereas Keynesian economics stressed that markets – and especially the labour market – would not be able to establish a sustainable equilibrium if left on its own, neo-classical economics argued that all the rules and regulations developed by welfare states to correct markets and market outcomes threatened to suffocate economic activity. Especially advocates of the so-called supply-side economics promoted less regulation in the labour market and more room for the incentives and disincentives of the price mechanism to do their job. Equilibrium could only be re-established again if the labour market were to become more flexible and less regulated. In the United States supply-side economists' ideas were picked up by the Reagan administration, while in Europe the United Kingdom government led by prime minister Thatcher was the main supporter of supply-side economics. However, in Europe also other countries took initiatives for the flexibilisation of their labour markets.

Following Atkinson (1984), many studies on labour market flexibility take the perspective of the organisation and distinguish four types of flexibility:

- Numerical flexibility
- Functional flexibility
- Outsourcing of work
- Flexible pay.

The first three forms of flexibility concern the quantity of labour. The fourth form concerns the price of labour. For each form of flexibility it can be argued why and under what conditions this form will be attractive from an organisational point of view. The overarching argument is that all forms of labour market flexibility offer the organisation an opportunity to shift the burden (and so the costs) of underutilisation of labour from their own payroll to the employee. While permanent workers get paid for their idle time (between two commissions, before the crop is ripe, and so on) different forms of flexibility offer organisations the opportunity to pay workers only for the time they actually contribute to the organisation's production. This can be done by hiring workers only for specific tasks, a limited period of time or negotiating a contract with a clause that someone does not get paid for 'idle hours'.

While the logic of different forms of flexibility seems clear – at least at first sight – from the perspective of the organisation, it is not immediately clear why an employee would be prepared to take over the burden of underutilisation from the employer (Horemans and Marx, 2017). The most simple explanation is that during some periods (for instance if unemployment is high and jobs are scarce) some workers have no other option than to accept a flexible job, as the alternative is no job at all. Another explanation could be that flexible jobs may have some attraction for individuals for whom paid work is not their prime activity. This may be because they are focusing on parenthood or other care tasks, or because they have already retired or are still in education and only want to work occasionally to earn some additional money (next to their main source of income). For this type of worker the time they are not engaged in paid work is no idle time or a form of underutilisation, as they are primarily engaged in other activities, which may be outside the labour market.

Those who are in flexible forms of employment like on-call work, a zero-hour contract, a min-max contract or working for a temp agency are not only dependent on an employer who decides when they will be hired, the employer also determines their wages and their working conditions. The employer has legal authority over the employee.

SELF-EMPLOYMENT: A GROWING BRANCH ON THE TREE OF FLEXIBILITY

For a group of individual workers the latter dimensions of the labour relation are not in line with their labour market preferences. They attach much importance to the opportunity to decide themselves on when to work, how to work, for whom to work and what kind of work they do. So, they are prepared to give up the security of a fixed monthly income for their independence and the freedom to be 'their own boss'. They prefer a kind of labour market flexibility in which there is no authority of the employer over the employee. Instead, they negotiate with the organisation on the price, the volume and the other conditions of the work the organisation wants them to do. And they enter into a legal contract only if both parties agree on the terms of the assignment.

Individuals with this type of preference may opt for a labour market position of (solo) self-employment. From a theoretical perspective (and other chapters in this volume will present empirical material supporting this theoretical perspective) this group of individuals that voluntarily chooses self-employment is not an accidental one. First, as already mentioned, they share high preferences for independence. Second, they are likely to have at least some confidence in the possibilities to acquire enough work to earn a decent living. This confidence includes both the idea that they have to offer 'something' (a product or a service) for which there is actually enough demand among organisations/employers as well as the conviction that they will be able to negotiate a proper price and other terms of the contract. If this confidence would be absent, it would not make much sense to start a career in self-employment. Of course, enough confidence in a good result does not automatically guarantee such a result. Expectations may be wrong or conditions may shift as the economy enters a downturn. Moreover, individuals who take up a position in self-employment do not let themselves be scared off by the paperwork and the red tape that comes with self-employment activities (in different amounts in different countries). This may vary from sending your own bills to arranging your own old age or disability pension and transferring VAT to the tax authorities. Even though this relatively new group of self-employed individuals shows a big variety of characteristics they are likely to share, at least to some extent, these two major common characteristics. These two characteristics also present the road towards part of the explanation for the growth of this branch of the flexibility tree. On the one hand educational levels have risen in most European countries, stimulating the appreciation for independence and self-control. On the other hand, modern organisations have become much more complicated and rule and regulation based, making an individual feel like a small cogwheel in the wheels of the organisation. So, both the opportunities and the need to break away from traditional organisations may have grown over the past decades.

THE LOSS OF TRADITIONAL SELF-EMPLOYMENT

The emergence of this new type of (often: solo) self-employed individual is quite the opposite from what has happened to a lot of individuals in traditional self-employment. Many of the independent shopkeepers, owners of a small farm, garage owners or independent pharmacists have experienced the effects of the increase in scale that characterises modern economies. They may have survived the first supermarket in the village or the first steps of land consolidation, but the establishment of a hypermarket or further automation of the process of land preparation, sowing and harvesting may have been a bridge too far. Some of them had to close down their small business and either retired or had to seek a job as an employee within an organisation. In some cases their small establishment was taken over by a larger group and instead of the owner they became the manager of their establishment in their new role of an employee of a bigger company. Of course, this was not the destiny of all traditional self-employed individuals as we shall see later on: a lot of them 'survived', adapted to new economic circumstances and still are the backbone of a lot of communities all over Europe.

THE RISE OF INVOLUNTARY SELF-EMPLOYMENT

Next to the two categories of self-employed persons discussed above, especially the first decade of this century witnessed the growth of a third category, that is, the category of involuntary self-employed. Of course, no one who is engaged in self-employment carries a sticker on his/her forehead saying 'voluntary' or 'involuntary self-employed'. Yet recent labour market history shows that the further growth of self-employment in several European countries is strongly connected with the economic crisis from the end of the first decade when quite a number of workers who had lost their job saw no other opportunity then to opt for self-employment. In several cases the involuntary nature of the decision to become self-employed was even more clear. Sometimes employers had or pretended to have so many problems that they burdened (part of) their employees with the dilemma: I cannot pay your current wage and the wage costs associated with the job any longer, so I will have to fire you, but if you are prepared to work in self-employment I could hire you again if you are willing to work for a lower wage than you earned before. Depending on the perceived alternatives (which were often limited due to the crisis) many workers accepted this proposal out of sheer necessity; not because they were longing to be self-employed. Some of them even had to buy or lease their own equipment that was previously provided by their former employer. As some of the following chapters will show, several individuals belonging to this category of (solo) self-employed find it hard to make a decent living. Now that the economy is booming again in many European countries one can wonder how many of them will try to find a new opportunity to re-enter employment with a 'traditional' company again.

A CHANGING INDUSTRIAL LANDSCAPE

In the meantime, the industrial landscape of Europe has been changing and may change even further in the decades ahead. Whereas we already mentioned the 'emancipation' of the ever-higher educated European population as one of the factors promoting a higher demand for working in self-employment, we should not forget also that the opportunities for self-employment have increased substantially. This has to do with the falling price of physical capital, due to technological innovation, the ICT-revolution and the technology involved in different branches of industry. Suppose someone wanted to start a travel agency somewhere in the sixties or seventies of the previous century. Most likely he or she would look for an office somewhere in a shopping centre where potential travellers could easily find the travel agency and he or she would hire people for several tasks like answering the phone, organising all booking forms, composing a travel brochure, printing it, displaying it in an attractive way in the shop window and so on. Of course this starting entrepreneur would need some office equipment like typewriters, phones and some furniture and then ask the local mayor to come and open the new travel agency. The whole plan would have required a serious amount of financial capital and most people starting such an enterprise could not do this without the help of a loan from the local bank. Nowadays, if one was to start a travel agency one could easily imagine doing this completely online with the help of a single laptop, a cell phone, a subscription to an Internet provider and some creativity. This principle does not only apply to starting a travel agency. For every activity that requires communication with potential customers and the processing of information one can argue that this has become much easier and much cheaper than in the past that one does not need the framework of an organisation anymore to engage in this activity. Whereas the price of a computer in the eighties was still (the equivalent of) many thousands of euros, you can buy a good one now for less than a thousand euros. And the Internet as a virtual and low-cost place to meet has replaced many offices and jobs, relieving entrepreneurs from the necessity to invest in bricks and mortar.

This argumentation also shows the logic why self-employment can be realised easier in some sectors than in others. Especially economic activities that primarily involve communication and administration require less capital than before. On the contrary, the manufacturing industry and agriculture require more capital – and less workers – than in the past (think of the robots that dominate most car plants or the enormous blast furnaces used for steel production). So, these are sectors where it is much more difficult to start in self-employment. This development may also explain why traditional self-employment in agriculture is losing ground. Modern agricultural companies that want to compete on the world market need high-tech machines and installations that require much more capital than most individuals can put on the table themselves. So, the growing number of self-employed individuals is not only a matter of preferences or (lack of) labour market opportunities, but also of changing structural conditions related to technological innovation and the falling prices of computers, cell phones and other ICT related facilities.

DIFFERENT NATIONAL INSTITUTIONAL ARRANGEMENTS

A final factor that should be taken into consideration when trying to explain the growing, but also diverging share between European countries of people in self-employment concerns national institutional arrangements. European countries differ substantially when it comes to rules and regulations that apply to self-employment. Some countries stimulate self-employment with beneficial fiscal arrangements for the self-employed, others de facto restrict the opportunities for starters in self-employment with rules on qualifications to operate in a specific sector. In some countries the self-employed can opt out from social security and pension arrangements, actually allowing them to work at lower costs and lower prices than employees for whom employers have to pay all kinds of additional labour costs. Consequently, it may not come as a surprise that above and beyond the factors mentioned before, institutional arrangements strongly contribute to national differences in the share and growth of the number of self-employed workers within the EU.

Table 2.1 shows that the average share of self-employed people in the European Union was 13.7 per cent of total employment in 2017, with the highest scores in Mediterranean countries like Greece and Italy and low scores in Scandinavian countries like Denmark and Sweden. Looking at the former communist countries of Eastern Europe there is no clear pattern. The same holds for the so-called continental corporatist countries, as distinguished by Esping-Anderson (1990). So, it looks like the type of welfare state is not dominant in determining the share of people in self-employment. Traditionally, the palette of economic activities in a country and specific national rules and regulations appear to be more important determinants of the share of self-employment.

Table 2.1 furthermore shows that even though the share of self-employed workers in the EU has been relatively stable since the turn of the century, there are a lot of diverging developments behind this European

Table 2.1   *The development of self-employment in the EU and a number of selected European countries, 2000–2017 (self-employment as a % of total employment)*

	2000	2005	2010	2015	2017
European Union	14.6	14.6	14.6	14.1	13.7
Austria	10.6	11.3	11.3	11	10.6
Bulgaria	13.8	12	11.3	11.1	10.8
Czech Republic	14.4	15.1	16.8	16.3	16.1
Denmark	8	7.6	8.4	7.8	7.4
Finland	12.6	11.7	12.2	12.7	11.7
France	10	9.7	10.7	10.8	10.9
Germany	9.7	10.8	10.5	9.6	9.1
Greece	31.4	28.9	29.3	29.6	29.4
Hungary	14.4	13.1	11.8	10.2	9.7
Ireland	16.7	15.4	15.1	14.1	13.3
Italy	23.6	24	22.8	21.9	20.8
Lithuania	15.7	14.1	9.1	10.8	10.9
Netherlands	10	11.3	13.8	15.3	15.5
Norway	6.9	6.9	7.2	6.2	5.8
Poland	21.8	20	18.7	17.9	17.4
Portugal	20.4	20.2	17.7	14.5	13.4
Romania	20.2	19	20.3	17.6	16.4
Slovakia	7.7	12.5	15.8	14.9	15
Spain	17.8	16.2	15.6	16.4	15.7
Sweden	9.9	9.6	9.8	8.9	8.6
Switzerland	15	13.4	12.8	11.7	11.6
United Kingdom	11.5	12.2	13	13.6	14

Source: Eurostat (2018), own calculations.

average. A group of countries shows a steady decline in the share of self-employed persons (Bulgaria, Ireland, Italy, Lithuania, Poland, Romania, Switzerland and especially Hungary and Portugal), while only few countries show a substantial increase (United Kingdom and especially the Netherlands and Slovakia). The other countries in the table show a more or less stable share of self-employed workers. Apart from what appear to be structural developments in several countries, many countries show a relatively high score for the years 2010 or 2015. This might be an effect of the economic crisis that urged part of the workforce to try their luck in self-employment.

SELF-EMPLOYMENT AND GENDER

Another motive to engage in self-employment activities that is sometimes brought forward is that self-employment would offer more and better opportunities to combine work and private life with more in particular care tasks for children and for example, dependent relatives like older (grand)parents or parents-in-law (see e.g. Boden, 1999; Wellington, 2006; Gurley-Calvez et al., 2009). As these tasks have traditionally been and still are often primarily women's responsibility in most European countries this could give rise to the hypothesis that self-employment would be particularly attractive for women. Figure 2.1, however, shows quite a different picture. While women's share in total employment is between 40 and 50 per cent in most European countries, their share in self-employment is lower (and sometimes substantially lower) in all countries selected for this figure. As a matter of fact only in five countries the differences is less than ten percentage points (Czech Republic, Greece, Italy, Latvia and Luxembourg). So, self-employment is by far not a form of employment that is particularly popular among women. This result is in line with, for example, Blanchflower (2000) and Verheul et al. (2012). One explanation might be that even though self-employment could offer better opportunities to schedule one's working hours in order to reconcile work and family life, self-employment may also require taking responsibility for administrative matters, perhaps acquisition of clients and a high degree of responsiveness to the desires of customers. These activities, of course, take time, but may also result in an unpredictable time schedule that does not easily match with family responsibilities. This argument is supported by Annink (2017). She shows that the way individual women in self-employment experience their work–life balance depends very much on the particular form of self-employment. She explains how these experiences are influenced by the interplay of work and business characteristics and also depend on the actual policy, economic and cultural context. Other studies have pointed to the fact that women and men are engaged in different sectors of industry as a possible explanation for the lower female participation in self-employment (e.g. Wharton, 1989; Van Es and Van Vuuren, 2011). Setting aside the wide variety between countries, there is indeed (sometimes strong) occupational and sectoral segregation between women and men in most European countries (Bettio and Veraschgagina, 2009). Focusing on the sectors where women seem to be overrepresented shows, however, that these are primarily capital-extensive sectors like commercial services where it is relatively easy to engage in self-employment. Men, on the contrary, are overrepresented in capital-intensive industries where it less easy to start your own small business. So, this potential explanation for lower female participation in self-employment does not

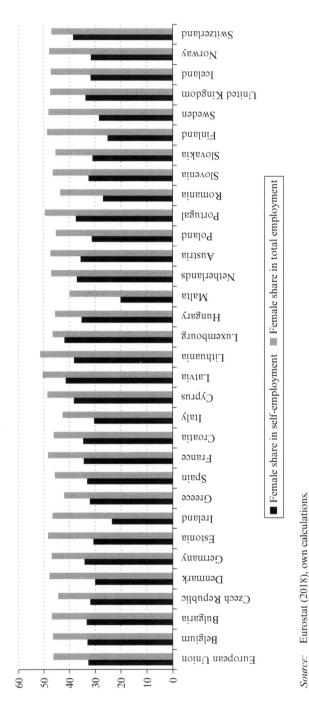

Source: Eurostat (2018), own calculations.

Figure 2.1 *Women's share in self-employment compared to women's share in total employment*

look very promising. Among others Schippers (1987) and Williams (2012) have pointed to self-employment as an 'escape strategy' for women. If they experience or perceive discriminatory behaviour by employers with respect to wages or career opportunities (think of the so-called 'glass ceiling') this may push them into self-employment to avoid this kind of discriminatory behaviour.

SELF-EMPLOYMENT AND PRECARIOUSNESS

One of the major issues in discussions on increasing labour market flexibility has been the social perspective (Horemans and Marx, 2017). While it may be perfectly understandable from an employers' point of view that he wants to reduce the risk of idleness of workers in his firm, the other side of the coin is the uncertainty and the limited social protection for flexible workers. First, flexible workers cannot be sure about their earnings. Depending on the kind of contract they have one month they will work many hours and have high earnings, while the next month things can be totally different. Accordingly, their social protection will be limited compared with the protection of full-time, permanent workers. Still, though depending on national or sectoral arrangements, flexible *employees* do have at least some social protection. In some countries this protection goes quite far. For instance, in the Netherlands even individuals who work for a temp agency and meet some specific conditions in terms of working hours and tenure nowadays have their own collective labour agreement, including entitlements to training facilities and pension rights.

In comparison, self-employed individuals are typically worse off. Not only do they experience the same insecurity in terms of earnings as their fellow flexible workers, but while flexible employees 'only' have to bother about the quantity of labour they will be able to supply, self-employed workers are not sure about the rate at which they can supply their labour either. When the economy is booming they can 'sell' many hours at a relative high price, but during an economic downturn not only the hours they can supply will be smaller, but probably the hourly rate will fall as well due to competition in the market. Of course, (temporary) employees may also experience the negative consequences of excess supply in the labour market, but collective bargaining through unions and institutional arrangements like minimum wage law and collective agreements may mitigate these negative consequences at the individual level. As a result the risk of in-work poverty is much higher for the self-employed than for employees (Eurofound, 2017). As can be seen from Figure 2.2, among the group of self-employed there also is a difference between solo self-employed

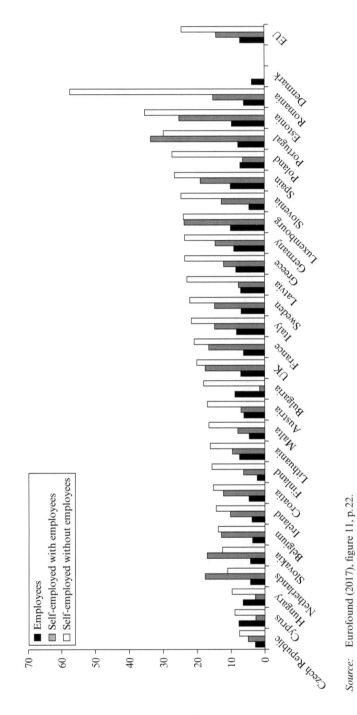

Source: Eurofound (2017), figure 11, p. 22.

Figure 2.2   In-work poverty risk rates (in %), self-employed and employees, EU Member States (2014)

and self-employed with employees. As Conen (2018) has demonstrated, solo self-employed are generally even more at risk than self-employed with employees. From a theoretical perspective one could argue that most self-employed will not decide overnight to hire an employee and take up not only the responsibility to pay wages, but also enter into all kinds of additional legal obligations one has as an employer. On the other hand, if your (small) business has to generate both your own earnings and also the wage for one or more employees this might make your enterprise more vulnerable for market contingencies. Of course – as Horemans and Marx (2017) argue – in-work poverty risk is just one dimension of the problem of precariousness. That is why they also discuss the issue of material deprivation, relate the two phenomena and try to estimate the relation with several socio-demographic characteristics.

When it comes to social protection, the situation of self-employed workers is usually even worse, as will be analysed in several of the following chapters in this volume. In many instances, but again depending on national or sectoral institutional arrangements, social protection is limited to employees (especially in the so-called continental corporatist welfare state regimes) and self-employed individuals often have to provide for their own arrangements. This brings along the risk that paying the rent, the electricity bill and the supermarket will require all of the budget when earnings are low and no means are left to pay for future-oriented provisions like a disability insurance or old age pension facilities. So, even though self-employed workers may currently get along and make ends meet, without proper arrangements for unemployment, disability or old age they may fall into precariousness when the odds turn against them. All kinds of social arrangements prevent or mitigate these risks for employees.

MAINTENANCE OF HUMAN CAPITAL AND SKILL DEVELOPMENT AS A NEW RISK

While the traditional welfare state primarily focuses on the risk of income loss due to illness/disability, unemployment and old age, several authors have pointed to a growing risk following from the fast process of technological transformation (WRR, 2013; Schippers, 2018). Rapid technological developments tend to increase the pace of depreciation of existing human capital. In the fifties or even sixties of the previous century an initial degree in intermediate vocational training in combination with growing experience was more or less enough for a productive career. However, the introduction of new technologies has rendered much existing knowledge obsolete and increased the necessity to invest in getting acquainted with and mastery of these new technologies. Once again, self-employed workers seem at a disadvantage here. If within an organisation the employer decides to introduce a new generation of computers and a new version of Windows or any other software program it is in his own advantage to offer his employees the opportunity to get acquainted with the new software. During the first month or so there may be even someone at a helpdesk available for the purposes of trouble shooting and helping employees on their way in the labyrinth of the myriad of possibilities the software offers. Someone who is self-employed will not only have to pay for the new hardware and software himself. He also has to rely on his own skills to find the right equipment and to develop the skills to work with it. Of course, he can turn to the supplier of the new equipment or the new software, but these services usually do not come for free. And again – just like in the case of low earnings and investments in arrangements for future income protection – the present may turn into the enemy of the future. If someone who is self-employed has to choose between the opportunity to write a proposal for a new client or to spend his time on new software training (for which he has to pay), which alternative will he choose: investing time with well-defined potential short term revenues or investing time in activities of which the revenues are uncertain and if they materialise it will be in the long term only? The likely answer is not reassuring, given the findings of Hyde and Phillipson (2014) that lack of time and financial constraints are consistently shown the most important barriers to lifelong learning. So, there is the risk that short-term priorities will have the upper hand on investments of which the revenues are uncertain and – by nature – lie in the more distant future. In more general terms self-employed individuals run the risk that they base their economic activities on existing knowledge and skills, but fail to invest (time and money) in the development of these skills, of new 'products', become 'a one trick pony' and lose their earning capacity if economic conditions and market demands change. A lack of unequivocal government policies does not help the self-employed to develop a clear and successful lifelong learning strategy (Lange et al., 2000).

Unfortunately Eurostat does not provide figures on lifelong learning or participation in adult learning/vocational training specifically for the self-employed (yet). However, figures that make a distinction between large companies and small companies show that the share of small companies providing training for their workers lags (substantially) behind that of large companies. In a similar vein much more workers with a permanent contract and/or working full time participate in adult learning than workers with a temporary contract and/or working part time (Fouarge et al., 2012; Sequeda et al., 2015). Based on data from the sixth European Working Conditions Survey (2015) Conen and De Beer (2019) find that compared to paid employed workers with temporary contracts who relatively often report to be in need of further training, self-employed workers relatively often report to have enough skills to deal with more demanding duties. Moreover, they found that 20 per cent of the (solo) self-employed participated in some form of training (paid for by themselves) during the past twelve months. This is less than half of the share of permanent workers that participated in some form of training (54 per cent) and substantially less than the share of temporary workers (39 per cent) too. For both permanent and temporary workers in employment it is usually the employer who pays for the training (Conen and De Beer, 2019, Table 3). Combining the theoretical arguments presented above and these empirical findings, it would not come as a surprise if figures on participation in lifelong learning for the self-employed were to be substantially lower than those for employees too.

The next chapters in this volume (especially in Part II) will provide more empirical information on different dimensions of precariousness in several European countries.

CONCLUSIONS

A conclusion of this chapter can be that self-employment is an important shoot at the trunk of flexibility. The chapter helps to understand both the attractiveness of self-employment for part of the working population as well as the (potential) problems related to self-employment, which is relevant for studying self-employment within the wider framework of (increasing) labour market flexibility. Still, self-employment is not growing everywhere in Europe, even though in general the opportunities to start a business in self-employment seem to be increasing. Some countries show a remarkable increase, but in other countries self-employment appears to be stable or decreasing. While overall labour market participation tends to become less gendered over the years, participation in self-employment is strongly gendered all over Europe: on average women make up one-third of the self-employed population. The following chapters will go into much more detail with respect to (the risk of) precariousness for those who work in self-employment, but it is safe to conclude here already that self-employment brings along several risks. Of course, there is the risk of low current income due to sometimes heavy competition and – compared with the employee-sector – relatively little institutional arrangements and low institutional protection. There are also risks related to future income, partly as a consequence of insufficient arrangements for sickness/disability, unemployment and old age, but also as a consequence of (too) limited investment in the development of new skills and the maintenance of existing human capital.

From a perspective of government policy (be it at the local, the national or the European level) self-employment constitutes a rather complicated issue, as the following chapters will show. Growth in some sectors and countries, decline in others, differences between solo self-employment and self-employed with personnel, differences between successful highly educated self-employed who preferred to start their own independent business and willy-nilly self-employed constitute a scattered picture of self-employment with different needs and preferences, that does not immanently give rise to a series of self-evident policy measures. So, it is also safe to conclude here already that self-employment will be on the policy agenda for quite some time to come.

REFERENCES

Annink, S.M. (2017). *Busyness around the business: a cross-national comparative research of the work-life balance of self-employed workers*. Rotterdam: Erasmus University Rotterdam.

Atkinson, J.S. (1984). Manpower strategies for flexible organisations. *Personnel Management*, 16, August, 28–31.

Bettio, F. and Veraschgagina, A. (2009). *Gender segregation in the labour market. Root causes, implications and policy responses in the EU*. European Commission's Expert Group on Gender and Employment (EGGE). Luxembourg: Publication Office of the European Union.

Blanchflower, D.G. (2000). Self-employment in OECD countries. *Labour Economics*, 7(5), 471–505.

Boden, R.J. (1999). Flexible working hours, family responsibilities, and female self-employment. *American Journal of Economics and Sociology*, 58(1), 71–83.

Conen, W.S. (2018). Do we have to worry about the 'new' solo self-employed? Self-sufficiency and precariousness among workers with different types of contract. *Mutual Learning Programme DG Employment, Social Affairs and Inclusion, Host Country Discussion Paper – the Netherlands*. Brussels: European Commission.

Conen, W.S. and De Beer, P.T. (2019). Human capital investments and the value of work: comparing employees and solo self-employed. In: Van der Lippe, T. and Lippényi, Z. (eds), *Investments in a sustainable workforce in Europe*. London: Routledge, forthcoming.

Esping-Anderson, G. (1990). *The three worlds of welfare capitalism*. Cambridge, UK: Polity Press.

Eurofound (2017). *In-work poverty in the EU*. Luxembourg: Publications Office of the European Union.

Eurostat (2018). *Labour Force Survey*. Luxembourg: Eurostat Database.

Fouarge, D., de Grip, A., Smits, W. and de Vries, R. (2012). Flexible contracts and human capital investments. *De Economist*, 160(2), 177–95.

Gurley-Calvez, T., Biehl, A. and Harper, K. (2009). Time-use patterns and women entrepreneurs. *American Economic Review*, 99(2), 139–44.

Horemans, J. and Marx, I. (2017). Poverty and material deprivation among the self-employed in Europe: an exploration of a relatively uncharted landscape. *IZA Discussion Paper No. 11007.*

Hyde, M. and Phillipson, C. (2014). *How can lifelong learning, including continuous training within the labour market, be enabled and who will pay for this? Looking forward to 2025 and 2040 how might this evolve?* Government Office for Science.

Lange, T., Ottens, M. and Taylor, A. (2000). SMEs and barriers to skills development: a Scottish perspective, *Journal of European Industrial Training*, 24(1), 5–11.

Schippers, J.J. (1987). *Beloningsverschillen tussen mannen en vrouwen (Wage differences between men and women)*. Groningen: Wolters-Noordhoff.

Schippers, J.J. (2018). On the need for universities to engage in lifelong learning. In: Heijnen, A. and van der Vaart, R. (eds), *Places of engagement. Reflections on higher education in 2040 – a global approach*, Amsterdam: Amsterdam University Press B.V., 65–68.

Sequeda, M.F., Grip, A. de and Velden, R. van der (2015). *Does informal learning at work differ between temporary and permanent workers? Evidence from 20 OECD countries.* Bonn: IZA.

Van Es, F. and Van Vuuren, D.J. (2011). A decomposition of the growth in self-employment. *Applied Economics Letters*, 18(17), 1665–9.

Verheul, I., Thurik, R., Grilo, I. and Van der Zwan, P. (2012). Explaining preferences and actual involvement in self-employment: gender and the entrepreneurial personality. *Journal of Economic Psychology*, 33(2), 325–41.

Wellington, A.J. (2006). Self-employment: the new solution for balancing family and career? *Labour Economics*, 13(3), 357–86.

Wharton, A.S. (1989). Gender segregation in private-sector, public-sector, and self-employed occupations, 1950–1981. *Social Science Quarterly*, 70(4), 923–40.

Williams, D.R. (2012). Gender discrimination and self-employment dynamics in Europe. *The Journal of Socio-Economics*, 41(2), 153–8.

WRR (2013). *Naar een lerende economie.* Rapport no. 90. Den Haag: Wetenschappelijk Raad voor het Regeringsbeleid (The Netherlands Scientific Council for Government Policy. Towards a learning economy. Investing in the Netherlands' earning capacity).

3. Social protection for the self-employed: an EU legal perspective

Hanneke Bennaars

INTRODUCTION

Self-employment dynamics are highly shaped by institutional conditions (Eichhorst et al., 2013). The institutional context is not only likely to affect the choice to become self-employed (Torrini, 2005), but also affects the extent to which the self-employed are able to gain sufficient income from a job in self-employment and have to deal with various types of social risk, including the risk of poverty in old age, the risk of disability and the risk of unemployment. This short *intermezzo* chapter aims to function as a contextual background and sketches the contours of the EU legal perspective to the social protection of the self-employed.

SOCIAL PROTECTION FOR THE SELF-EMPLOYED: A CONTRADICTORY CONCEPT

The essence of self-employed workers is that they are independent entrepreneurs and are rather to be seen as a 'business' or an enterprise than as a worker. Social protection can be perceived as a synonym for employee protection, consisting in a system of labour law, employment law and social security law and thus not obviously linked to self-employed workers. Nevertheless, in the past decades the social protection of the self-employed has become a frequently discussed issue in the legal academic debate. This increase in interest in the self-employed worker is often explained by the rise of self-employment in Europe. Data shows, however, that in Europe the share of total employment that is self-employment has been relatively stable for the past decade in the EU-28; at least at the aggregated level. However, the composition of the group seems to be fundamentally changing, for instance, in terms of growth in the service sector and decline in the agricultural sector and an increase in the proportion of the self-employed without employees and a decrease of the self-employed with employees

(Williams and Lapeyre, 2017; Eurofound, 2017; see also Chapter 2 of this volume). It is especially the group of self-employed without employees that shows more and more commonalities with employees, breaking down the traditional divide between employees and self-employed (Barnard, 2012). This raises the question of whether or not this sharp distinction is still viable and whether the large difference in social protection is still justified. Current developments show also that the EU institutions have an increased awareness of the position of the self-employed workers, especially for the *dependent* self-employed worker or *false* self-employed.

EU CONCEPT OF WORKER, SELF-EMPLOYED, DEPENDENT SELF-EMPLOYED AND FALSE SELF-EMPLOYED

EU legislation does not define worker or 'self-employed' although both terms are used in the Treaty on the Functioning of the EU (TFEU) and in secondary EU legislation (regulations and directives). The terms 'dependent self-employed' or 'false self-employed' are also used in literature and sometimes even by the EU Court of Justice (ECJ) (see below).

Worker

The notion of worker is referred to in two ways. First of all, the ECJ has developed in various cases a definition of the concept of worker in Article 45 TFEU. Article 45 stipulates the right to free movement of workers, one of the fundamental freedoms of the EU. The definition by the ECJ is an autonomous definition, which means that it is irrelevant how individual member states have defined worker or employee. The term 'worker' in Article 45 TFEU has a Community meaning: a worker is any person who pursues activities which are real and genuine, to the exclusion of activities on such a small scale as to be regarded as purely marginal or ancillary. The essential feature of an employment relationship is that for a certain period of time a person performs services for and under the direction or another person in return for which he receives remuneration (ECJ case 66/85 *Lawrie-Blum* [1986] and case 53/81 *Levin* [1982], amongst others).

Second, the personal scope of social policy regulations and directives very often refers to the member state's definition of 'employee' or 'worker'. That is, those who are protected by employment law in the national member state, falls under the scope of the relevant regulation or directive. However, in order to ensure the *effet utile* of the EU legislation, member states are not fully free to decide through their own definitions what EU legislation is applicable and what isn't. There can be seen a tendency that when it comes to social policy legislation the scope is more and more tailored to the Lawrie-Blum definition of the Article 45 TFEU worker (e.g. ECJ case 428/09 *Union Syndicals Solidaries Isère* [2010])

Self-employed

The term is used in the TFEU, for example, Article 49 regarding the freedom of establishment and Article 53 regarding the recognition of diplomas. Secondary EU regulation also contains the term 'self-employed'. We can find a similar definition structure as for workers. In Article 49 TFEU the ECJ explained that the self-employed work outside a relationship of subordination, they bear the risk for the success or failure of their employment and they are paid directly and in full (ECJ case 268/99 *Jany* [2001]). Furthermore, the self-employed can conduct activities of an industrial or commercial character, activities of craftsmen, or activities of the professions of a member state (ECJ case 257/99 *Barkoci and Malik* [2001]).

The term self-employed is also used in secondary EU law, reference can be made to the Citizen's Rights Directive (2004/38) and the Directive on the equal treatment of the self-employed (2010/41). In the secondary EU legislation often reference is made to national law for a definition of self-employment. See for instance Article 2 of Directive 2010/41: 'all persons pursuing a gainful activity for their own account, under the conditions laid down by national law. All member states have different ways of defining the self-employed and different ways of regulating their position. A 2017 study on national policies of 33 European countries shows that not every jurisdiction provides for a definition and if it does, it often concerns various definitions in labour law, tax law, civil law and social security law (Spasova et al., 2017). In the *Allonby* case, the ECJ stipulated that formal classification of a self-employed person under national law did not exclude the possibility that a person had to be classified as a worker within the meaning of Article 157 (1) TFEU (equal pay for male and female workers). This could be the case if the independence is merely notional, thereby disguising an employment relationship in the sense of Article 157 TFEU (ECJ Case 256/01 *Allonby* [2004]).

In short: whether social protection applies or not is a matter of classification and that classification is not a clear cut exercise. EU law refers to both national law and to autonomous concepts of worker and self-employed, piercing the veil by taking the reality of the case into account and not only looking at wording or labels.

False Self-employment/Dependent Self-employment

In the *FNV Kiem* case, the ECJ has introduced the term 'false self-employed'. The case revolves around the substitutes for musicians in orchestras. They are classified as independent service providers, but nevertheless in a collective labour agreement a minimum fee is agreed upon. This is allowed for employees, but not for the self-employed from a competition law perspective. The Court considers that this is different if the service providers are in fact 'false self-employed', that is to say, service providers in a situation comparable to that of employees (ECJ Case 413/13, *FNV Kiem* [2014]). This is a somewhat confusing consideration. It seems that, even if there is no misclassification, there is a category of self-employed who are comparable to employees. Under certain circumstances apparently these 'false self-employed' can make use of the right to conclude collective agreements as if they were employees. See Barenberg and Grosheide (2016) for an extensive analysis of this decision.

EU LEGISLATION PROVIDING SOCIAL PROTECTION FOR THE SELF-EMPLOYED

Leaving aside the definition issues and the blurring boundaries between employees and self-employed, a number of EU social policy regulations deal with the self-employed, albeit scarcely. Below these regulations are summarized, dividing social policy in to four topics: working conditions, social security, health and safety and equal treatment.

Working Conditions

The following directives have been analyzed:

- Directive 91/533/EEC (Written statement directive on the employer's obligation to inform employees of the conditions applicable to the contract or employment relationship),
- Directive 2003/88/EC (concerning certain aspects of the organization of Working Time) and
- Directive Council 99/70/EC (Fixed-term work).

None of these directives refer to the self-employed. However, the Commission proposed in December 2017 to replace the Written Statement directive. In the proposal, the self-employed are granted some rights, see below under recent developments.

Social Security

With respect to social security, the EU legislation coordinates the national systems of social security to support the free movement of workers. It is important to realize that this regulation only coordinates and does not establish a standard or norms. This is a difference with the other fields of social policy where EU legislation does establish standards.

The relevant regulation is Regulation 883/2004. This regulation is based on the following four principles:

- EU citizens are covered by the legislation of one country at a time and the decision of which legislation applies is taken by social security authorities.
- Principles of equal treatment and non-discrimination apply and a person moving to another member state has the same rights and obligations as the nationals of the country.
- There is an aggregation of periods as when claiming a benefit, the previous periods of insurance, work or residence in other countries are taken into account if necessary.
- Benefits are exportable and EU citizens are entitled to receive cash benefits from one country while living in another under certain conditions.

Regulation 883/2004 has a broad scope and applies to all member state citizens including workers and the self-employed.

Health and Safety

In accordance with Article 153 TFEU, the EU is responsible for supporting and complementing the activities of the member states with regard to the improvement of the working environment to protect workers' health and safety. In pursuance of this goal, the European Framework Directive 89/391/EEC, sets out the general framework for health and safety at work. The scope of the directive is broad and, pertaining to ECJ case law, coincides largely with the scope of Article 45 TFEU (ECJ case 428/09, *Union Syndicals Solidaries Isère* [2010]). The directive also requires the employer to take appropriate measures so that employers of workers from any outside undertakings and/or establishments engaged in work in his undertaking and/or establishment receive, in accordance with national laws and/or practices, adequate information concerning:

- The safety and health risks and protective and preventive measures and activities in respect of both the undertaking and/or establishment in general and each type of workstation and/or job.
- The measures on first aid, fire-fighting and evacuation of workers, serious and imminent danger.

This directly concerns the self-employed as this means that in the case where a self-employed person works in the same work space as other workers, the self-employed must at least dispose of the same information of risks and benefit from the same protective and preventive measures established by the national law.

Equal Treatment

The Directive on the equal treatment of the self-employed (2010/41) prohibits discrimination on the basis of sex. Article 2 proclaims that equal treatment means that there shall be no discrimination whatsoever, for instance, in relation to the establishment, equipment or extension of a business or the launching or extension of any other form of self-employment. An important step towards social protection of the self-employed can be found in Article 8: the member states must take the necessary measures to ensure that female self-employed workers 'may in accordance with national law, be granted a sufficient maternity allowance enabling interruptions in their occupational activity owing to pregnancy or motherhood for at least 14 weeks'. It is up to the member states to decide whether the maternity allowance is granted on a mandatory or voluntary basis. Although this rather noncommittal provision can be seen as social protection for the self-employed, an evaluation has showed that the directive was unsuccessful in delivering improved maternity and social benefits to the self-employed (Barnard and Blackham, 2015).

CURRENT DEVELOPMENTS

European Commission

In November 2017, President Juncker of the EU proclaimed the European Pillar of Social Rights. The Pillar builds upon 20 principles of which principle 12 is important: 'Regardless of the type and duration of their employment relationship, workers, and, under comparable conditions, the self-employed, have the right to adequate social protection.'

On 21 December 2017 the European Commission submitted a proposal for a directive of the European Parliament and of the Council on transparent and predictable working conditions in the European Union. The proposal updates and replaces Directive 91/533/EEC (the Written Statement Directive which gives employees the right to be notified in writing of the essential aspects of their contract or employment relationship). The interesting part is that the scope is extended to the Article 45 TFEU definition. This means that although the directive is still targeting the employee and not the self-employed, there might be room for the ECJ to extend the scope.

The European Commission, on 13 March 2018, proposed a Council Recommendation on access to social protection for workers and the self-employed (COM(2018) 132 final) as a follow up to the aforementioned principle 12 of the European Pillar of Social Rights. The recommendation is applicable to workers and the self-employed on the issues of:

a)   unemployment benefits;
b)   sickness and health care benefits;
c)   maternity and equivalent paternity benefits;
d)   invalidity benefits;
e)   old-age benefits;
f)   benefits in respect of accidents at work and occupational diseases.

The recommendation aims to establish minimum standards in the field of social protection of workers and the self-employed. Social protection can be provided through a combination of schemes, including public, occupational and private schemes and can involve contributions, in accordance with the fundamental principles of national social protection systems. Member states are competent to define the level of contributions and decide which combination of schemes is appropriate. The proposal is still pending.

FINAL REMARKS

As already pointed out in the introduction, the position of the self-employed from an EU legal perspective is rather ambiguous. On the one hand, self-employed workers are considered as entrepreneurs, on the other hand they are sometimes very dependent and not fully meeting the EU 'definition' of self-employed. From a realistic point of view there is no reason to deal with the self-employed differently from a social protection point of view, although they would not meet the criteria of being a worker. However, the current EU classification system, and most legal systems, make a very binary clear cut between 'workers' (in the EU perspective) and the self-employed. Considering the disparities between national member state definitions of self-employment and the ongoing discussions on the future of work, the step of the European Commission in its recent recommendation is a bold move towards a more unified appreciation of 'labour as a production factor'.

A complicating factor is the role of competition law when it comes to 'dependent self-employed' and their possibilities to negotiate on working conditions. As long as the self-employed are considered a 'business' or an 'enterprise', they face competition law: agreements on minimum fees are not accepted by competition law. This puts the dependent self-employed in a difficult position.

Whether or not this legal context encourages the self-employed or drives them to employment is a matter of empirical evidence.

REFERENCES

Barenberg, M. and Grosheide, E.F. (2016). Minimum fees for the self-employed: a European response to the Uber-ized economy. *Columbia Journal of European Law*, 22, 193–236.

Barnard, C. (2012). *EU Employment Law*. Oxford: Oxford University Press.

Barnard C. and Blackham A. (2015). *The implementation of Directive 2010/41 on the application of the principle of equal treatment between men and women engaged in an activity in a self-employed capacity, report of the European network of legal experts in the field of gender equality*, commissioned by the Directorate-General Justice of the European Commission.

Eichhorst, W. et al. (2013). *Social protection rights of economically dependent self-employed workers*. Brussels: European Union.

Eurofound (2017). *Exploring self-employment in the European Union*. Luxembourg: Publications office of the European Union.

Spasova S., Bouget D., Ghailani, D. and Vanhercke, B. (2017). *Access to social protection for people working on non-standard contracts and as self-employed in Europe. A study of national policies. European Social Policy Network (ESPN)*. Brussels: European Commission.

Torrini, R. (2005). Cross-country differences in self-employment rates: the role of institutions. *Labour Economics*, 12(5), 661–83.

Williams, C.C. and Lapeyre, F. (2017). *Dependent self-employment: trends, challenges and policy responses in the EU*. International Labour Organization.

4. Self-employment, pensions and the risk of poverty in old age

Uwe Fachinger

BACKGROUND

It is a common understanding in the literature that many self-employed people do appreciate their professional life (Blanchflower and Oswald, 1998; Hundley, 2001; Benz and Frey, 2004; Blanchflower, 2004; Benz and Frey, 2008; Binder and Coad, 2016; Manyika et al., 2016; see for a critical view Hanglberger and Merz, 2011). Yet, some of them feel pushed into self-employment and find it hard to make a proper living, in particular those without personnel (Fachinger 2016; Burmester 2017; Fachinger and Frankus, 2017). Especially those who find it hard to earn a proper living are often not able to finance insurances against social risks such as sickness, disability due to a work accident and/or occupational diseases, invalidity or longevity, that is, the risk of running out of money due to increasing life expectancy. Policy debates about entrepreneurship and fostering self-employment pay little attention to the potential problems which arise from a lack of social security. In fact, a large number of self-employed people have to live with unsteady working careers and high income mobility, which make them vulnerable with regard to social risks.

The occurrence of a social risk during working life leads inter alia to a break of employment, loss of income, and in some cases (such as illness or disability) to additional financial burdens. In several European countries, the self-employed are free to choose whether to insure themselves against various social risks or not and/or they can decide about the extent of the protection. However, some social risks are partially covered by social security systems whereas others, for example, lack of orders, shortfall in payment, and bankruptcy are not covered at all by any such system. To cope with such a situation, to maintain one's living standard and to avoid social exclusion, one option is to acquire ancillary insurance in addition to the country-specific general protection scheme.

In general, social security systems are very heterogeneously constructed, with different goals – maintaining one's living standard or avoiding poverty and social exclusion – and measures (Directorate-General for Employment, 2014; Directorate-General for Employment, 2017). Therefore, when analysing different insurance schemes to cover social risks for self-employed people, one has to consider the specific design of the system, the purpose why the system has been established and its specific arrangements. Against this background, this chapter is centred around the protection against the risk of poverty due to longevity. One reason to focus on longevity is that those security systems have the largest share of expenses for social security. For example, the expenditures of the statutory old age pension system in Germany comprise 30.8 per cent of the entire social budget (Bundesministerium für Arbeit und Soziales 2017, p. T3). Another reason is that on the micro level, self-employed people have to save a large amount of income during their working life if they want to maintain their living standard during retirement.

In this chapter, the two sides of the coin of 'social security' will be discussed: the financing of the systems and the benefits. Regarding financing, the aspects of willingness and ability so save are problematised. Regardless of the specific structure of the social security system – whether it is private or public or whether the system is pay-as-you-go or capital funded – people have to save money if they want to be insured against the risk of longevity. With respect to the phase of accumulation of entitlements, the risk of poverty entails the problems of financing an adequate pension. The different aspects of the arrangement of the social security system like assessment basis, contributions and tariff rates, guarantee of regularly recurring payments, and problems of premium adjustments will be discussed in more detail.

Once someone is retired, difficulties lie in guaranteeing the stability and security of pensions to maintain one's living standard. Therefore, concerning the pensions the focus will lie on aspects of the replacement rate or the equivalence of pensions, on the security of the entitlements and on adjustments of pensions during retirement. All three issues pose special problems as they can cause an increase of inequality in later life which goes hand in hand with an increased risk of becoming poor. The absence of adjustment to inflation or development of average income will counteract the goal of maintaining one's living standard and gradually increases the risk of poverty.

GENERAL ASPECTS OF SAVING FOR OLD AGE PROVISION

To reduce the risk of poverty in old age, self-employed people have to save, as they cannot rely on earned income for all of their life. Though most of them can decide about when to retire by themselves, due to the process of ageing their physical and cognitive abilities will diminish and they ultimately will have to give up their business. Therefore, after retiring from work earned income has to be substituted by other means. In general, such income sources will be generated by saving during working life.

To shed some light on savings for old age provision and the risk of poverty, two very important aspects have to be considered. The saving behaviour for old age provision encompasses the ability to save and the willingness to save (Katona, 1951; Venti and Wise, 1998; Berverly and Sherraden, 1999, p. 459 ff.; Traut-Mattausch and Jonas, 2011; Nyhus, 2017).

The *ability to save* foremost requires an appropriate income. In case of low income, the ability to save will also be low. Even with a high savings rate, the absolute amount of savings will be too low to accumulate enough wealth or entitlements to finance a decent living in old age. However, it has to be taken into account that not one single income source is relevant – for example, earnings out of self-employment – as the ability to save depends not only on the individual, but on the household income, which may differ substantially (Fachinger and Frankus, 2017, p. 251 ff.). Therefore, when analysing the ability to save, the household context has to be taken into account.

Furthermore, the ability to save is not only determined by the financial situation of private households, but relies also on the conditions of the financial or capital markets. Within insurance markets for example, typically risk selections take place. Therefore, not only the prices or premiums differ between the insurance companies and between the various risk groups, but also it is possible that for certain people no insurance at all is available.

The *willingness to save* depends inter alia on the awareness of the necessity of old age provision. People may be myopic, not thinking in time categories of decades (Thaler and Benartzi, 2004; Ratner et al., 2008; Andersen and Bhattacharya, 2011). Solving everyday problems may seem more important. Thinking of retirement that lies twenty or even thirty years in the future, seems not to be an urgent problem. Therefore, especially younger people may not be aware of the relevance of savings for old age. Instead, other aspects within a short time perspective seem to be more important such as paying for education, starting a family or setting up a house. Furthermore, at a younger age, one may underestimate the effects of not saving and may believe that it is possible to make up for it later in life. In this context two aspects are discussed in the literature: underestimation of future needs and a high preference for the present. With a given willingness to save money both effects would reduce the amount of savings for old age ceteris paribus.

Furthermore, knowledge about the social security system is necessary and will influence the willingness to save (Berverly and Sherraden 1999, p. 463 ff.; Sherraden et al., 2003). An adequate old age provision strategy can only be created on the basis of profound knowledge about the institutional and legal regulations. So for the self-employed it is necessary to know whether being insured in the statutory pension scheme is mandatory or not. If the insurance is mandatory, self-employed people can rely on the statutory old age pension system accumulating entitlements. In such cases, only additional savings could be necessary depending on the desired level of living in old age. Otherwise people have to plan their old age provision by themselves, sometimes with the aid of specialised advisers. In both cases specific knowledge about how to do it is required – often called financial literacy (Lusardi and Mitchell, 2011; Bongini et al., 2015; Brounen et al., 2016) – and this knowledge will impact the willingness to save. People choose a specific portfolio of old age provision concerning their anticipated needs and on the basis of their knowledge about the possibilities of investment forms.

Additionally, the problem of miscalculation of the performance of the savings portfolio exists. For the self-employed it is not possible to adapt the portfolio to the future development and even the best experts are sometimes wrong, which is especially true for old age provision with respect to the distant future. However, it may be possible to adjust to the current and recent situation, but those adjustments will go hand in hand with inter alia transaction costs and therefore a loss of income and/or wealth.

Moreover, trust in the reliability of the chosen product and/or institution is important. The assumptions of long-term development are a matter of trust assuming that the future will develop in the same positive or negative way as the past. Events like crashes of financial markets, economic downturns, high inflation or wars will reduce trust and therefore the willingness to save.

Overall, if the ability to save is low – especially in case of low income – even a high degree of willingness to save will not lead to enough accumulated wealth and will not prevent self-employed people from low entitlements to old age provision.

Due to the aforementioned aspects, old age provision is mandatory for most employees in almost all developed economies. It is seen as a prophylactic measure to avoid old age poverty and to reduce social costs, for example social assistance, because of insufficient saving. Contrary to that, self-employed people are mostly not covered by statutory pensions schemes (European Commission, 2014; Spasova et al., 2017) but rely on social assistance if the individual efforts for building up adequate retirement entitlements fail (Fachinger and Frankus, 2015; Fachinger and

Frankus, 2017). However, to get an idea of the risk of poverty in old age, one has to take a look at the influencing factors.

In general, factors determining the material situation in old age can be divided into factors that can be influenced partly by the individuals themselves and those factors which are independent of individual actions or behaviour. In the following, some of the main factors which determine the material situation in old age are elaborated. Especially contributions and tariff rates, the guarantee of regularly recurring payments, assessment basis, and problems of premium adjustments will be discussed in more detail.

RISK OF POVERTY IN OLD AGE: SPECIAL ASPECTS

Personal Determinants

The accumulation of entitlements depends on two factors:

a) the length of time, and
b) either on the amount of payments or premiums[1] or in earnings related pension systems on the height of the assessment basis over this time span.

Normally self-employed people are not mandatorily insured in statutory old age pension systems (European Commission, 2014; Spasova et al., 2017). Therefore, they have to decide when to start saving for old age pensions and to what extent. Both factors – duration and amount of savings – generally depend on individual decisions and any contributions have to be paid out of the disposable income.

If the disposable income is low, the ability to save is low even if the willingness to save is high. This holds true especially when the contributions are flat rated as is the case in capital funded private insurance systems with defined contributions. The financial burden of flat rate payments increases disproportionally the lower the income gets, as shown in Figure 4.1.

Paying contributions may decrease the disposable income below the social minimum existence level. This will increase the current risk of poverty and additionally could result in higher risk of poverty in old age because people may decide not to save for old age provision at all.

To avoid such problems, the contributions could be calculated as a percentage of the disposable income. This would keep the contributions in a constant relationship to the disposable income and would most likely not overtax people. However, in the case of low income, the absolute amount

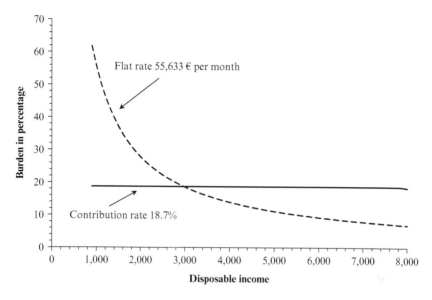

Financial burden of flat rate contributions

Note: * The numbers refer to the German situation as an example.

Source: Own calculations.

Figure 4.1   Financial burden of flat rate contributions,* in percentage

of savings would also be low as shown in Figure 4.2. This would lead to low pensions due to low entitlements and would increase the risk of poverty in old age. From an individual point of view, saving does not make a lot of sense in such a case when it can be foreseen that the pensions are below the minimum existence level and people will be in need of social assistance during retirement anyway. As a consequence, people may not save for old age at all, which increases the risk of becoming poor in old age even more.

Another problem results from the potentially high mobility and insecurity of income out of self-employment. This makes it difficult for self-employed people to guarantee regularly recurring payments.

High income mobility is characterised by large up- and downturns of income which occur frequently. In phases of low or even with no income, it may be very difficult or actually impossible to keep up the savings for an old age pension. The consequences of such circumstances depend on the special form of the contracts. In cases of life insurance the contributions could be waived or the insured could convert a life policy into a paid-up policy. Cancellation of contributions or even the termination of contracts may occur more often in such cases. Nonetheless, whatever people do may

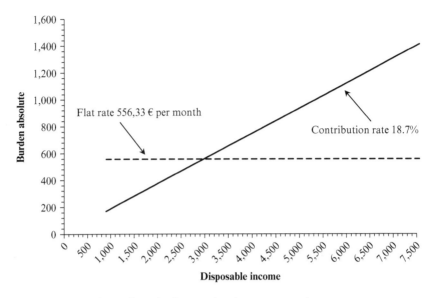

Note: * The numbers refer to the German situation as an example.

Source: Own calculations.

Figure 4.2   Financial burden of flat rate contributions,* absolute

lead to lower entitlements in old age and therefore increases the risk of poverty.

Additionally, the uncertainty about the income situation even in the near future will influence the saving decision. The contractual agreement on a flat rate payment means that the same amount of income has to be payed continually over a long period of time. As income insecurity makes it problematic to oversee future income developments, it makes people hesitant to commit themselves to paying a specific amount over a larger time span, especially when it is difficult or costly to adjust premiums in a short time. Therefore, there is a high probability that self-employed people may decide not to take up any form of old age provision.

Trying to solve these problems, especially the low willingness to save, by introducing a mandatory system or integrating the self-employed into an existing statutory old age pension system, will cause many problems. One of the issues that have to be addressed is the assessment basis for paying contributions. This could be net or gross earnings. Net earnings are problematic to determine. Especially for self-employed people, many country-specific tax regulations exist which reduce the taxable income and therefore the assessment basis. This is problematic in earnings-related pension systems, where this leads to low entitlements and as a result to higher poverty risk in old age. Another problem is that the total amount of net earnings is known only after taxation. For practical reasons it could therefore be more reasonable to use gross earnings as the assessment basis.

Beside those individual determinants, the risk of poverty in old age depends on factors, which cannot be influenced by individuals, that is, non-personal determinants. The institutional and legal framework as well as the development of the capital market can by no means be influenced by individual behaviour. It is thought that people will adjust their old age provision to changes of these non-personal determinants.

Non-personal Determinants

The institutional and legal framework is, in most analyses, seen as constant over time. However, in most cases this is not true. Over the last decades, adjustments were made referring to the demographic changes, particularly the ageing of societies. The main goals of the measures taken were to reduce the financial burden – especially of the state and enterprises – and to reach a more sustainable way of financing old age pension systems. However, in cases where the benefit level of pension schemes was reduced, the risk of poverty in old age will increase.

The pension level before taxation of the statutory old age pension system in Germany (GRV), for example, will decrease over the next decades, starting in 2009, as is shown in Figure 4.3. The pension level before taxation is defined as the relation of the so-called standard pension and the gross average income of all dependent workers per year ('durchschnittliches Jahresarbeitsentgelt', Deutsche Rentenversicherung Bund 2017, S. 315). The standard pension is calculated by multiplying the current pension value (Aktueller Rentenwert, ARW) by 45, as the standard pension is seen as a benchmark with people working for 45 years and earning in each year a gross average income. For example, in 2017 the ARW for West Germany is 31.03 € which gives a standard gross pension of 1,396.35 € per month. As the average income in 2017 for West Germany is 37,103 €, the actual gross pension level in 2017 is 45.16.

Subtracting the contributions to the statutory health and long-term care insurance from the standard pension yields the so-called disposable standard pension. Subtracting the contributions to the social security systems from the gross average income results in the disposable gross income.[2] Dividing the disposable standard pension by the disposable gross income results in the pension level before taxation, which is shown in Figure 4.3.

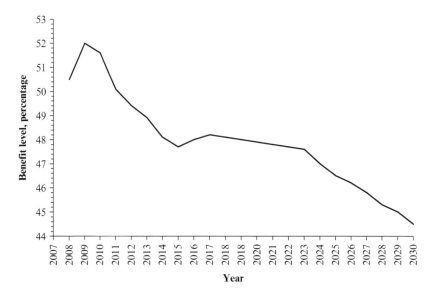

Source: Author's own based on Bundesministerium für Arbeit und Soziales (2016), p. 39.

Figure 4.3   Pension level before taxation in percentage, Germany

The pension level before taxation is often interpreted as the indicator of the efficiency of the GRV.

Figure 4.3 reveals the potential overall reduction of pensions. This development will reduce not only the pensions of retirees but also the value or purchasing power of entitlements of people who are still working. For people near retirement age or already retired there is no possibility to counteract these reductions.

Self-employed people who are mandatorily or voluntarily insured in the GRV organised their old age provision due to the regulations which were in place at the time of the decision. People may address such changes by modifying their additional measures for old age pension provisions. But such adjustments will be costly or even not possible from an individual point of view, depending on the specific characteristics of their contracts, especially in advanced age. Additionally, the inner logic or construction logic of the capital funded systems regarding, for example, the calculation of pensions is not compatible with the calculation of pensions out of the GRV. Therefore, compensation by other old age pension systems is only possible to a very limited extent, if at all. Consequently, the risk of becoming poor in old age increases through the reduction of the pension level of the statutory pension scheme.

Another aspect is the development of capital markets which is especially relevant for capital funded old age pension systems. Even highly experienced experts are not fully able to assess the future development of these markets always adequately – as can be seen regarding the financial crises in recent times. An example is the depreciation of the existing capital stock due to the event on 11 September 2001, the so-called dot.com crisis, or the crisis in 2008 (Meyer, 2015, p. 190), with a loss in value of shares of more than 49 per cent (Börsch-Supan et al., 2010, p. 386; see Organisation for Economic Co-Operation and Development (OECD), 2009, p. 32 ff., regarding the loss of pension funds). All problems concerning the instability of capital markets and the insecurity of the entitlements increase the risk of old age poverty for self-employed people, as old age provisions of large parts of this group are based on capital funded systems.

A third aspect which has to be considered is adjustments of the contributions. Whereas in pay-as-you-go financed systems, the contribution rate may change over time, in theoretical or conceptual analysis, contributions are mostly seen as constant over time, especially in capital funded systems, which is not always the case. For example, in defined benefit systems, the rise in life expectancy may lead to an increase in contributions to adjust for a longer period of pension payments.

As is shown in Figure 4.4 exemplarily for self-employed people, who are mandatorily insured in the old age statutory pension system in Germany,

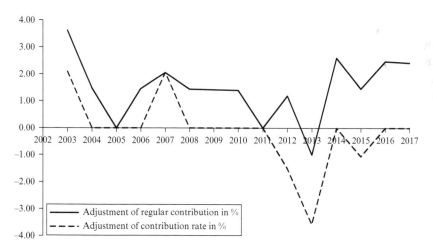

Source: Own calculations on the basis of Deutsche Rentenversicherung Bund (2017), pp. 262, 266.

Figure 4.4   Adjustment of payments in percentage

the contributions are not stable over time. The solid line reflects the adjustments of regular contributions[3] since 2003. The dotted line describes the changes of the earnings-related contribution rate. Over the time span of 16 years, the regular contribution, which is not income-related, increases by 24.2 per cent, whereas the contribution rate for income related contributions decreases by 2.1 per cent.

To deal with such contribution adjustments, income and substitution effects will occur, whereby the net effect is unclear. Nevertheless, the disposable income would also have to increase otherwise the current living standard cannot be contained. Where this may be possible for the changes of income-related contribution rates, the increase of the regular contribution of around 24.2 per cent is a general problem to overcome particularly for self-employed people with low income.

Overall, not only the income out of self-employment could be instable over time but also the contributions either in absolute or in relative terms. Therefore, even if self-employed people have a continuous income stream, the variation of contributions can lead to an increase of the financial burden, which may overload the financial capacities. As a consequence, the reaction could be the same as in the case of high income mobility.

A fourth factor which cannot be influenced by individuals themselves is the adjustment of pensions during retirement. Inflation or a general increase in income leads to a decline of the living standard either in absolute terms regarding a decrease in the purchasing power or in relative terms concerning the reduction of the income position. Therefore, adjustments are important as otherwise the standard of living cannot be maintained.

In statutory old age pension systems, adjustments take place with respect to price or income indexation (Kröger, 2011, p. 380; Organisation for Economic Co-Operation and Development (OECD), 2015, p. 129; Directorate-General for Employment, 2017). If self-employed people are not or only partially insured in such systems, they have to rely on the capital funded private old age pension systems. Such systems have no inherent mechanism for adjustments of pensions with respect to inflation or to the development of average income (Diamond, 1977, p. 280). In capital funded old age pension systems, the pensions depend on the development of the capital market, the success of the enterprise, for example insurer or bank, the administration and marketing costs, and so on. There is no connection between earned income and the pensions but between the (sum of) contributions and the accumulated entitlements. How those entitlements will be annualised to replace the earned income is determined contractually and depends not on inflation rate or income development. Regarding the annualisation of accumulated entitlements, it is impossible to anticipate the future development of prices or average income over a long time period.

Overall the rates of return are uncertain and the security of the entitlements is not given (Diamond, 1977, p. 279),[4] which leads to the persistent risk of poverty in old age. This leads, according to Bodie (2008) to the conclusion ". . . that capital funded old age pension system should carry a guarantee of a minimum level of income, wealth, or rate of return provided by the firm managing the assets . . ." (Bodie, 2008, p. 253). Although such a guarantee would reduce the risk of poverty in old age, with such regulations it is not possible to fully avoid poverty in old age even when people have adequately saved due to the missing adjustment with respect to inherent dynamics of the economic process, for example inflation or increase of wealth.

SUMMARY

The risk of poverty in old age entails the problems of financing and receiving an adequate pension. Some of the risk is determined by factors which can be affected by individuals and by factors which cannot be influenced by individual actions or behaviour. The first group of factors have to be seen in the context of the ability and willingness to save. Regarding the ability to save among other things, the high instability of income out of self-employment, the tariff rate, and the guarantee of regularly recurring payments pose problems for adequate saving. The willingness to save is a more complex matter. Starting with the individual time preference up to the point of trust in the capital market mechanism, all these factors may negatively affect the willingness to save and therefore increase the risk of poverty in old age.

The second group refers mainly to the institutional and legal framework and to the development of capital markets. Here the stability and security of the entitlements, the replacement rate, and the adjustment of pensions during retirement to maintain one's living standard poses special problems to avoid poverty in old age.

The discussion focuses on theoretic-conceptual aspects of pensions and the risk of poverty in old age of self-employed people. However, regarding self-employed people's knowledge about social security, currently only limited information is available and reliable data are lacking (Fachinger and Frankus, 2015; Fachinger and Frankus, 2017). Therefore, the state of knowledge on the social security provisions which self-employed people acquire in order to insure themselves against social risks, especially old age poverty, is far from satisfying. However, even with the limited information, the situation is not encouraging. Given the increasing extent of self-employment, insufficient social protection within this group inevitably leads to a rise in the number of people exposed to social risks. This will result in increasing poverty and a rise in the number of people suffering from social exclusion. Alongside the difficulties posed for social policy, these factors will contradict social policy aims in Europe and counteract the goal of the European Commission and of most member states to foster self-employment (Organisation for Economic Co-operation and Development (OECD) 2017; Organisation for Economic Co-operation and Development (OECD) and European Union, 2017).

NOTES

1. In what follows the generic term contributions is used.
2. The tax is not subtracted.
3. Lump sum payment to the GRV, which is not income related ('Regelbeitrag').
4. However, there may exist country-specific regulations with respect to the pensions like the Pension Benefit Guaranty Corporation (PBGC) in the US, which was created on the basis of the Employee Retirement Income Security Act of 1974, or the Pensions-Sicherungs-Verein on the basis of § 14 'Gesetz zur Verbesserung der betrieblichen Altersversorgung' (BetrAVG) for Germany.

REFERENCES

Andersen, T.M. and Bhattacharya, J. (2011). On Myopia as Rationale for Social Security. *Economic Theory*, 47(1), 135–58.

Benz, M. and Frey, B.S. (2004). Being Independent Raises Happiness at Work. *Swedish Economic Policy Review*, 11(2), 95–134.

Benz, M. and Frey, B.S. (2008). Being Independent Is a Great Thing: Subjective Evaluations of Self-Employment and Hierarchy. *Economica*, 75(298), 362–83.

Berverly, S.G. and Sherraden, M. (1999). Institutional Determinants of Saving: Implications for Low-Income Households and Public Policy. *Journal of Socio-Economics*, 28(4), 457–73.

Binder, M. and Coad, A. (2016). How Satisfied Are the Self-Employed? A Life Domain View. *Journal of Happiness Studies*, 17(4), 1409–33.

Blanchflower, D.G. (2004). Self-Employment: More May Not Be Better. *NBER Working Paper Series*, 10286, National Bureau of Economic Research, Cambridge, MA.

Blanchflower, D.G. and Oswald, A.J. (1998). What Makes an Entrepreneur? *Journal of Labor Economics*, 16(1), 26–60.

Bodie, Z. (2008). Pension Guarantees, Capital Adequacy and International Risk Sharing. In: Broeders, D., Eiffinger, S. and Houben, A. (eds), *Frontiers in Pension Finance*. Cheltenham, UK and Northampton, MA, USA: Edward Elgar Publishing, pp. 243–54.

Bongini, P., Colombo, L. and Iwanicz-Drozdowska, M. (2015). Financial Literacy: Where Do We Stand? *Journal of Financial Management, Markets and Institutions*, 3(1), 3–12.

Börsch-Supan, A., Gasche, M. and Ziegelmeyer, M. (2010). Auswirkungen Der Finanzkrise Auf Die Private Altersvorsorge. *Perspektiven der Wirtschaftspolitik*, 11(4), 383–406.

Brounen, D., Koedijk, K.G. and Pownall, R.A.J. (2016). Household Financial Planning and Savings Behavior. *Journal of International Money and Finance*, 69, 95–107.

Bundesministerium für Arbeit und Soziales (2016). *Bericht Der Bundesregierung Über Die Gesetzliche Rentenversicherung, Insbesondere Über Die Entwicklung Der Einnahmen Und Ausgaben, Der Nachhaltigkeitsrücklage Sowie Des Jeweils Erforderlichen Beitragssatzes in Den Künftigen 15 Kalenderjahren Gemäß § 154 Sgb Vi (Rentenversicherungsbericht 2016)*. Berlin: Rentenversicherungsbericht.

Bundesministerium für Arbeit und Soziales (2017). *Sozialbericht 2017*. Berlin: Sozialbericht Bundesministerium für Arbeit und Soziales.

Burmester, I. (2017). *Einkommenssituation Selbständiger in Der Europäischen Union*. Baden-Baden: Nomos.

Deutsche Rentenversicherung Bund (ed.) (2017). *Rentenversicherung in Zeitreihen. Oktober 2017*. Berlin: Deutsche Rentenversicherung Bund.

Diamond, P.A. (1977). A Framework for Social Security Analysis. *Journal of Public Economics*, 8(3), 275–98.

Directorate-General for Employment, S.A.a.I. (2014). *Social Protection in the Member States of the European Union, of the European Economic Area and in Switzerland. Social Protection of the Self-Employed. Situation on 1 January 2014*. MISSOC. Mutual Information System on Social Protection European Commission. Brussels: Directorate-General for Employment, Social Affairs and Inclusion, Unit D/3.

Directorate-General for Employment, S.A.a.I. (2017). *Comparative Tables on Social Protection – Results. 1. January 2017*. MISSOC – Mutual Information System on Social Protection European Commission. Brussels: Directorate-General for Employment, Social Affairs and Inclusion.

European Commission (2014). *Employment Policy Beyond the Crisis*. Social Europe guide European Commission, Brussels: Directorate-General for Employment, Social Affairs and Inclusion.

Fachinger, U. (2016). Self-Employment and the Distribution of Income – Increasing Divergence? *Discussion Paper*, 25/2016, Fachgebiet Ökonomie und Demographischer Wandel. Vechta: Institut für Gerontologie.

Fachinger, U. and Frankus, A. (2015). Freelancers, Self-Employment and the Insurance against Social Risks. *International Review of Entrepreneurship*, 13(2), 117–28.

Fachinger, U. and Frankus, A. (2017). Self-Employment and Pensions – Is Old Age Poverty the Inevitable Dark Side of an Entrepreneurial Society? In: Bonnet, J., Dejardin, M. and De Lema, D.G.P. (eds), *Exploring the Entrepreneurial Society. Institutions, Behaviours and Outcomes*. Cheltenham, UK and Northampton, MA, USA: Edward Elgar Publishing, pp. 245–56.

Hanglberger, D. and Merz, J. (2011). Are Self-Employed Really Happier Than Employees? An Approach Modelling Adaptation and Anticipation Effects to Self-Employment and General Job Changes. *Discussion Paper*, 5629. Bonn: Institute for the Study of Labor.

Hundley, G. (2001). Why and When Are the Self-Employed More Satisfied with Their Work? *Industrial Relations: A Journal of Economy and Society*, 40(2), 293–316.

Katona, G. (1951). *Psychological Analysis of Economic Behavior*. New York: McGraw-Hill.

Kröger, K. (2011). Pension Adjustment and Its Problems. A Critical Overview of the Measures, Exemplified on the Basis of the German Pension Scheme. *International Journal of Behavioural and Healthcare Research*, 2(4), 375–94.

Lusardi, A. and Mitchell, O.S. (eds) (2011). *Financial Literacy. Implications for Retirement Security and the Financial Marketplace*. Oxford: Oxford University Press.

Manyika, J., Lund, S., Bughin, J., Robinson, K., Mischke, J. and Mahajan, D. (2016). *Independent Work: Choice, Necessity, and the Gig Economy*. San Francisco/ Washington/Brussels/Zurich: Highlights McKinsey Global Institute (MGI).

Meyer, T. (2015). Die Dritte Säule in Der Alterssicherung – Brauchen Wir Eine Neubewertung Nach Der Finanz- Und Wirtschaftskrise? Deutschland Im Europäischen Vergleich. *Sozialer Fortschritt*, 64(8), 189–95.

Nyhus, E.K. (2017). Saving Behaviour: Economic and Psychological Approaches. In: Ranyard, R. (ed.), *Economic Psychology*. Newark: John Wiley & Sons, pp. 206–21.

Organisation for Economic Co-Operation and Development (OECD) (2009). *Pensions at a Glance 2009. Retirement-Income Systems in OECD and G20 Countries*. Paris: Organisation for Economic Co-Operation and Development.

Organisation for Economic Co-Operation and Development OECD (2015). *Pensions at a Glance 2015. OECD and G20 Indicators*. Paris: Organisation for Economic Co-Operation and Development.

Organisation for Economic Co-operation and Development (OECD) (2017). *Financing SMES and Entrepreneurs 2017*. Paris: Financing SMEs and Entrepreneurs.

Organisation for Economic Co-operation and Development (OECD) and European Union (2017). *The Missing Entrepreneurs 2017: Policies for Inclusive Entrepreneurship*. Paris: Organisation for Economic Co-operation and Development, European Union.

Ratner, R.K., Soman, D., Zauberman, G., Ariely, D., Carmon, Z., Keller, P.A., Kim, B.K., Lin, F., Malkoc, S., Small, D.A. and Wertenbroch, K. (2008). How Behavioral Decision Research Can Enhance Consumer Welfare: From Freedom of Choice to Paternalistic Intervention. *Marketing Letters*, 19(3), 383–97.

Sherraden, M., Schreiner, M. and Beverly, S. (2003). Income, Institutions, and Saving Performance in Individual Development Accounts. *Economic Development Quarterly*, 17(1), 95–112.

Spasova, S., Bouget, D., Ghailani, D. and Vanhercke, B. (2017). *Access to Social Protection for People Working on Non-Standard Contracts and as Self-Employed in Europe. A Study of National Policies 2017*. Brussels: European Social Policy Network (ESPN).

Thaler, R.H. and Benartzi, S. (2004). Save more tomorrow™: Using behavioral economics to increase employee saving. *Journal of Political Economy*, 112(S1), S164–S187.

Traut-Mattausch, E. and Jonas, E. (2011). Why Do People Save? *Zeitschrift für Psychologie*, 219(4), 246–52.

Venti, S.F. and Wise, D.A. (1998). The Cause of Wealth Dispersion at Retirement: Choice or Chance? *The American Economic Review*, 88(2), 185–91.

PART II

Self-employment and precarious work in
Europe: empirical results

5. Self-employment: independent 'enterprise', or precarious low-skilled work? The case of the UK

Nigel Meager

INTRODUCTION

This chapter looks at the evolution of self-employment in the UK in recent decades, which encompass two periods (the 1980s and the post-2000 period) of remarkable growth in the numbers of self-employed.

Self-employment now accounts for more than 15 per cent of the employed workforce in the United Kingdom and, at the time of writing (mid-2018), is continuing to grow. In particular the rapid expansion of self-employment since 2000, during periods of both economic growth and recession, is historically unprecedented, and raises important questions about the role of this form of work in the modern labour market. Self-employment in the UK now affects not only larger numbers of workers, but includes different groups of workers and affects different occupations and sectors than was the case in previous decades. This has generated a debate in the economic and social research literature about the implications of these changes for the income levels and well-being of the workers affected, as well as the necessary legislative and institutional infrastructure which needs to be put in place as this form of work becomes a larger part of the labour market landscape. More recently the debate has been given further impetus by the emergence of apparently hybrid forms of work in the so-called 'gig' economy (freelance work facilitated through online platforms), which appear to share some characteristics with self-employment and others with employees, raising important questions about how such jobs should be classified and regulated. This debate shares some similarities with the previous debate about bogus self-employment in the construction and other sectors during the 1990s, which led to policy changes (discussed further below) aimed at discouraging such forms of work; however, the more recent debate about the gig economy and its relationship to self-employment has been more nuanced, with a growing recognition that some aspects of these developments are positive and provide flexible opportunities to people who wish to be able to work in this manner, with some recent studies suggesting relatively high levels of satisfaction with these forms of work (see for example Lepanjuuri et al., 2018; Broughton et al., 2018). The current emphasis of much of the policy debate now focuses on efforts to disentangle or 'segment' the self-employed population (Williams et al., 2017) to identify which groups of self-employed and types of self-employment are closer to bogus self-employment and thus require policy support to reduce their vulnerability or regulation to change their status from self-employed to employee or 'worker' (an intermediary status), without discouraging or inhibiting the growth of self-employment which offers higher quality economic opportunities. This debate has been a key contributory factor leading to the UK government commissioning the independent 'Taylor Review' (led by Matthew Taylor: BEIS, 2017), to which the government has subsequently responded (BEIS, 2018) with a number of policy and legislative proposals (yet to be implemented), including proposals to improve the clarity of employment status of employees, self-employed and workers in UK legislation.

This chapter reviews both the literature on these questions and the recent statistical evidence from the UK, drawing also on the author's recent work on the job quality of the self-employed,[1] to address the question of how far the recent trends in self-employment can be interpreted as a positive development for the UK economy, reinforcing entrepreneurship, flexibility and economic growth, and how far they have more negative implications reinforcing labour market inequalities and generating a new form of labour market disadvantage for certain segments of the 'new self-employed'.

THE DEVELOPMENT OF SELF-EMPLOYMENT IN THE UK SINCE 1980

As can be seen from Figure 5.1, the recent trajectory of self-employment falls into three distinct periods. During the first of these periods in the 1980s, self-employment was on a strong upward trend.[2] Indeed, as noted elsewhere by the author (Meager, 2008), during this period the level and rate of self-employment almost doubled from 1.8 million (7 per cent of those in work) at the beginning of the decade to 3.5 million (13 per cent of those in work). This growth was unprecedented, both historically and in comparison with other European countries, and was independent of the economic cycle (the growth was equally strong during the deep recession of the early 1980s and during the economic upturn during the second half

Source: Labour Force Survey, Office for National Statistics.

Figure 5.1   UK self-employment trends 1984–2017

of the decade). The consensus from the research literature of that period (see Meager, 1993; Acs et al., 1994) is that this growth reflected the coming together of a range of factors conducive to self-employment growth. In particular it seems that the aggregate growth in self-employment reflected increasing inflow rates to self-employment (rather than changes in the average duration of self-employment spells) due to a combination of: the rapid structural change from manufacturing to services which took place in the UK economy; the growth of sub-contracting (particularly in the construction sector which saw a rapid growth in self-employment as 'disguised wage employment' (as noted in Nisbet, 1997; Winch, 1998; Nisbet and Thomas, 2000)); franchising and privatisation of public services; an unrestricted regulatory framework for business start-up and easy access to financial capital; and an expansion of government support for the unemployed to enter self-employment.[3]

The second period, essentially covering the 1990s, is one in which the level of self-employment was fairly static (fluctuating within the range of 3.25m to 3.5m), and although there was strong economic and employment growth in the second half of this decade, this did not filter through to growth in self-employment. Indeed, the share of self-employment in total employment fell back again from 14 to 12 per cent in this period. As Meager (2008) notes, the explanation for the stagnation in self-employment during the 1990s appears to lie partly in increased outflows from self-employment (especially in the recession during the early 1990s, as many of the new start-ups which had been established during the 1980s boom turned out not to be resilient to economic downturn), and partly in sector-specific factors. In particular, while self-employment in the construction sector had expanded strongly in the 1980s (due to a growth in sub-contracting arrangements), it fell back strongly in the 1990s in response to a clamp-down on bogus self-employment in this sector by the tax and social security authorities (Green, 1998; Briscoe et al., 2000; Behling and Harvey, 2015).

Since the turn of the century, around 2000–2001, however, self-employment in the UK has entered a third phase and resumed a strong upward trend. This has continued unabated throughout the period and as with the surge in self-employment in the 1980s has been apparently unaffected by the economic cycle. As Figure 5.1 shows, the upward trend in self-employment was equally strong both during the period of economic growth of 2000–2007 and during the major recession following the financial crisis of 2007–2008 and thereafter. At the time of writing (mid-2018), UK self-employment stands at an unprecedented level of 4.8 million (15 per cent of the employed workforce).

WHAT IS KNOWN ABOUT THE NATURE OF UK SELF-EMPLOYMENT FROM PREVIOUS RESEARCH?

Before looking at this most recent period in a little more detail, however, it is worth outlining what the research literature tells us about the changing characteristics of self-employment. Many of these 'stylised facts' about self-employment in the UK have been outlined in earlier works by the author (see in particular Meager, 2008 and Baumberg and Meager, 2015, for more details and a fuller account of the earlier research literature). In summary, we know the following from the previous research:

Self-employment has changed dramatically from the picture which pertained between the end of the Second World War, and the late 1970s, when it could be characterised as a small, stable or declining segment of the workforce, dominated by occupations in agriculture, traditional crafts and parts of the liberal professions as well as traditional small business owner/proprietors:

- Over the period since 1980 self-employment has (Meager and Bates, 2001 and 2004):

    ○ become more dynamic, with larger inflows to and outflows from self-employment;

    ○ affected a larger segment of the workforce such that a larger proportion of the population now experiences spells of self-employment at some point during their working life;

    ○ become more heterogeneous both in the sense of encompassing a wider range of work types (occupations and activities), and in the sense of affecting a broader range of the working population (with a growing share of women and young people entering self-employment, for example).

- Compared with employees, the self-employed population is a very polarised group on some indicators. In particular, while average earnings of the self-employed tend to be lower than that of employees, the earnings distribution of the self-employed is considerably more polarised than that of employees, with larger proportions of the self-employed at both extremes of the distribution (very high and very low earnings) than is the case for employees (Parker, 1997). Additionally, research from the 1980s and 1990s (Meager and Bates, 2001; Meager, 2008) found that, in the UK, being self-employed (after controlling for other personal and work-related variables) increased the risk of poverty in the sense that spells of self-employment increased an individual's likelihood of falling into the lowest end of the earnings distribution (but not the highest end). There was also some evidence of a 'scarring' effect, in that this likelihood of low earnings persisted after the individual had left self-employment, and indeed after leaving work altogether, with lower levels of income and wealth through poorer pension entitlements and savings levels in later life.

- The self-employed tend to work much longer hours on average than employees (Meager et al., 2011), and when this is taken alongside the lower average earnings of the self-employed, the 'typical' self-employed worker earns considerably less per hour than their waged counterparts.

- The self-employed are much less likely than employees to receive work-related training or to be studying for a qualification than comparable workers who are employees (Meager et al., 2011), raising questions about how the self-employed are able to develop and update their work-related skills during their working lives.

Overall, as noted in Baumberg and Meager (2015), a picture emerges from the previous research of UK self-employment, in which a large and possibly growing proportion of the UK self-employed are in relatively insecure work with a high risk of a poor level of financial well-being, alongside long working hours and little ability to develop their human capital. As a result:

> There has been a long-standing debate about the intrinsic job quality of self-employment, and whether it represents "good work" (new opportunities for autonomy and fulfilling work) or "bad work" (the erosion of security among marginalised workers). (Baumberg and Meager, 2015, p. 106)

It is worth noting also that these issues and debates are not confined to the UK. Indeed, it is commonly observed in many countries that, on average, and compared with employees, the self-employed work longer hours,[4] earn less[5] and enjoy in many respects poorer working conditions and job security (Pedersini and Coletto, 2010).

Despite this apparent weight of evidence on the negative aspects of job quality associated with self-employment, it is also observed in many data sets in many countries that the self-employed report higher levels of job (and life) satisfaction than comparable employees.[6] Typically this apparent paradox of the self-employed being happier than employees despite being in worse jobs, is (at least partly) explained in the research through some kind of selection effect, namely that those who enter self-employment are more likely to value the autonomy, independence and flexibility associated with 'being their own boss', and these factors tend to offset the more negative aspects of job quality in self-employment.[7] However, there remains a number of issues arising from the heterogeneity of the unemployed as a group which remain unresolved in this discussion about 'good jobs' and 'bad jobs' for the self-employed. For example, it is also well documented in the research literature from many countries, going back to the 1980s at least, that a significant proportion of the self-employed are not 'volunteers' in the sense of choosing self-employment over alternative forms of work; rather many of them (and this is particularly true in times of high unemployment and economic crisis) may be 'pushed' into self-employment by lack of alternatives in wage employment. There is a large literature which highlights the distinction between 'opportunity' and 'necessity' entrepreneurship, and the relative balance between the two as a motivation for individuals to choose self-employment (Dawson et al., 2009, for example), and it is not clear, for necessity entrepreneurs, that a psychological preference for autonomy will play the same role in explaining job satisfaction differences between the self-employed and employees as it does for opportunity entrepreneurs. Indeed Binder and Coad (2013) report an observed relationship between job satisfaction and whether an individual is a 'necessity' or an 'opportunity' entrepreneur with the latter generally recording higher levels of satisfaction than the former. It might, therefore, be expected that average levels of job satisfaction among the self-employed would fall during an economic downturn as the proportion of self-employed who are 'pushed' into self-employment through necessity, rather than 'choosing' self-employment in response to opportunity, increases. In a subsequent section of this chapter, we look at this hypothesis in the context of the economic downturn following the financial crisis of 2007–2008.

SELF-EMPLOYMENT POST-2000: BEFORE AND AFTER THE FINANCIAL CRISIS

Following this review of changes in the volume and composition of self-employment in earlier decades, we now turn to examine the most recent (post-2000 period), which exhibits further important developments, some of which continue the trends observed in previous history, but others of which contain significant new elements.

Aggregate Trends in Self-employment Since 2000

Turning to the most recent period, Figure 5.2 shows clearly that aggregate self-employment has returned to strong growth in around 2000, and this growth has continued unabated thereafter. This has reignited a debate in academic and policy circles (D'Arcy and Gardiner, 2014), very similar to that which took place in the 1980s, about whether the growth represents

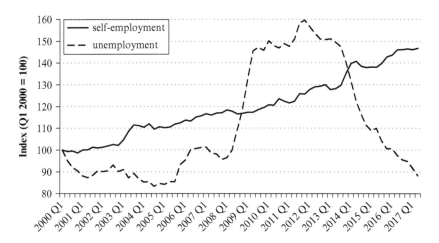

Source: Labour Force Survey, Office for National Statistics.

Figure 5.2   UK self-employment and unemployment, 2000–2017

a genuine entrepreneurial upsurge in the labour market, or whether (particularly since the financial crisis) it represents a growth in poor quality, precarious work, driven by a lack of traditional employment opportunities and workers trying to keep a foothold in the labour market by undertaking insecure work on a freelance basis. Or indeed, is it some combination of these two phenomena? The debate has been given a further twist in the most recent period by the controversial emergence of jobs (many notionally categorised as 'self-employed' in the so-called 'gig economy' (Donovan et al., 2016), involving workers whose employment relationships (with both the contracting enterprise and the ultimate consumer of services/goods) are mediated by a variety of new IT platforms (drivers for the Uber taxi service are a well-known example: Eisenbray and Mishel, 2016).

In analysing the recent growth in self-employment, the first striking point is that there is no relationship between the self-employment trend and the overall economic environment. The early part of the period to 2006 was one of economic growth and low unemployment. Following the financial crisis, unemployment surged, more than doubling between 2007 and 2011, before the labour market recovered strongly in the more recent (2012–2017) period. As has been well-documented elsewhere (Coulter, 2016) the UK labour market as a whole performed much better in the most recent recession than in previous recessions in the 1980s and 1990s. The fall in GDP post-2007 was larger than in any recession since the Great Depression of the 1930s, and it took longer for GDP to recover from the downturn than in any previous recession. As Figure 5.2 shows, however, the impact on unemployment was relatively short-lived (and indeed much less severe than would have been expected from previous recessions). This lack of a clear relationship between aggregate self-employment and the economic cycle was also observable in the 1980s and 1990s, and as has been noted in the literature for many years (Meager, 1992), this does not negate the distinction between opportunity and necessity entrepreneurs, rather the balance between the two in self-employment flows can vary over the cycle, so it is perfectly possible for the trend in the stock of self-employment to be largely independent of the cycle. Thus self-employment increases in the upturn as opportunity entrepreneurs predominate in the inflows, and outflows shrink as economic conditions are good for small firm survival; in the downturn outflows may increase, but this increase could be more than offset by a surge in necessity entrepreneurs in the inflows, so self-employment continues to increase. Looking at both recent periods of strong self-employment growth which persisted throughout complete economic cycles (the 1980s and the post-2000 period) it is clear that the aggregate growth in self-employment concealed important compositional differences in self-employment growth between the upturn and downturn parts of the cycle (this was documented for the 1980s period in Meager (1993), and is illustrated further in the present chapter below for the post 2000 period).

A second point of note, particularly in the period following the financial crisis of 2007, is that the continuing growth of self-employment has been a key contributor to the overall growth in UK employment, despite the poor GDP performance. Of course there are also many other explanations put forward for the apparent resilience of the UK labour market following the financial crisis (see Coulter, 2016), including: a greater tendency for employers to 'hoard' labour (e.g. through negotiating working time reductions) than in previous recessions, in order to avoid the re-emergence of skill shortages following the recession; a weakening of trade union power since the 1980s (facilitating a reduction in real wages, such that jobs were protected at the expense of lower wages); and more extensive and effective active labour market policies, introduced in the UK since the early 1990s, which facilitated a faster return to work among the unemployed.

Nevertheless it is clear that the remarkable growth in self-employment has itself been a key additional factor contributing to overall employment growth (and hence lower unemployment) during and after the recession. As can be seen in Figure 5.3, of the 3.1m extra jobs created in the UK between 2009 and 2017, almost 1m (32 per cent) were self-employed jobs

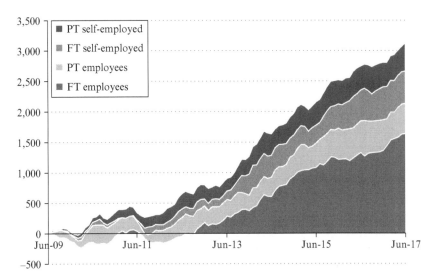

Source: Labour Force Survey, Office for National Statistics.

Figure 5.3   Sources of employment growth in UK economic recovery since 2009

(with the significance of self-employment particularly marked in the earlier years of recovery), and even more noteworthy is the fact that nearly half (47 per cent) of the increase in self-employment was among people working part-time (and the share of part-time self-employment growth was also most marked in the early years of the recovery). Traditionally, as has been noted above, self-employment is characterised (in the UK and elsewhere) by long working hours, with part-time work very much the exception rather than the rule, and the average working hours of the self-employed are typically much longer than those of employees. This traditional pattern has shifted dramatically in the period after the recent financial crisis.

In summary, then, it is clear that one of the key reasons that the UK has created more employment in the recent economic recovery than following previous downturns is the exceptional growth in self-employment, particularly part-time self-employment. This recent and extremely unusual surge in part-time self-employment in the UK is very much a feature of the post financial crisis period, and has been a key element of the changing composition of the self-employed in the most recent period.

The Changing Composition of Self-employment Since 2000

Looking more generally at the composition of self-employment in the post-2000 period, it is changing in a number of important ways. Figure 5.4 shows how the gender balance and the working time patterns of the self-employed have been changing. Thus Figure 5.4 panel *a* shows clearly how, at the start of the most recent period of self-employment growth in 2001, self-employment was dominated by men (nearly three quarters of the self-employed), and by people working relatively long hours (nearly 40 per cent had working time longer than 45 hours per week on average).

Panel *b* documents changes in these patterns in two sub-periods: the period before 2008 (overall self-employment grew by 15 per cent between Q3 2001 and Q3 2008), and the post-2008 period of recession and slow economic recovery (during which self-employment continued to grow, by 25 per cent between Q3 2008 and Q3 2016).

Looking first at gender, the growth pattern of self-employment in the first period was rather similar between men and women (female self-employment grew slightly faster than male self-employment). After 2008, however, the growth was much faster among women: female self-employment grew by around 50 per cent over the eight years, three times faster than male self-employment. When it comes to working time, there were similarly dramatic differences between the growth patterns of self-employment in the two periods: in particular, it can be seen that self-employed jobs involving relatively short hours of work per week grew

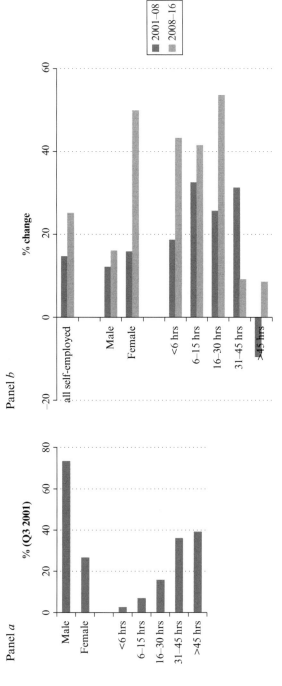

Source: Labour Force Survey, Office for National Statistics.

Figure 5.4   Gender and working time distribution of the self-employed in 2001 (panel a) and self-employment growth, pre- and post-2008 (panel b)

much faster in the second period than in the first period. So we can see a shift towards female self-employment and short-hours working in the post-financial crisis period, from 2008 onwards.

Figure 5.5 presents a similar analysis of the changing occupational distribution of the self-employed during this period. From panel *a* it can be seen that, at the beginning of the period, the self-employed were concentrated in particular in skilled manual occupations, a traditional source of self-employment which accounts for nearly a third of the self-employed, while there are also significant concentrations in professional and managerial occupations. The striking feature of panel *b*, which compares occupational trends in self-employment before and after the financial crisis, is the extent to which both highly skilled (managerial, professional and technical) occupations and low skilled and service occupations (caring, processing and elementary occupations) are over-represented in the growth of self-employment after 2008. In the post-2008 period the lack of self-employment growth in the traditional skilled craft occupations is particularly marked. In the pre-2008 period, by contrast, the growth is more evenly distributed across the occupational spectrum (the exceptions being 'managerial' self-employment and sales/customer services).

Similarly, when we look at the sectoral breakdown of self-employment growth before and after the financial crisis (Figure 5.6), there are once again important differences between the two periods. In 2001, while there are self-employed in significant numbers in all sectors of the economy (panel *a*), the largest concentrations are found in the traditional areas of construction (a fifth of the self-employed in this sector), distribution, retailing and related activities (13 per cent of the self-employed), and professional, scientific and technical activities (one in eight of the self-employed are in this sector). These sectors are not, however, the sectors experiencing rapid growth either before or after the financial crisis (panel *b*). Rather, there is a strong growth of self-employment in both periods in what are predominantly public sector activities (public administration and education), where self-employment is not traditionally found, reflecting perhaps growing levels of outsourcing in these sectors. Additionally, in the post-2008 period there is strong growth in self-employment in the financial sector, in information and communication and the generic 'other services' sector, the first two of which in particular are also not sectors which traditionally include a significant share of self-employed workers.

Migration and Self-employment

There is a large volume of work in the international literature (going back to debates in the US in the mid-eighties: Borjas, 1986), on the

Panel *a*

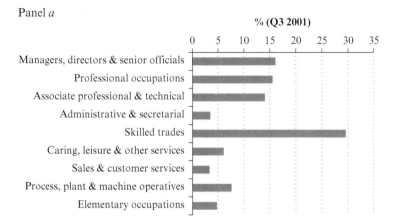

Panel *b*

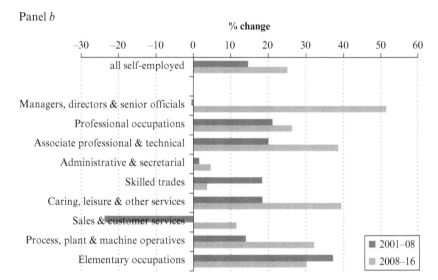

Source: Labour Force Survey, Office for National Statistics.

*Figure 5.5   Occupational distribution of the self-employed in 2001 (panel
               a) and self-employment growth by occupation, pre- and post-
               2008 (panel b)*

relationship between migration and self-employment, which highlights
both the diversity of self-employment rates and patterns between different
migrant groups and an ambiguity about the economic and social aspects
of this relationship (particularly whether self-employment among migrant

Panel *a*

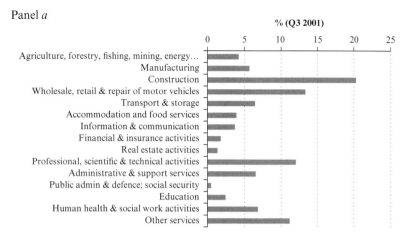

Panel *b*

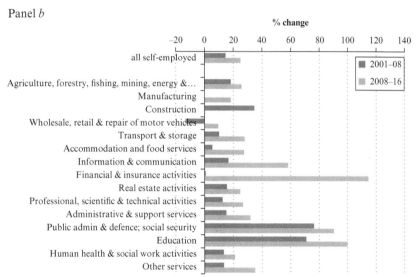

Source: Labour Force Survey, Office for National Statistics.

Figure 5.6 Sectoral distribution of the self-employed in 2001 (panel a) and self-employment growth by sector, pre- and post-2008 (panel b)

groups is a response to exclusion from the 'regular' labour market or whether it offers a valuable route to integration as well as adding to the entrepreneurial dynamics of the host economy). Given the recent significant increase in net migration to the UK (particularly since the accession of the A8 countries to the European Union in 2004), there has also been considerable interest in the UK to what, if any, role migration has played in the strong growth of self-employment during this period and in the experiences and characteristics of self-employed immigrants. The relevant evidence from previous research, together with new population census data analysis, is helpfully summarised in Clark et al., 2017. This study confirms earlier research showing much higher rates of self-employment among specific traditional immigrant groups (e.g. Pakistani men) than among other immigrant groups and the native population. However it also shows high rates among migrants from the newer member states of the EU, and highlights significant differences in the factors driving these rates: among traditional migrants from 'New Commonwealth' countries (former British colonies) high self-employment largely reflects poor opportunities for waged work and discrimination in the labour market; while among the more recent EU migrants it is more influenced by policy changes which allowed or encouraged migrant entrepreneurs. The authors conclude:

> Taken together, the findings suggest that recent changes in migration policy have had an impact, both directly and more indirectly, on self-employment and entrepreneurship in the UK. This applies both in relation to boosting rates of self-employment, given the high levels observed for some groups of (recent) migrants compared to the UK born – especially amongst women, as well as for the probability of employing others. (Clark et al., 2017, p. 1062)

It is, at the time of writing (mid-2018), too early to ascertain what impact Brexit will have on these developments. However, it seems likely that the high rates of net migration from EU countries will fall from the levels seen in recent years, and while the extent of any such change will inevitably depend on the terms of the Brexit settlement, and the post-Brexit migration regulations to be introduced by the UK government, it will inevitably affect self-employment as well as all other areas of the labour market and types of work which had benefited from the migration surge in the years following 2004.

Other Aspects of Self-employment in the Most Recent Period: Job Quality and Earnings

It was noted earlier in this chapter that in comparison with employees the self-employed tend to report greater job satisfaction, but this is despite the lower apparent quality of their jobs. However, there is some interesting, and more nuanced evidence on job quality in self-employment emerging from more recent UK research (Baumberg and Meager, 2015) which suggests:

a) That the previous emerging consensus about the 'quality' of self-employed jobs may have been overly negative; and

b) That the economic cycle may be relevant both to the quality of self-employed jobs and to individuals' reported satisfaction with the quality of self-employed jobs, with a tendency for both to fall in an economic downturn (as implied by some of the 'necessity/opportunity' literature referred to above).

A key observation from this recent work is that the earlier literature has typically relied on rather limited measures of 'job quality', or on indices of quality which are more appropriate to those in wage employment than to the jobs of the self-employed. Thus Baumberg and Meager (2015) were able to make use of data from a series of cross-section surveys repeated on a regular basis in the UK since the 1980s, which found more consistency between the job quality and satisfaction indicators for the self-employed.

Further, their study found not only that the self-employed, after controlling for a range of personal and job-related characteristics through multivariate statistical analysis, reported *higher* levels of (subjective) job satisfaction than employees (being more satisfied with all aspects of their job except for job security than were employees), but that this also applied to most indicators of (objective) job quality. The latter included, for example, greater task discretion at work, greater variety at work, a better match between their skills and the job, and a slower pace of work. There were, additionally, a few 'quality' indicators on which the self-employed fared less well (they worked harder, and received less work-related training than employees, for example). However, the study also found considerable heterogeneity among the self-employed: thus, for example, the self-employed who had staff tended to work harder than sole traders, but reported more satisfaction with various aspects of their job.

Additionally, the repeated survey evidence suggested that the job quality enjoyed by the self-employed in the UK had tended to increase decade on decade, on most indicators, up until the mid-2000s. However, a further finding, comparing data over the 2006 to 2012 period, was that the average 'quality' of self-employment had, on most indicators, deteriorated (although still remained above that of comparable employees), as had nearly every measure of job satisfaction. When taken together with the evidence above of the changing gender, working time, occupational and sectoral patterns of self-employment pre- and post-recession, this provides further support for the hypothesis that the continuing surge in self-employment in the period following the crisis differed in important ways from the growth prior to the recession. In particular, it raises the question of whether the decline in the average quality of self-employment jobs may be associated with the changing composition of self-employment observed during the same period.

Alongside this apparent decline in quality of work, there is evidence of important changes taking place to the average earnings of the self-employed, both in absolute terms and relative to employees. While it needs to be acknowledged that there are serious difficulties in making robust estimates of self-employed earnings (difficulties which are well explained in Athow, 2017), the most reliable source of trend data for the UK on self-employed earnings (the Family Resources Survey), reports a significant decline in median self-employed annual earnings over the period since the financial crisis in 2007/2008 (a much smaller decline was apparent in the median earnings of employees). Thus as reported in BIS (2016), between the six year period 2007/2008 to 2013/2014, the median earnings of the self-employed fell by 26 per cent in real terms[8] while the real earnings of employees fell by only 11 per cent over the same period. This decline can be only partly explained by the growth in part-time self-employment outlined above, as a similarly large decline in earnings was found among self-employed full-timers (working 30 or more hours per week).

CONCLUDING REMARKS

The huge heterogeneity of self-employment in the UK, as in other countries, makes it hard to draw robust conclusions about the causes and implications of the historically unparalleled recent growth in self-employment. Nevertheless, the following points can be tentatively highlighted on the basis of the evidence presented in the present chapter.

First, while the growth in self-employment since 2000 has persisted unabated throughout a period of economic growth before 2007, and a recession and (muted) economic recovery since 2007, there do seem to be some important changes taking place to the nature and composition of self-employment in the post 2007 period. In particular:

- The growth in self-employment in the **early part of the period** (2000–2007) while the economy was expanding and unemployment was low, was in many ways typical of the more familiar pattern of self-employment growth in previous economic upturns (fairly evenly spread across occupational groups, including significant numbers in traditional skilled craft and professional occupations; as well as growth in the construction sector, again a traditional source of self-employment). In other ways, however, the self-employment growth in this period had some less familiar characteristics: in particular the rapid growth in part-time self-employment began to be apparent, alongside self-employment growth in some non-traditional sectors (including public administration and education)

- In the **second part of the period**, following the financial crisis in 2007 (and during the recession and recovery which followed that crisis), the characteristics of the ongoing growth in self-employment further diverged from the more traditional patterns. In addition to the continued growth in part-time self-employment and short-hours working among the self-employed, the growth of self-employment among women was particularly rapid, and there was fast growth among self-employment in occupations at both the top and bottom ends of the occupational hierarchy (managerial and professional on the one hand, along with unskilled, routine, caring and leisure occupations on the other), while the sectors in which self-employment growth was most marked included financial and public services and education (not traditional sources of self-employment). By contrast, during this period self-employment in more traditional occupations (e.g. skilled craft jobs) and sectors (e.g. construction) was relatively stagnant.

The second key conclusion from the evidence presented in this chapter is that some of the concerns emerging from previous research about the 'quality' of self-employed jobs may have been overly pessimistic. Indeed, more recent evidence suggests that on many indicators, after controlling for other factors, the self-employed report higher quality of work than their employee counterparts in similar jobs (this is also consistent with their higher levels of reported job satisfaction, which could previously be explained only by some kind of 'selection effect' and preference for independence and autonomy among the self-employed). However, there is also evidence that this quality advantage may have been reduced in the recent period following the financial crisis, with survey evidence suggesting that the quality of self-employed jobs has fallen in recent years, and fallen faster than among employees. Alongside this latter evidence, this period saw not only the changes in composition of self-employment (more short-hours working, different occupations and so on) but also emerging findings that the median earnings of the self-employed fell rapidly (and to a greater extent than employee earnings).

It is clear that the continuing growth of self-employment in countries like the UK means that it must increasingly be taken seriously as a significant and permanent part of the labour market. It is clear also that the heterogeneity of self-employment means that the aggregate trends conceal some of the highly dynamic aspects of the self-employed population, the composition of which continues to change rapidly. There is much that can be seen as positive about self-employment growth, which has helped the UK labour market survive a massive economic depression with relatively little sustained impact on unemployment.

However, although most self-employed are still in the traditional occupations and sectors and still working long hours, it seems that the recent recession may have pushed a much wider group of people into self-employment, many doing small bits and pieces of work in a much wider range of occupations, perhaps because they are unable to find employee jobs, and this is consistent with the survey evidence of a recent fall in the job quality of the self-employed. Hence, while acknowledging its many positive aspects, it is also necessary to paint a balanced picture which recognises that the growth of self-employment is not simply an economic and socially beneficial entrepreneurial upsurge, and which acknowledges that some of the possible downsides of a world in which more people spend more of their working lives in self-employment, and which were highlighted in the research from the 1980s and 1990s, are still present, and still pose a challenge for public policy makers. These include low pay, insecurity, low levels of social protection (including, particularly, pensions), and low levels of training and human capital development during their working lives.

NOTES

1. Baumberg and Meager (2015).
2. Note that this trend started around 1979, but the official Labour Force Survey series used in the chart started in the current form only in 1984.
3. For a discussion of the growth and impact of self-employment schemes for the unemployed during this period, in the UK and other European countries, see Meager (1996).
4. See, for example, the discussion of working time patterns of the self-employed in: Pedersini and Coletto (2010).
5. See: Hamilton (2000) and Koellinger et al. (2015). As Koellinger et al. note: "When entrepreneurs say that they are 'not in it for the money', the data seem to support them" (Koellinger et al., p. 137).
6. See: Blanchflower (2000), Hundley (2001), Taylor (2004), Benz and Frey (2008).
7. See, for example, two studies which use European-level data to examine this question of job-satisfaction: Lange (2012), Millán, J. et al. (2013).
8. Calculated at constant 2013/2014 prices.

REFERENCES

Acs, Z., Audretsch, D. and Evans, D. (1994). Why does the self-employment rate vary across countries over time? *CEPR Discussion Paper*, no. 871, London.
Athow, J. (2017). *Why is measuring self-employed income so hard?*, Office for National Statistics, online blog August 2017. https://blog.ons.gov.uk/2017/08/14/why-is-mea suring-self-employed-income-so-hard/ (accessed 15 June 2018).

Baumberg, B. and Meager, N. (2015). Job quality and the self-employed: is it still better to work for yourself? In: Felstead, A., Gallie, D. and Green, F. (eds), *Unequal Britain at Work: The Evolution and Distribution of Intrinsic Job Quality in Britain*. Oxford: Oxford University Press, 105–29.

Behling, F. and Harvey, M. (2015). The evolution of false self-employment in the British construction industry: a neo-Polanyian account of labour market formation. *Work, Employment and Society*, 29(6), 969–88.

BEIS (2017). *Good Work: The Taylor Review of Modern Working Practices*. London: Department for Business, Energy and Industrial Strategy, July 2017. https://assets. publishing.service.gov.uk/government/uploads/system/uploads/attachment_data/ file/627671/good-work-taylor-review-modern-working-practices-rg.pdf (accessed 15 June 2018).

BEIS (2018). *Good Work: A Response to the Taylor Review of Modern Working Practices*. London: Department for Business, Energy and Industrial Strategy, February 2018. https://assets.publishing.service.gov.uk/government/uploads/sys tem/uploads/attachment_data/file/679765/180206_BEIS_Good_Work_Report. pdf (accessed 15 June 2018).

Benz, M. and Frey, B. (2008). Being independent is a great thing: subjective evaluations of self-employment and hierarchy. *Economica*, 75(298), 362–83.

Binder, M. and Coad, A. (2013). Life satisfaction and self-employment: a matching approach. *Small Business Economics*, 40, 1009–33.

BIS (2016). *The Income of the Self-employed*. London: Department for Business, Innovation and Skills, February 2916. https://www.gov.uk/government/uploads/ system/uploads/attachment_data/file/500317/self-employed-income.pdf (accessed 15 June 2018).

Blanchflower, D. (2000). Self-employment in OECD countries. *Labour Economics*, 7(5), 471–505.

Borjas, G. (1986). The self-employment experience of immigrants. *Journal of Human Resources*, 21, 485–506.

Briscoe, G., Dainty, A. and Millett, S. (2000). The impact of the tax system on self-employment in the British construction industry. *International Journal of Manpower*, 21(8), 596–613.

Broughton, A., Gloster, R., Marvell, R., Green, M., Langley, J. and Martin, A. (2018). *The Experiences of Individuals in the Gig Economy*. London: Department for Business, Energy and Industrial Strategy, February 2018. https://assets.publishing. service.gov.uk/government/uploads/system/uploads/attachment_data/file/679987/ 171107_The_experiences_of_those_in_the_gig_economy.pdf (accessed 15 June 2018).

Clark, K., Drinkwater, S. and Robinson, C. (2017). Self-employment amongst migrant groups: new evidence from England and Wales. *Small Business Economics*, 48(4), 1047–69.

Coulter, S. (2016). The UK labour market and the 'great recession'. In: Myant, M., Theodoropoulou, S. and Piasna, A. (eds), *Unemployment, Internal Devaluation and Labour Market Deregulation in Europe*. Brussels: European Trade Union Institute, 197–227.

D'Arcy, C. and Gardiner, L. (2014). *Just the Job – or a Working Compromise? The Changing Nature of Self-employment in the UK*. London: Resolution Foundation. http://www.resolutionfoundation.org/app/uploads/2014/05/Just-the-job-or-a-wor king-compromise.pdf (accessed 15 June 2018).

Dawson, C., Henley, A. and Latreille, P. (2009). Why do individuals choose self-employment? *IZA Discussion Paper* no. 3974. http://ftp.iza.org/dp3974.pdf (accessed 15 June 2018).

Donovan, S., Bradley, D. and Shimabukuro, J. (2016). What does the gig economy mean for workers? Congressional Research Service, *CRS Report R44365*. https://www.fas.org/sgp/crs/misc/R44365.pdf (accessed 15 June 2018).

Eisenbray, R. and Mishel, L. (2016). *Uber Business Model Does Not Justify a New 'Independent Worker' Category*. Employment Policy Institute, 17 March 2016. http://www.epi.org/publication/uber-business-model-does-not-justify-a-new-independent-worker-category/ (accessed 15 June 2018).

Green, B. (1998). Survey reveals effects of fewer self-employed. *Construction News*, 5, November, 6–7.

Hamilton, B. (2000). Does entrepreneurship pay? An empirical analysis of the returns to self-employment. *Journal of Political Economy*, 108, 604–31.

Hundley, G. (2001). Why and when are the self-employed more satisfied with their work? *Industrial Relations*, 40(2), 293–316.

Koellinger, P., Mell, J., Pohl, I., Roessler, C. and Treffers, T. (2015). Self-employed but looking: a labour market experiment. *Economica*, 82(325), 137–61.

Lange, T. (2012). Job satisfaction and self-employment: autonomy or personality? *Small Business Economics*, 38(2), 165–77.

Lepanjuuri, K., Wishart, R. and Cornick, P. (2018). *The Characteristics of those in the Gig Economy*. London: Department for Business, Energy and Industrial Strategy, February 2018. https://assets.publishing.service.gov.uk/government/uploads/system/uploads/attachment_data/file/687553/The_characteristics_of_those_in_the_gig_economy.pdf (accessed 15 June 2018).

Meager, N. (1992). Does unemployment lead to self-employment? *Small Business Economics*, 4(2), 88–103.

Meager, N. (1993). Self-employment and labour market policy in the European Community (1993), a report to the European Commission (DGV) under the MISEP programme, Berlin, WZB (Published as *WZB Discussion Paper* FSI 93–201).

Meager, N. (1996). Self-employment as an alternative to dependent employment for the unemployed. In: Schmid. G., O'Reilly, J. and Schömann, K. (eds), *International Handbook of Labour Market Policy and Evaluation*. Aldershot, UK and Brookfield, VT, USA: Edward Elgar Publishing, 489–519.

Meager, N. (2008). Self-employment dynamics and transitional labour markets. In: Muffels, J. (ed.), *Flexibility and Employment Security in Europe*. Cheltenham, UK and Northampton, MA, USA: Edward Elgar Publishing, 195–222.

Meager, N. and Bates, P. (2001). The self-employed and lifetime incomes: some UK evidence. *International Journal of Sociology*, 31(1), 27–58.

Meager, N. and Bates, P. (2004). Self-employment in the United Kingdom during the 1980s and 1990s. In: Arum, R. and Müller, W. (eds), *The Reemergence of Self-Employment*. Princeton: Princeton University Press, 135–69.

Meager, N., Martin, R. and Carta, E. (2011). *Skills for Self-employment*, Evidence Report 31, London: UK Commission for Employment and Skills. http://webarchive.nationalarchives.gov.uk/20140108111346/http://www.ukces.org.uk/publications/er31-skills-for-self-employment (accessed 15 June 2018).

Millán, J., Hessels, J., Thurik, R. and Aguado, R. (2013). Determinants of job satisfaction: a European comparison of self-employed and paid employees. *Small Business Economics*, 40(3), 651–70.

Nisbet, P. (1997). Dualism, flexibility and self-employment in the UK construction industry. *Work, Employment and Society*, 11, 459–80.

Nisbet, P. and Thomas, W. (2000). Attitudes, expectations and labour market behaviour: the case of self-employment in the UK construction industry. *Work, Employment and Society*, 14(2), 353–68.

Parker, S. (1997). The distribution of self-employment income in the United Kingdom, 1976–1991. *The Economic Journal*, 107(441), 455–66.

Pedersini, R. and Coletto, D. (2010). Self-employed workers: industrial relations and working conditions. Dublin: European Foundation for the Improvement of Living and Working Conditions. http://www.eurofound.europa.eu/sites/default/files/ef_files/docs/comparative/tn0801018s/tn0801018s.pdf (accessed 15 June 2018).

Taylor, M. (2004). Self-employment in Britain: when, who, what and why. *Swedish Economic Policy Review*, 11(2), 139–73.

Williams, M., Broughton, A., Meager, N., Spiegelhalter, K., Johal, S. and Jenkins, K. (2017). *The True Diversity of Self-employment*. London: Centre for Research on Self-employment, November 2017. http://www.crse.co.uk/sites/default/files/The%20true%20diversity%20of%20self-employment_0.pdf (accessed 15 June 2018).

Winch, G. (1998). The growth of self-employment in construction. *Construction Management and Economics*, 16, 531–43.

6. Micro-entrepreneurship and changing contours of work: towards precarious work relations? Empirical findings from Austria

Dieter Bögenhold, Andrea Klinglmair, Zulaicha Parastuty and Florian Kandutsch

SELF-EMPLOYMENT AND CHANGING CONTOURS OF WORK

As labour markets are closely linked to the settings of societies, they are also facing massive structural changes which affect the composition of labour markets and, in particular, the self-employed part thereof. One section of the chapter will take a closer look at the changing contextual factors with a focus on implications for the labour market, in particular for the (solo) self-employed. This chapter deals with a special group within the sector of self-employment, which is receiving increasing interest from scholars in that field: the hybrid (solo) self-employed. Within this group, we are facing a great heterogeneity with respect to different aspects and we can see a rise of blurred boundaries between dependent work and self-employment. Increasingly we find a variety of different forms of work behaviour and of social security due to different economic and social status groups (European Commission, 2018). The majority of the self-employed are working as a one-man- or one-woman-firm, which raises the need for challenging established views on self-employment and entrepreneurship. Too often the general changing contours of work are overlooked (Sweet and Meiksins, 2017). Accordingly, the division of occupations is analysed as if the social and economic world is stationary. Especially, trends towards deindustrialisation in Western countries and tendencies of globalisation at the same time coincide with new phenomena which we commonly call digitalisation. In fact, digitalisation raises new questions about the interaction of self-employment, economic change and the conditions of occupational and social structures. The so-called new 'gig economy' (McKinsey Global

Institute, 2016; McGovern, 2017; Morgan and Nelligan, 2018; Prassl, 2018) is exactly about those interactions in new times of the world of work. Talking about self-employment implies acknowledging a broader framework of factors influencing the configuration of employment categories, economic processes, and social and labour market realities (Bögenhold et al., 2014a).

Entrepreneurship has become a central issue when discussing ways to promote job creation and growth. Especially in the context of IT technologies and ideas on innovative regional clusters, entrepreneurship has evolved to be a pivot for a sustainable economic and social future (Audretsch, 2007; Bonnet et al., 2010; Bonnet et al., 2012). However, critical discourse shows that entrepreneurship as a *terminus technicus* in scientific discussion is not always precisely defined. In particular, the socioeconomic heterogeneity of the human actors and their different occupational and biographical careers and orientations are not sufficiently acknowledged. Taking the labour market category of self-employment as a proxy for entrepreneurship, which is often practised – and discussed critically – one realises that the majority of entrepreneurs is associated with the category of micro-firms, which are mainly one-(wo)man firms. Their entrepreneurial activities are 'under transition' (Chepurenko, 2015). The complex processes of interplay between technological change, globalisation and the labour market leading to a shift towards a service sector economy are mirrored by the emergence of new patterns of employment and the related institutional context. Viewing the issue of self-employment, a growing trend towards part-time self-employment and one-(wo)man firms can be found. These newly emerging firms are increasingly regarded as an alternative to wage- or salary-dependent working. While Schumpeter (1912) portrayed the actor of entrepreneurship as 'captain of industry', most of these small business owners do not fit this metaphor: They do not operate with different hierarchy levels and they work in their companies without any employees. Occasionally, their work situations show a hybrid status between dependent employed working and the idealised idea of autonomy associated with the semantic of entrepreneurship (Folta et al., 2010; Bögenhold and Klinglmair, 2016 and 2017). Economies worldwide are going through the profound process of structural change, which alters established employment relationships. As one consequence the proportion of people in precarious working arrangements rises and at the same time, a rise in solo self-employment can be observed. New forms of small self-employment (Bögenhold and Fachinger, 2007; Bögenhold, 2019) are heterogeneous and sometimes contradictory, ranging from good positions in terms of income and security down to new kinds of modern day labourers who are permanently in search of 'gigs' to realise income. Those actors

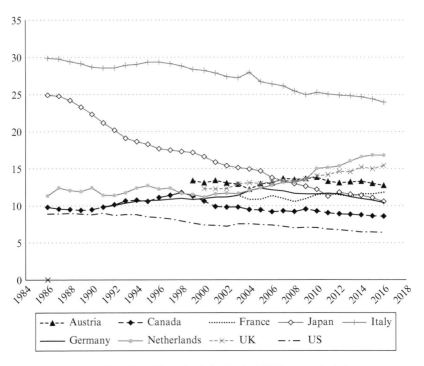

Source: OECD (2018). Labour Force Statistics, Paris: OECD, own calculations.

Figure 6.1   Self-employment rate in OECD countries from 1986 to 2016

were conventionally labelled as freelancers (Kitching and Smallbone, 2012; Meager, 2015) and nowadays they are increasingly coined independent professionals (IPROS) (McKeown, 2005; McKeown, 2015).

Looking at the development of self-employment ratios in selected OECD countries (Figure 6.1) shows very divergent developments for the last 25 years. Some countries like Italy and Japan have a strong decline which seemingly has not come to an end. This decline started from a comparatively high level in the eighties when the self-employment ratios were at 25 and 30 per cent. Other countries like Canada or the US indicate a moderate decline resulting from a low initial level of less than 10 per cent already in the eighties. In opposition to these countries, the UK and the Netherlands give an example of self-employment increases which are quite substantial in terms of percentages while France and Germany show somehow indifferent patterns of stability.

Changing the observation from the self-employment ratio of men and women together to the self-employment ratio of women (figure available

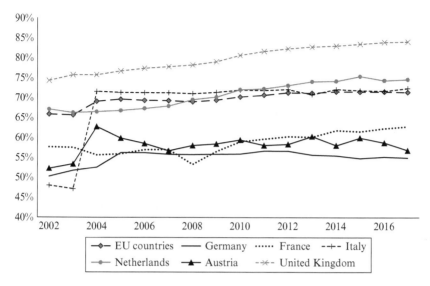

Source: Eurostat, various years, own calculations.

Figure 6.2   Ratio of solo self-employment per total self-employment

upon request) shows that the female self-employment ratios are slightly lower than the general self-employment ratios. However, the trends of development seem to be quite similar. As Figure 6.2 indicates, the share of solo self-employed people is remarkably high in regard to the total amount of self-employed persons. In this figure only a few member states were picked to show the relevance of the solo self-employed, but it should be stated here that no country within the EU has a share below 50 per cent, while the average for the European Union is higher than 70 per cent. The share of solo self-employment increases in all countries observed with the exceptions of Germany and Austria. The UK and the Netherlands have comparatively high and increasing ratios of solo self-employment. In the UK the ratio is between 80 and 85 per cent which raises a series of further questions of research interest regarding quality and nature of those economic activities: Is it possible that many of these activities exist due to a comparatively lower net of social welfare and labour law regulations so that some of those actors are just dependent workers without the appropriate status? Our findings just provoke those questions without offering answers at this level. However, a deeper analysis can also show that women have a higher representation in solo self-employment than men.

SOLO SELF-EMPLOYMENT AS A SPECIAL CASE OF ENTREPRENEURSHIP: THEORETICAL CONSIDERATIONS

The findings of our study try to shed light on the issue of the real world of smallest businessmen and woman to gain new information to fill a knowledge gap. As seen above, more than 70 per cent of all self-employed people in Europe (EU-28) fall into the category of independent businessmen who work without further employees. These one-(wo)man firms do not share the conventional portrait of economic and social features which is conventionally reported as stereotypical of big companies. What is the rationality of actors being involved in these micro-firms, what are their economic and social intentions, which occupational biographies can be reported, and how can the phenomenon of micro-self-employment be interpreted most adequately? Classic and modern definitions of entrepreneurship concentrate mostly on some very restrictive aspects: The classic ones, for example those definitions derived from Schumpeter (1987) or Kirzner (1979), see the entrepreneur as a person with a special role in the economy. Present-day definitions, for the most part, see the self-employed woman and man as opportunity finders, therefore the connection between the entrepreneur and a lucrative opportunity is pointed out (Shane and Venkataraman, 2000). They all have one aspect in common, namely that they assume certain requirements: On the one hand those are the special functions and abilities a person has to have to become an entrepreneur. On the other hand lucrative entrepreneurial opportunities must exist in order to exploit them. In reality it is not as simple as it is in theory. Behind the decision to become a self-employed man or woman, various social and economic processes have to be respected. Different forms of entrepreneurship can be found behind the aggregated data, so therefore a critical point of view can give fruitful insights into the working and living conditions of the self-employed, in particular the solo self-employed. The chapter is based upon findings of a representative survey in one federal region in Austria (Carinthia) as a pilot-study for further investigation of this phenomenon.

The research question focuses on these forms of micro-entrepreneurship asking for diverse aspects of economic and social performance like income, motives for self-employment, well-being, job satisfaction or prospects for the future. The chapter will identify one-person enterprises that are self-employed due to missing chances in the labour market ('precarious' forms). Then, this group of companies will be compared with their non-precarious counterparts with respect to various factors like job satisfaction, business performance or future prospects. The rest of this chapter is structured as follows. In this section, the theoretical background will be explored further, the next section addresses the role of one-person enterprises in Austria based on data from official statistics, followed by the design of the empirical study in Austria and the major empirical findings. The concluding section tries to sum up the findings.

Academic discussion has no doubt that new self-employment has a necessary impact for the vitality of our modern economies. It is argued that increasing self-employment contributes to wealth, increasing jobs and to a better integration of society (OECD and The European Commission, 2013; Amorós and Bosma, 2014). Although this view is convincing for many reasons, not enough stress is put upon the fact of the considerable heterogeneity of self-employment. "This heterogeneity and modest-majority dominance is a challenge for researchers" (Davidsson, 2014, p. 22). Most of them show very limited ambitions, resources and novelty. Very few will ever embark on a trajectory of growth (Davidsson et al., 2010). Therefore, we must acknowledge a broad range of social and economic situations within the scope of entrepreneurship where the majority belongs to the category of smallest firms. In principle, two competing interpretations of the phenomenon of one-(wo)men enterprises are on the agenda: One is a negative-critical perspective and the other is a positive-optimistic one. The first interpretation views the phenomenon in combination with new tendencies of instabilities on the labour market (Kalleberg, 2009 and 2011), when many labour market participants are *pushed* into micro self-employment due to a lack of (paid) jobs and tendencies of flexibilisation in order to find a niche in the employment system. On the other hand, it is argued that an economy is permanently dependent upon new business entries, which – by their nature – start as small and smallest. These new entries represent fertile ground for firms, which potentially grow and subsequently provide impulses for the labour market and technological development. In this last view, micro-firms are regarded as a bridge to positive spillover effects. However, a third – intermediating – perspective refers to the point that several one-person firms engage consciously within the smallest size sector and do not have ambitions for growth, for various reasons. These business owners are satisfied if they can realise a sufficient income through freelance work or micro-entrepreneurship, and they do not want to replace further growth with less leisure time or other different packages of work duties.

According to Shane and Venkataraman (2000) three sets of research questions about entrepreneurship are central:

1. Why, when, and how do opportunities come into existence?
2. Why, when, and how do some people and not others discover and exploit these opportunities?
3. Why, when, and how are different modes of action used to exploit entrepreneurial opportunities?

Additionally, to this tableau of research domains one may raise the question of where the entrepreneurs come from, how they sustain themselves, and what their occupational and social biographies are within the division of work. Related to this question, one may continue with specific social issues of relevance: Which divergent social networks can people instrumentalise to operate their strategies and to maximise their social positions (Davidsson and Honig, 2003; Burt et al., 2013; Bögenhold 2013)? Reasoning about the future of entrepreneurship (Wiklund et al., 2011) shall include these sociological questions (Bögenhold et al., 2014a). Nevertheless, we are increasingly in a world society with a puzzle of labour market patterns and biographical careers in which the clinical dichotomy between wage- or labour-dependent work on the one side and self-employed activities on the other side is muddied since hybrid forms of combinations arise, where people have more than one job at one time, or along the biographical axis of individual careers so that we observe patterns of multiplicity and parallelisms in which entrepreneurship seems to be a complex process, often a long duration which alters established black and white thinking (Davidsson, 2014).

If we employ the labour market category of self-employment as a proxy for entrepreneurship, which may occasionally be questioned but which most closely resembles actual practice, it becomes evident that in many countries the majority of entrepreneurs belong to the category of micro firms, which effectively exist as one-(wo)man companies, with many of their number not even being registered in the yellow pages or having their own premises or sign above the door (Bögenhold et al., 2014b). Generally, the complex interaction of technological development, globalisation, decentralisation and socio-demographic change accelerated a structural change in the economy resulting in a changing working environment and new forms of employment. In the field of self-employment, an emerging trend towards part-time self-employment and one-person enterprises can be observed. These new forms of entrepreneurship are increasingly regarded as an important alternative to dependent employment (Korunka et al., 2011).

In some way, their current status and their biographies display a somewhat hybrid nature, positioned between wage or salary dependency and the freedom of entrepreneurs in their stereo-type (Folta et al., 2010). 'Die-hard entrepreneurs' (Burke et al., 2005) are those actors who are portrayed in public discourse and also in economics as those agents who are dynamic, willing to expand and to engage in risk taking. Conversely, those self-employed actors who do not meet with this image, but who are the majority of people in terms of self-employment numbers, seem to be rather neglected (Bögenhold et al., 2001; Bögenhold and Fachinger, 2007).

Since most of the theories in economics are based upon the observation of a dozen giant firms (Stigler, 1949), one has to turn attention to the real world of the economy with the majority of firm owners who are part-time workers and part-time entrepreneurs.

THE ROLE OF ONE-PERSON ENTERPRISES IN AUSTRIA AND IN CARINTHIA

In Austria as well as the European Union as a whole (EU-28) an increase in self-employment has been observed for several years. In particular, the number of self-employed people in Austria rose from 439,100 in 2004 to 476,900 in 2013, which represents an increase of 8.6 per cent.[1] Especially female self-employment went up with significant ratios of increase, when their numbers rose by 14.1 per cent; the increase in male self-employment was just 5.9 per cent (Statistik Austria, 2014). In the EU-28, total self-employment increased in the same time period by merely 1.3 per cent. As in Austria, female self-employment has risen disproportionately by 8.1 per cent since 2004, while the number of male self-employed went down by 1.6 per cent (Eurostat-Database, 2017).

The category of self-employment can be split into two subcategories. On the one side, self-employed people hire additional labour in their companies, and on the other side there are those who just work on their own without any further employees in their companies. According to Eurostat-Database (2017), the category of solo-entrepreneurs with micro-enterprises without further employees in their firms is about 59.9 per cent of all self-employed people in Austria. In the EU-28, by contrast, the share of solo self-employed to total self-employment is even higher and amounts to 71.3 per cent. Furthermore, the Austrian statistics indicate the high relevance of one-(wo)man firms. According to the Austrian public census of company units ('*Arbeitsstättenzählung*'), 329,481 firms are led only by a solo-entrepreneur, representing 52.9 per cent of all Austrian firms (Statistik Austria, 2013a). Statistics of the Austrian Chamber of Commerce ('*Wirtschaftskammer Österreich*' = WKÖ) reveal a lower level of one-person enterprises with 266,910 units, which is due to the fact that a variety of freelancers are not included in the data.[2] Compared to the total number of firms registered in the Chamber of Commerce, the share of one-person enterprises thus amounts to 57.3 per cent (see Table 6.1). Since 2008 the number of one-person enterprises in Austria has risen by 30.0 per cent. During the last year alone (2013), an increase of 6.3 per cent was observed. In the federal state of Carinthia there are 16,446 one-person firms listed in the register of the Chamber of Commerce. Here, the share

*Table 6.1   Key figures for one-person enterprises in Austria and Carinthia,
2013*

Indicator	Austria	Carinthia
Number of one-person enterprises	266,910	16,446
Share among all enterprises	57.3 %	55.6 %
Δ per cent 2008–2013	30.0 %	30.8 %
Δ per cent 2012–2013	6.3 %	9.5 %

Source: WKÖ (2013a); WKK (2014); own calculations and depiction.

of one-person entrepreneurs among all enterprises amounts to 55.6 per
cent. The development over time is very close to the whole of Austria.
Hence, since 2008 the number of one-person enterprises in Carinthia has
increased by 30.8 per cent. In 2013 the rise was slightly higher than in
Austria (9.5 per cent).

Solo-firms have their domains in the business and craft sector, as well
as the information and consulting branch, where the share of one-person
enterprises among all enterprises is higher than 60 per cent. Additionally,
with a share of 47.5 per cent the trade sector has a high ratio of one-person
enterprises (WKK, 2013; WKÖ, 2013b).

When reasoning about micro-firms operated by solo self-employed
individuals, a critical question is if this remarkably high representation
of one-person enterprises is a new phenomenon, or if it has always
existed, without being taken into theoretical and empirical account in the
academic sphere. Part of an answer must be that small business owners
with shops or in small handicraft production have a very long tradition,
but in recent times new technological developments have opened up new
grounds for new firms, many of these being very small. The related structural change in the labour market towards a service-sector-dominated
economy, changing behaviour and life-styles and related new demands
and new occupations have contributed to a push towards new forms of
self-employment (Gatterer and Kühmayer, 2010; Mandl et al., 2009).
Finally, classic jobs in wage- or salary-dependent work (e.g. in the IT and
consulting sector, but also in wide fields of health care) are continuously
replaced by self-employed activities (Korunka et al., 2011).

Our hypothesis is that one-person enterprises and their owners can
be divided into two subgroups: On the one hand, there are one-person
entrepreneurs who are primarily governed by motives of self-reliance and
autonomy, flexible working times and a related positive work–family–life

balance (Bank Austria, 2012; Mandl et al., 2007). On the other hand, the second subgroup may be primarily pushed into self-employment due to unemployment or precarious labour market situations.

In general, self-employment can also be considered as a driver of poverty. Statistical figures for annual gross incomes of dependent employees and self-employed people show that the incomes in self-employment are lower and that the indices for median and mean figures differ considerably in self-employment, which means that volatility and divergencies amongst self-employed incomes are very strong. Comparing the medians of incomes indicates that self-employment incomes are less than half of the incomes of employees. These figures suggest that many incomes are close to poverty and/or are not sufficient to allow single subsistence but must be combined with further sources of income.

Moreover, the risk of becoming poor is significantly higher for self-employed people than for wage- or salary-dependent employees. People who have a household income below the 60 per cent line of the median are counted as poverty-vulnerable. The ratio of poverty vulnerability marks the risk of getting poor for specific social and economic status categories. For the dependent working people this ratio is at approximately 17 per cent and for self-employed people it is at 23 per cent. In addition, the equivalised incomes of the self-employed people are on average 26 per cent below the at-risk-of-poverty threshold; under the employees this poverty gap is only 18 per cent (see Table 6.2). The comparison between employees and self-employed people further shows that the self-employed are more highly affected by financial deprivation, which mirrors the inability to participate in the defined minimum standard of living. Accordingly, 26 per cent of all self-employed people are financially deprived compared to 20 per cent for the category of employees (Statistik Austria, 2013a). Additionally, the durability of the poverty risk is much higher for entrepreneurs than for employees. While 85 per cent of the employees were never close to poverty, the ratio for the category of entrepreneurs is significantly lower at 59 per cent (Statistik Austria, 2013a).

Table 6.2   Poverty rate and poverty gap by primary source of income, 2012 (in per cent)

Primary source of income	Annual gross income Median	Annual gross income Mean	Poverty rate	Poverty gap
Employment	€24,843	€29,017	17 %	18 %
Self-employment	€11,553	€24,077	23 %	26 %

Source: Statistik Austria (2013b), Rechnungshof (2012); own depiction.

Public statistics for bankruptcies also highlight the partially precarious situations of solo entrepreneurs: In 2012 6,267 company bankruptcies were registered, of which nearly half (55.3 per cent) belonged to solo-entrepreneurs and one-person companies (AKV, 2013). Also, Statistik Austria (2013d) shows that one-person firms are overrepresented in relation to bankruptcies. More than three quarters (77.1 per cent) of all business company exits in 2011 were one-(wo)man firms, which is significantly higher than their representation within the population of all companies (66.5 per cent).

EMPIRICAL RESULTS FOR AUSTRIA

Design of the Empirical Survey

Although self-employed people generate lower incomes on average, are increasingly affected by poverty and financial deprivation, as well as insolvencies and company closures, an upward trend in the field of self-employment can be observed. This development is mainly due to factors like technological development ('digital age'), the structural change of the labour market towards a service economy, or changing social preferences. Especially one-person enterprises play an important role in the Austrian business sector. But what are the economic and social rationalities of these micro entrepreneurs; what are their motives for being self-employed? How satisfied are the one-person enterprises with their professional situation; what about their economic and financial situation and finally, is their emergence due to missing chances in the labour market? In order to answer these questions, a comprehensive online survey has been implemented in cooperation with the Chamber of Commerce in Carinthia. The survey is based on a questionnaire containing 52 questions in total. This questionnaire has been developed and tested in a process lasting several months and has finally been adapted for the online survey with the help of appropriate software (LimeSurvey). The contents of the questionnaire refer to the extent and motives of self-employment, client relations, success and satisfaction with self-employment, future prospects of the one-person enterprises, and socioeconomic characteristics.

In February 2014, a total of 9,002 one-person enterprises were contacted by the Carinthian Chamber of Commerce and invited to participate in the online survey. The response rate was 7.0 per cent, resulting in a sample size of 626 one-person enterprises. The generated sample is representative with respect to the legal form (over 90 per cent individual entrepreneurs),

Table 6.3   *Sector of one-person enterprises in the sample compared to the basic population*

Economic sector	Sample (n=626)	Basic population	
		absolute	in per cent
Business and craft	37.4 %	7,654	48.5 %
Industry	1.8 %	190	1.2 %
Trade	17.7 %	3,640	23.1 %
Transport	1.6 %	407	2.6 %
Tourism and leisure	8.1 %	1,389	8.8 %
Information and consulting	30.2 %	2,494	15.8 %
Banking and insurance	0.0 %	1	0.0 %
Other	2.2 %	0	0.0 %
Don't know	1.0 %	0	0.0 %
In total	**100.0 %**	**15,775**	**100.0%**

Source: Wirtschaftskammer Kärnten (2014); own calculations.

age (mean age in the sample and in the total population: 47 years) and gender, with males being slightly overrepresented in the sample compared to the total population. Regarding the economic sector, Table 6.3 shows that one-person enterprises from the information and consulting branch are considerably overrepresented (sample: 30.2 per cent, basic population: 15.8 per cent). This result may be due to the higher affinity for technology of this group of entrepreneurs and the associated familiarity with online surveys. Conversely, business and craft enterprises are represented less in the sample (37.4 per cent) than in the total population (48.5 per cent). Moreover, gender-related differences can be observed. While business and craft enterprises are mainly female (share of women: 51.1 per cent), the information and consulting sector is dominated by men (share of men: 73.5 per cent).

Additionally, the information and consulting sector exhibits a high share of academics (46.6 per cent), while one-person enterprises in the remaining economic fields are significantly less educated. Hence, in these economic sectors, the share of one-person enterprises with a school education below high school level (Matura) is greater than 50 per cent.

Identification of Precarious Forms of One-person Enterprises Based on the Collected Data

As indicated above, the empirical survey covers a wide range of issues related to self-employment as a one-person enterprise. The empirical

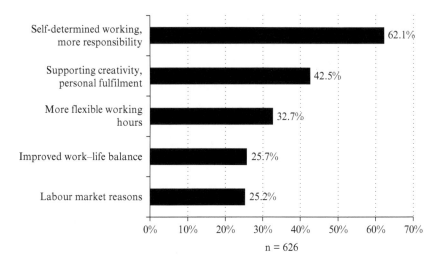

Source: Own calculations and depiction.

Figure 6.3   Motives for self-employment (multiple answers; in per cent)

results of this chapter focus on the motives for being self-employed and the associated identification of precarious forms of one-person enterprises.

The main motives for self-employment are shown in Figure 6.3. The most-often cited argument for being self-employed (62.1 per cent of the respondents) is the possibility of self-determined working and the associated higher level of responsibility. In addition, 42.5 per cent of the respondents think that self-employment represents the best way to develop their own creativity and achieve personal fulfilment. Finally, more flexible working hours and the associated improved work–life balance rank among the major rationalities for setting up a business. Regarding the motives for being self-employed, we also observed gender-related differences. Both the improved reconciliation of work and family life, as well as the more flexible working time play a greater role for women than for men, while higher income opportunities are a major incentive for male entrepreneurs.

Beside these non-economic factors, economic motives play an increasingly important role for the decision to become self-employed. Hence, about one quarter (25.2 per cent) of the one-person enterprises decided to work as an entrepreneur due to labour market reasons.[3] Labour market reasons refer to:

- the individual inability to find dependent employment,
- the precarious labour market situation that requires self-employment, or

- the representation of self-employment as an alternative to or escape from unemployment.

Based on the collected data, the main objective of this chapter is to identify these precarious forms of one-person enterprises (self-employment due to the above mentioned labour market reasons) and analyse whether this group of solo-entrepreneurs differs from the one-person enterprises that started their business activities based on non-economic factors with regard to age, job satisfaction, the economic situation or future prospects. For this purpose, the whole sample was divided into two subsamples:

- Subsample (1): One-person enterprises for which we found evidence that they are crowded out from the dependent labour market (n=158).
- Subsample (2): One-person enterprises that are driven by non-economic factors (n=468).

Subsequently, we analysed whether the frequency distribution of certain characteristics differs between the two groups. The results of this comparative analysis are shown in Table 6.4.

First of all, we found out that in the subgroup of precarious micro-entrepreneurs (self-employed due to labour market reasons) the share of individuals aged older than 45 years is significantly higher (69.0 per cent) as compared to the reference group which become self-employed based on other, non-economic factors (53.6 per cent). Consequently, labour market reasons as a motive for self-employment are predominantly given in the age group greater than 45 years, rather than in the younger reference group. Hence, about 30.3 per cent of the one-person entrepreneurs older than 45 years decided to become self-employed due to labour market factors, whereas this is only true for 18.4 per cent of the younger counterparts up to an age of 45 years (statistical significance of the correlation: Pearson-χ^2=11.397, p-value=0.001). This result may relate to the fact that elderly people (> 50 years) principally face problems in the labour market. According to that, older employees are intensively affected by unemployment and are more often unemployed for a longer period (long-term unemployment).[4] Self-employment may represent a way out of their precarious labour market situation.

Regarding job satisfaction, we also found significant differences based on the motives for becoming self-employed. In the subsample of the precarious one-person enterprises (labour market reasons), the share of respondents that is dissatisfied with the professional situation is more than twice as high as in the reference group (see Table 6.4). This

Table 6.4 Results of the comparative statistical analysis

Variable	Attribute levels	Subgroup: labour market reasons (n=158)	Subgroup: other motives (n=468)	Statistical relationship: Cramers V	Pearson-χ^2 (p-value)
Age	≤ 45 years	31.0 %	46.4 %	0.135	11.397***
	> 45 years	69.0 %	53.6 %		(0.001)
Job satisfaction	Very/rather satisfied	71.5 %	85.9 %	0.164	16.741***
	Rather/very unsatisfied	28.5 %	14.1 %		(0.000)
Monthly net income	≤ €1,500	74.7 %	65.4 %	0.086	4.673**
	> €1,500	25.3 %	34.6 %		(0.031)
Future prospects	Very/rather optimistic	77.8 %	88.9 %	0.139	12.033***
	Rather/very pessimistic	22.2 %	11.1 %		(0.001)

Significance: *** 1 per cent level ** 5 per cent level * 10 per cent level

Source: Own calculations.

difference was also found to be statistically significant at the 1 per cent level (Pearson-χ^2=16.741, p-value=0.000).

Moreover, the economic situation of individuals in one-person businesses who decided to work as entrepreneurs due to labour market reasons is comparatively poor. As can be seen from Table 6.4, nearly three quarters (74.7 per cent) of the 'precarious' forms of one-person enterprises generate a monthly net income of up to €1,500. In the reference group this share amounts to merely 65.4 per cent. Hence, one-person enterprises driven by non-economic factors perform comparatively better, and thus generate higher incomes (Pearson-χ^2=4.673, p-value=0.031).

Finally, one-person entrepreneurs that decided to be self-employed due to labour market reasons are less optimistic regarding their entrepreneurial future. In total, 22.2 per cent assess the future perspective of their business as rather or very pessimistic, a share that is twice as high as in the reference group of the non-precarious one-person enterprises (see Table 6.4). Moreover, the correlation between future prospects and motives for self-employment is highly statistically significant (Pearson-χ^2=12.033, p-value=0.001).

CONCLUDING REMARKS

Data from official statistics show a clear growth trend in the field of self-employment resulting from factors like the structural change of the labour market towards a service economy, or changing social preferences and living conditions. Closely related to this, is an emerging trend towards one-person enterprises, which already represent more than 50 per cent of all Austrian companies. Although the working life of an individual entrepreneur or one-person enterprise is associated with advantages like more self-responsibility, working without hierarchies and more flexible working hours, the business activity is subject to major disadvantages. Many one-person enterprises are struggling to survive economically. Evidence can be found in the data from official statistics, which indicate that self-employed people earn – based on yearly median incomes – significantly less as compared to employed wage earners. Moreover, self-employed persons are more often affected by poverty, financial deprivation and insolvencies.

In fact, about one quarter (25.2 per cent) of the respondents from our survey chose the way into self-employment for one or more economic or labour-market relevant reasons. Hence, these people are working as a one-person enterprise because they were unable to find dependent employment, wanted to escape from unemployment, or found themselves in an economic situation that required self-employment. On the basis of statistical comparison analyses we found evidence that these one-person enterprises are more frequently dissatisfied with their professional situation, are less optimistic regarding their entrepreneurial future, earn less and mainly belong to the older age group (> 45 years). However, this does not mean that individuals in one-person enterprises that started their business from a precarious labour market situation are unable to perform successfully as an entrepreneur. On the contrary, precarious labour market conditions may also open opportunities for the persons affected. In any case, one-person enterprises represent a very heterogeneous group in the field of self-employment. This can be shown on the basis of the collected data. Beside the established and economically successful one-person enterprises, one-person enterprises may also represent sideline businesses in the sense of a combination between independent and dependent employment (hybrid forms of entrepreneurs). Finally, there also exist necessity-driven one-person enterprises that were crowded out from the (dependent) labour market. Due to this heterogeneity, it is extremely important to differentiate: One-person enterprises may be driven by different motives and may exhibit diverging social constellations and professional biographies. In this respect, empirical research is required in order not to remain in the realm of speculation.

Beside the limitations of the chapter regarding its focus on Carinthia, we see some very general evidence that in contrast to stereotypical assumptions, the phenomenon of entrepreneurship may look totally different when it is studied as a phenomenon embedded in the labour markets and specific occupational contexts, applications and sectors (see e.g. Welter and Lasch, 2008). Some types of small businessmen and independent professionals belong to a category which does not fit with the 'clean' image of entrepreneurship. They do not show ambition for growth and they are sometimes very close to low income ranges, occasionally to poverty (Kautonen et al., 2010; Shane, 2008). Empirical studies on diverse groups of self-employed individuals in larger societal and labour market contexts produce alternative pictures, challenging stereotypical assumptions and rhetoric related to entrepreneurship (see Blackburn and Kovalainen, 2008). As Baumol (1990, p. 894) puts it straight: ". . . entrepreneurs are always with us and play some substantial role. But there are a variety of roles among which the entrepreneur's efforts can be reallocated, and some of those roles do not follow the constructive and innovative script that is conventionally attributed to that person".

Especially being in an entrepreneurial society (Audretsch, 2007) must be furnished sociologically. One has to upgrade it with the challenge of an appropriate definition of entrepreneurship at least. Baumol (1990), Zahra (2006) and Welter (2011) have brought to attention that researchers are faced by a multiplicity of contexts and that one has to distinguish between those institutional variables. Therefore it is necessary to take the historical, institutional and social context into account when examining entrepreneurship, so the dichotomous distinction between regularly employed and self-employed has to be questioned. Aiming to understand the formation of markets and the inherent competition processes (Freeman et al., 1983) one needs not only empirical studies but also a theoretical framework of socioeconomics helping to investigate entrepreneurship formation seriously in a wider context.

Besides the necessity of more empirical studies, the discussion on solo self-employment has to be brought to a more in depth theoretical discussion. Due to the great heterogeneity of those self-employed actors, comparisons of entrepreneurs and entrepreneurship among different countries – even in the EU – is almost difficult to undertake. In a first step it would be necessary to shape an internationally accepted definition of the term, so that every more or less entrepreneurial self-employed actor can find themselves in this category. Legal business owners can convert themselves intentionally or non-intentionally to paid managers who are formally wage- or salary-dependent in their own company, just in order to realise tax or other social security benefits (Bögenhold and Klinglmair, 2016 and 2017). Of course, these circumstances hint at analytical problems of coherence when using a formal labour market category of being dependent or self-employed. The same is true for the unclear borderlines between dependent work and self-employment which is very often oscillating and never precise.

Last but not least, looking at the categories of social stratification and the labour market, self-employment shows such a heterogeneity in different terms that divergences within the category are sometimes higher than divergences to other social employment groups (Bögenhold, 2019). It is not only the issue of income, which makes a difference, but segmentation lines also go along dimensions of working time, which is not necessarily an equivalent to income. A further interesting aspect is how many sources of income contribute to the monthly or annual income of a person, and which bits of income through self-employment, wage- or salary-dependent work and welfare system payments can be found.

NOTES

1. In the same period, the number of dependent employees increased by 10.8 per cent.
2. In this sense, freelancers have no business licence and are not organised in a legal representation.
3. Additionally, 16.9 per cent of the respondents stated that they started their business activities as a one-person enterprise during or subsequent to a period of unemployment. These results are also in line with the young business survey from Statistik Austria (2007,

83 ff). In this survey, preventing unemployment represents one of the main motives for the formation of one's own company.

4. In the age group greater than 50 years the unemployment rate in Austria amounts to 8.2 per cent; by contrast, the total Austrian unemployment rate is 7.6 per cent and thus below this value (AMS-Database, 2014).

REFERENCES

AKV – Alpenländischer Kreditorenverband (2013). Insolvenzstatistik, vollständige Übersicht aller Insolvenzfälle in Österreich, Gesamtjahr 2012. Vienna.

Amorós, J. E. and Bosma, N. (2014). *Global Entrepreneurship Monitor, 2013 Global Report. Fifteen Years of Assessing Entrepreneurship Across the Globe.* Santiago de Chile.

AMS-Database (2014). *Arbeitslosigkeit, Beschäftigung und Arbeitslosenquoten nach Bundesländern* (Date: 2013). http://iambweb.ams.or.at/ambweb/ (downloaded 21 March 2014).

Audretsch, D.B. (2007). *The Entrepreneurial Society.* Oxford: Oxford University Press.

Bank Austria (2012). *Ein-Personen-Unternehmen. Charakteristika, Rahmenbedingungen und der Weg zum Erfolg.* UniCredit Bank Austria AG: Vienna.

Baumol, W.J. (1990). Entrepreneurship: productive, unproductive, and destructive. *Journal of Political Economy*, 98(5), 893–921.

Blackburn, R. and Kovalainen, A. (2008). Researching small firms and entrepreneurship: past, present and future. *International Journal of Management Review*, 11(2), 127–48.

Bögenhold, D. (2013). Social network analysis and the sociology of economics: filling a blind spot with the idea of social embeddedness. *American Journal of Economics and Sociology*, 72(2), 293–318.

Bögenhold, D. (2019). From hybrid entrepreneurs to entrepreneurial billionaires: observations on the socioeconomic heterogeneity of self-employment. *American Behavioral Scientist*, 63(2), 129–46.

Bögenhold, D. and Fachinger, U. (2007). Micro-firms and the margins of entrepreneurship: the restructuring of the labour market. *The International Journal of Entrepreneurship and Innovation*, 8(4), 281–92.

Bögenhold, D. and Klinglmair, A. (2016). Independent work, modern organizations and entrepreneurial labor: diversity and hybridity of freelancers and self-employment. *Journal of Management & Organization*, 22(6), 843–58.

Bögenhold, D. and Klinglmair, A. (2017). One-person enterprises and the phenomenon of hybrid self-employment: evidence from an empirical study. *Empirica. Journal of European Economics*, 44(2), 383–404.

Bögenhold, D., Fachinger, U. and Leicht, R. (2001). Entrepreneurship, self-employment, and wealth creation. *The International Journal of Entrepreneurship and Innovation*, 2(2), 81–91.

Bögenhold, D., Fink, M. and Kraus, S. (2014a). Integrative entrepreneurship research – bridging the gap between sociological and economic perspectives. *International Journal of Entrepreneurial Venturing*, 6(2), 118–39.

Bögenhold, D., Heinonen, J. and Akola, E. (2014b). Entrepreneurship and independent professionals. Social and economic logics. *International Advances in Economic Research*, 20(3), 295–310.

Bonnet, J., García-Pérez-de-Lema, D. and van Auken, H. (eds) (2010). *The Entrepreneurial Society: How to Fill the Gap between Knowledge and Innovation.* Cheltenham, UK and Northampton, MA, USA: Edward Elgar Publishing.

Bonnet, J., Dejardin, M. and Madrid-Guijarro, A. (eds) (2012). *The Shift to the Entrepreneurial Society: A Built Economy in Education, Support and Regulation.* Cheltenham, UK and Northampton, MA, USA: Edward Elgar Publishing.

Burke, A.E., Fitz Roy, F.R. and Nolan, M.A. (2005). What makes a die-hard entrepreneur? Trying, or persisting. In: *Selfemployment.* Max-Plank Foundation, Discussion Papers on Entrepreneurship, Growth, and Public Policy, Jena.

Burt, R.S., Kilduff, M. and Tasselli, S. (2013). Social network analysis: foundations and frontiers on advantage. *Annual Review of Psychology*, 64, 527–47.

Chepurenko, A. (2015). Entrepreneurial activity under 'transition'. In: Blackburn, R., Hytti, U. and Welter, F. (eds), *Context, Process and Gender in Entrepreneurship.* Cheltenham, UK and Northampton, MA, USA: Edward Elgar Publishing, 6–22.

Davidsson, P. (2014). The field of entrepreneurship research: some significant developments. Unpublished Research Paper.

Davidsson, P. and Honig, B. (2003). The role of social and human capital among nascent entrepreneurs. *Journal of Business Venturing*, 18(3), 301–31.

Davidsson, P., Achtenhagen, L. and Naldi, L. (2010). Small firm growth. *Foundations and Trends® in Entrepreneurship*, 6(2), 69–166.

European Commission (2018). *Behavioural Study on the Effects of an Extension of Access to Social Protection for People in All Forms of Employment.* Brussels: Directorate General for Employment, Social Affairs and Inclusion.

Eurostat-Database (2017). *Selbstständigkeit nach Geschlecht, Alter und Beruf* (lfsa_ esgais). http://epp.eurostat.ec.europa.eu/portal/page/portal/statistics/search_data base (downloaded 21 March 2017).

Folta, T., Delmar, F. and Wennberg, K. (2010). Hybrid entrepreneurship. *Management Science*, 56(2), 235–69.

Freeman, J., Carroll, G.R. and Hannan, M.T. (1983). The liability of newness: age dependence in organizational death rates. *American Sociological Review*, 48(5), 692f.

Gatterer, H. and Kühmayer, F. (2010). EPU machen Zukunft. Trenddossier zur Zukunft von Ein-Personen-Unternehmen. Zukunftsinstitut Österreich GmbH: Vienna.

Kalleberg, A.L. (2009). Precarious work – insecure workers: employment relations in transition. *American Sociological Review*, 74(1), 1–22.

Kautonen, T., Down, S., Welter, F., Vainio, P. and Palmroos, J. (2010). Involuntary self-employment as a public policy issue: a cross-country European view. *International Journal of Entrepreneurial Behaviour and Research*, 16(2), 112–29.

Kirzner, I. (1979). *Wettbewerb und Unternehmertum.* Tübingen: J.C.B. Mohr.

Kitching, J. and Smallbone, D. (2012). Are freelancers a neglected form of small business? *Journal of Small Business and Enterprise Development*, 19(1), 74–91.

Korunka, G., Kessler, A., Frank, H. and Lueger, M. (2011). Conditions for growth in one-person-startups: a longitudinal study spanning eight years. *Psicothema*, 23(3), 446–52.

Mandl, I., Dörflinger, C., Gavac, K., Hölzl, K., Kremser, S. and Pecher, I. (2007). *Ein-Personen-Unternehmen in Österreich.* Endbericht. KMU Forschung Austria: Vienna.

Mandl, I., Gavac, K. and Hölzl, K. (2009). Ein-Personen-Unternehmen in Österreich. *Wirtschaft und Gesellschaft*, 35(2), 215–36.

McGovern, M. (2017). *Thriving the Gig Economy: How to Capitalize and Compete in the New World of Work*. Wayne, NJ: Career Press.

McKeown, T. (2005). Non-standard employment: when even the elite are precarious. *Journal of Industrial Relations*, 47(3), 276–93.

McKeown, T. (2015). What's in a name? The value of 'entrepreneurs' compared to 'self-employed' . . . but what about 'freelancing' or 'IPro'? In: Burke, A. (ed.), *The Handbook of Research on Freelancing and Self-Employment*. Dublin: Senate Hall, 121–34.

McKinsey Global Institute (2016). *Independent Work: Choice, Necessity, and the Gig Economy*. San Francisco: McKinsey Global Institute.

Meager, N. (2015). Job quality and self-employment: is it (still) better to work for yourself? In: Burke, A. (ed.), *The Handbook of Research on Freelancing and Self-employment*. Dublin: Senate Hall, 35–46.

Morgan, G. and Nelligan, P. (2018). *The Creativity Hoax: Precarious Work in the Gig Economy*. London: Anthem Press.

OECD and The European Commission (2013). *The Missing Entrepreneurs. Policies for Inclusive Entrepreneurship in Europe*. Paris: OECD.

Organisation for Economic Co-operation and Development (OECD) (2018). *Labour Force Statistics*. Paris: OECD.

Prassl, J. (2018). *Humans as a service: the promise and perils of work in the gig economy*. Oxford: Oxford University Press.

Rechnungshof (2012). *Bericht des Rechnungshofes über die durchschnittlichen Einkommen der gesamten Bevölkerung* (Allgemeiner Einkommensbericht 2012). Vienna.

Schumpeter, J.A. (1912). *Theorie der wirtschaftlichen Entwicklung*. Tübingen: J.C.B. Mohr.

Schumpeter, J.A. (1987). *Theorie der wirtschaftlichen Entwicklung. Eine Untersuchung über Unternehmergewinn, Kapital, Kredit, Zins und den Konjunkturzyklus*, 7. Berlin: Auflage, Drucker und Humboldt.

Shane, S. (2008). *The Illusions of Entrepreneurship*. New Haven: Yale University Press.

Shane, S. and V. Venkataraman (2000). The promise of entrepreneurship as a field of research. *Academy of Management Review*, 25(1), 217–60.

Statistik Austria (2007). *Erfolgsfaktoren österreichischer Jungunternehmen*. Vienna.

Statistik Austria (2013a). *Census 2011 Arbeitsstättenzählung, Ergebnisse zu Arbeitsstätten aus der Registerzählung*. Vienna.

Statistik Austria (2013b). *Statistisches Jahrbuch 2014*. Vienna.

Statistik Austria (2013d). *Ergebnisse im Überblick: Statistik zur Unternehmens demografie 2004 bis 2011, Untergliederung nach Rechtsform*. Vienna.

Statistik Austria (2014). *STATCube Datenbank: Mikrozensus Arbeitskräfteerhebung – Jahresdaten*. Vienna.

Stigler, G.T. (1949). A survey of contemporary economics. *Journal of Political Economy*, 57(2), 93–105.

Sweet, S. and Meiksins, S. (2017). *Changing Contours of Work: Jobs and Opportunities in the New Economy*. Los Angeles: Sage.

Welter, F. (2011). Contextualizing entrepreneurship – conceptual challenges and ways forward. *Entrepreneurship Theory and Practice*, 35(1), 165–84.

Welter, F. and Lasch, F. (2008). Entrepreneurship research in Europe: taking stock and looking forward. *Entrepreneurship Theory and Practice*, 32, 241–8.

Wiklund, J., Davidsson, P., Audretsch, D.B. and Karlsson, C. (2011). The future of entrepreneurship research. *Entrepreneurship Theory and Practice*, 35(1), 1–9.

WKK – Wirtschaftskammer Kärnten (2013). *Fachgruppenkatalog.* Klagenfurt.
WKK – Wirtschaftskammer Kärnten (2014). *EPU-Statistik, Sonderauswertung.* Klagenfurt.
WKÖ – Wirtschaftskammer Österreich (2013a). *Ein-Personen-Unternehmen (EPU) 2013, EPU-Anteil nach Bundesländern* (EinzelunternehmerInnen, GmbH). Vienna.
WKÖ – Wirtschaftskammer Österreich (2013b). *Ein-Personen-Unternehmen (EPU) 2013, EPU-Anteil nach Sparten (Mehrfachmitgliedschaften)* (Einzelunter nehmerInnen, GmbH). Vienna.
Zahra, S.A. (2006). Contextualizing theory building in entrepreneurship research. *Journal of Business Venturing*, 22(3), 443–52.

7. Precariousness and social risks among solo self-employed in Germany and the Netherlands

Wieteke Conen and Maarten Debets

INTRODUCTION

Recent decades show an increase in solo self-employment in many European countries (Eurostat, 2017). While self-employment has long been associated with occupations in agriculture (e.g. farmers) and trade (e.g. shopkeepers), the 'new self-employed' include a rather heterogeneous category of workers, covering a broad bandwidth of branches and occupations. The 'new' self-employed work for instance as IT-experts and business consultants, but also as carpenters, mail carriers or in domestic care. They are often own-account workers active in occupations with low capital requirements. Many of these new solo self-employed appreciate their position, although some feel forced and find it hard to make a proper living. Amongst other experts, policy makers and unions show growing concerns about the increase of solo self-employed and their labour market position and a substantial part does not seem to earn enough money to cover social risks.

Compared to other European countries, the Netherlands constitutes an interesting case when it comes to developments in solo self-employment; in almost no other European country has the proportion of solo self-employed as a share of total employment increased so strongly since the 1990s (from 6.3 per cent in 1992 to 11.5 per cent in 2016). Whereas the Netherlands has a rather flexible labour market and an economy that is strongly orientated towards trade and commercial services, Germany has a different tradition in labour market relations and a different industry mix, such as a relatively large industry sector. Germany also experienced an increase in the number of solo self-employed, but at a much more moderate pace. Since 2012, the number of self-employed has even declined slightly in Germany. Although the two countries share similarities in terms of several socio-demographic features of the self-employed (such as gender, age and in both countries the proportion of highly educated solo self-employed is among the highest in Europe), they fundamentally differ in their labour market structures, industrial relations and welfare state frameworks. Against this background, the question arises of how well the 'new self-employed' thrive in both countries. Particularly the discrepancies between the two countries may provide more insight into how industrial and institutional frameworks relate to potentially different developments in solo self-employment as precarious work.

Traditionally, self-employed workers are viewed as 'insiders' on the labour market who meet the criteria of an independent entrepreneur. However, self-employment and especially solo self-employment is increasingly associated with what has been termed 'involuntary', 'dependent' and 'precarious' employment (Schulze Buschoff and Schmidt, 2009; Westerveld, 2012). Nevertheless, governments of EU countries intend to further promote self-employment as means to enhance national and regional economic sustainability (European Commission, 2010). This may be problematic as there is only limited quantitative empirical knowledge about the extent and dimensions of precarious solo self-employment (D'Amours and Crespo, 2004; Stone, 2006). At the same time, unions express their worries about the related drawbacks to recent developments in self-employment (ETUC, 2016; Haake, 2016). Policy makers and politicians in both countries have started to consider the question of how to deal with the rise of solo self-employment in more depth (Dutch National Government, 2015; Brenke and Beznoska, 2016), but thus far seem not to have taken a clear stance.

While some concepts and typologies of precariousness rely solely on extrinsic dimensions such as financial rewards and social security provisions, others also include aspects like autonomy, control over the labour process and degree of work uncertainty (cf. D'Amours and Crespo, 2004; Stone, 2006; Vosko, 2006; Kalleberg, 2011; Scott-Marshal and Tompa, 2011). In this chapter, we analyse precariousness among solo self-employed by examining four dimensions: financial resilience, social protection, autonomy and control and degree of work uncertainty (see also the 'Data and Methods' section). We address the following research questions:

1. To what extent and on what dimensions can solo self-employed be classified as 'self-sufficient' or 'precarious' in Germany and the Netherlands?
2. To what extent and on what dimensions do solo self-employed differ – both within and between countries?

In the following section, we briefly address the institutional context with respect to social security programmes in Germany and the Netherlands. Next, an introduction to the methodology employed and the concept of precariousness used in this chapter is further explained. Based on the findings in this chapter, we present recommendations for researchers and practitioners on how to include self-employed interests adequately into socio-economic policy making in Germany and the Netherlands.

INSTITUTIONAL CONTEXT

> Notwithstanding the evident trend towards privatisation, the Dutch model (still) provides the most comprehensive social security [as compared to the British and German] for all self-employed people in terms of a basic pension system with universal coverage. (Schulze Buschoff and Schmidt, 2009, p. 156)

The institutional context is not only likely to affect the decision to become solo self-employed (Torrini, 2005; Baumann and Brändle, 2012), but also affects the extent to which solo self-employed are (a) able to gain sufficient income from a job in self-employment and (b) have to deal with various social risks (including the risk of poverty in old age, the risk of disability and the risk of unemployment). Regarding the institutional context, we discuss the national income tax system and coverage for various social risks in the Netherlands and Germany respectively.

Whether solo self-employed gain sufficient net income from a job in self-employment is partly related to the national income tax system. The Dutch income tax system has several fiscal facilities for solo self-employed workers, including the small business tax deduction and profit exemption for small and medium-sized enterprises, both lowering the taxable income of self-employed substantially. As the small business tax deduction does not depend on profit size, solo self-employed with a lower profit have a relative advantage. In addition, all Dutch residents – including the self-employed – are entitled to a basic pension after retirement age (see Table 7.1). The amount of benefits of this retirement pension is poverty-avoiding. In the context of universal access and relatively high replacement rates, especially for low-income earners, the protection of solo self-employed against age poverty is comprehensively ensured (Schulze Buschoff, 2007; Westerveld, 2016). Besides, self-employed in the Netherlands are covered by compulsory social health insurance, which is contribution-based and based on residency.

However, there are also substantial potentially uncovered social risks in the Netherlands when it comes to the solo self-employed. For instance,

Table 7.1   Comparison of old-age insurance schemes in Germany and the Netherlands

	Germany	Netherlands
Basic, national state insurance (first pillar)	Statutory pension insurance (GRV). Compulsory insurance for dependent employees; compulsory insurance systems exist for about a quarter of the self-employed	Basic system with universal coverage for all residents, including all self-employed
Occupational retirement provision (second pillar)	About half of the workforce (55% in co-determined companies, Baumann and Blank 2016) are included in occupational pension schemes; solo self-employed cannot join as they do not belong to a company	Occupational pensions play a dominant role (coverage of over 90% of employees); solo self-employed cannot join as they do not belong to a company
Private retirement provision (third pillar)	Voluntary private pension products; Riester pensions are subsidised by the state, but they are only available for dependent employees and a few groups of self-employed persons; solo self-employed persons can conclude a contract for the (also subsidised) Rürup pension	Voluntary private pension products, often with tax advantages

Source: Own composition, from Conen et al. (2016).

self-employed workers are largely expected to protect themselves against the risk of disability and save for additional retirement income via the private insurance market. In practice, however, only about a quarter of self-employed persons in the Netherlands indicate they have disability insurance and about one third thinks their pension savings and other sources of income will be sufficient to live comfortably after retirement (Conen et al., 2016, p. 82; Statistics Netherlands, 2017). Furthermore, in the case of maternity self-employed women are entitled to 100 per cent of a minimum income for a period of 16 weeks after birth, while women in paid employment are entitled to the full replacement of their regular income (Conen et al., 2016, p. 12).

In Germany, the income tax burden is in principle higher than in the Netherlands, but the system differs in its tax-deductible items. Whether a solo self-employed is 'better off' using the Dutch or German national tax system seems to depend upon the individual situation. Coverages of social risks in Germany are more or less comparable to the situation in the

Netherlands. For instance, German solo self-employed also have to deal with the risk of incapacity for work and additional pension savings via the private market[1] – with similarly low insurance rates. In addition, since 2009 Germany has an insurance obligation in the health insurance system for the entire population and thus also for the self-employed (Schulze Buschoff, 2016). However, Germany also has some special features with respect to social protection for self-employed persons. Maybe the most striking aspect is that some compulsory insurance (e.g. disability and poverty in old age) is limited to a few special groups of self-employed persons according to the tradition of Bismarck's social insurance.[2] Behind this duality is the idea that – in principle – the self-employed can provide for themselves and do not need the collective protection of the insured persons' solidarity. However, for some groups of self-employed the absence of a need for protection was not considered justified and they were gradually integrated into the state pension system, for instance. Today, about a quarter of the self-employed are in compulsory special schemes, with the conditions differing widely depending on the profession. These special schemes, as well as the statutory pension insurance are strongly oriented to the equivalence principle. Gaps in the occupational biography and low incomes are reflected in pensions. As a consequence, age poverty is being feared not only in the case of uninsured solo self-employed, but also among those who are integrated into the state pension system but are among the low-paid.

Overall, comparing the Dutch and German institutional context, the solo self-employed in the Netherlands seem to be more integrated into the state social insurance systems and more socially secure than the solo self-employed in Germany. This is, for instance, reflected in long-standing legislation in the areas of social health insurance and entitlement to a basic pension after retirement age. However, in the Netherlands there are also substantial gaps in social security for solo self-employed individuals, such as in the areas of disability insurance and additional retirement income savings.

DATA AND METHODS

The research questions were answered by using both survey data and interviews with solo self-employed. We elaborate on the collection of the survey data and qualitative interviews as well as on the applied methods in the following subsections.

Data

Survey data on behaviour and attitudes among solo self-employed were collected in Germany and the Netherlands in 2014. The total number of completed questionnaires amounts to 1,550, of which 757 are from Germany and 793 from the Netherlands. The response rate in Germany was 19 per cent and in the Netherlands 40 per cent, which is comparable to other surveys in organisational research and among solo self-employed (e.g. Baruch and Holtom, 2008; Zandvliet et al., 2013; Ybema et al., 2013).[3] At the country level, a random sample was drawn from a group of online panelists who are registered as being solo self-employed. The data collection was carried out by TNS Nipo and the method used was computer-assisted web interviewing (CAWI). The questionnaires used in both countries were identical and a double translation procedure was followed. At the start of the questionnaire, screening questions were posed to check whether respondents were (still) solo self-employed.

In-depth interviews with solo self-employed were held in 2015–2016 in both countries. In-depth interviewing is an appropriate method for collecting data on individuals' personal histories, perspectives and experiences. All interviews were recorded electronically and were fully transcribed. To ensure that we covered the same aspects of the qualitative research in both countries, a topic list for interviews was developed (semi-structured form). We used 'purposive sampling' or 'purposeful selection' for the recruitment of participants for this study. The selection criteria for inclusion were the following. Foremost, solo self-employed had to be active in a sector that was highly significant for the structural change and growth of self-employed labour; in both countries self-employment growth mainly seems attributable to a growth in 'construction' and different kinds of 'services' in both the public and the private sector (Conen et al., 2016). In addition, we wanted two groups of solo self-employed to be able to contrast their status in terms of freedom and insecurity. We therefore chose to focus on solo self-employed from 'construction' and 'creative industries' (with the exception of the 'art and heritage sector'). We recruited participants for whom solo self-employment was the main job from various age groups and with different self-employment durations. We followed the principles of informed consent and assigned each participant a unique code number and pseudonym (see Table 7.2).

Measuring Precariousness

Based on previous research on typologies of own account workers in Canada (D'Amours and Crespo, 2004; Vosko, 2006) and the United States

*Table 7.2   Participating solo self-employed by age, sector, occupation and
            country*

No.	Pseudonym	Age group	Sector	Occupation	Country
1	Megan	40-49	Construction	Painter	NL
2	Liam	50-59	Construction	All round construction	NL
3	Adam	50-59	Construction	Painter and glazier	NL
4	Matthew	20-29	Construction	Specialised welder	NL
5	Connor	50-59	Construction	All round construction	NL
6	George	30-39	Construction	Construction of stands/ stages	NL
7	Jack	50-59	Construction	Carpenter	NL
8	Thomas	20-29	Construction	Contractor	NL
9	Ann	40-49	Construction	All round construction	NL
10	Owen	50-59	Construction	Carpenter	NL
11	Richard	50-59	Construction	All round construction	NL
12	Patrick	50-59	Construction	Kitchen renovator	NL
13	Dian	30-39	Creative	Illustrator	NL
14	Phoebe	40-49	Creative	Communications	NL
15	Sansa	40-49	Creative	Producer/programme maker	NL
16	Kyle	30-39	Creative	Musician	NL
17	Rachel	40-49	Creative	Photographer	NL
18	Suzan	40-49	Creative	Interior styling and design	NL
19	Ned	40-49	Creative	Photographer	NL
20	Rob	40-49	Construction	Carpenter	DE
21	Scott	40-49	Construction	Architect	DE
22	Jeff	40-49	Construction	Heating engineer	DE
23	Sam	40-49	Construction	Parquet floor layer	DE
24	Brandon	40-49	Construction	Architect	DE
25	Abigail	40-49	Construction	Heating, gas and water engineer	DE
26	Matt	50-59	Construction	Construction consultant/ manager	DE
27	Anthony	40-49	Creative	Film editor	DE
28	Benjamin	40-49	Creative	Camera man	DE
29	Brandon	40-49	Creative	Music journalist	DE
30	Ella	50-59	Creative	Textile designer	DE
31	Jimmy		Creative	Producer advertising industry	DE
32	Chloe	40-49	Creative	Make-up artist	DE

(Stone, 2006) we examined four dimensions of precariousness – in both the survey and the interviews:

1. *Financial resilience* – Income may be the most definable dimension of precarious employment. Workers need sufficient earnings to maintain a decent standard of living. In the case of the solo self-employed, we chose to broaden the measurement of 'low pay' at the occupational level to a measurement of what we called 'low financial resilience' at the household level (see Box 7.1 for how 'financial resilience' is measured). We did so because income from self-employment is notoriously hard to measure (Parker, 2004; Crettaz, 2013), and because a substantial share of individuals who have a job in self-employment are – probably more often than is the case with wage and salary workers in low income jobs – not or not completely dependent on this income. Other sources of income may come for instance from a spouse, a second job or 'financial windfalls' (Taylor, 2001; Delmar et al., 2008; Conen et al., 2016).

2. *Social protection* –Social security provisions are another important part of an employment package, including, for example, life and disability insurance, pensions and health and dental coverage. In Europe, there is a large divide between self-employed who do and do not participate in disability insurance as well as pension savings (Schulze Buschoff, 2007; Schulze Buschoff and Schmidt, 2009; Choi, 2009).

3. *Autonomy and control* – This dimension refers to workers' control over the labour process, which is linked to control over working conditions and wages.

4. *Degree of work (un)certainty* – Although self-employed almost by the nature of their employment form have a relatively high degree of work uncertainty, they still may experience different degrees of uncertainty, for instance due to the level of competition or the size of the (potential) clientele base.

Given that the conceptualisation of precariousness consists of multiple facets, precariousness or self-sufficiency does not necessarily have to be conceived as a gradational matter. This chapter assesses – based on these four features of precariousness – how different types of solo self-employed can be identified.

Methods

To get to a typology a cluster analysis was performed based on the four dimensions of precariousness outlined in the previous subsection. Box 7.1

BOX 7.1   MEASUREMENT OF THE FOUR DIMENSIONS WITH SURVEY DATA

Financial resilience of solo self-employed was measured by three items. First, respondents reported their total gross yearly household income, which was adjusted to the household composition. A seven-point response format was used ('1' Minimum income (less than €12,500) to '7' More than two times average income (more than €78,500)). Besides, respondents were asked to indicate whether they have financial means to bridge a period without work ('1' No, I don't have financial means to '6' Yes, I can overcome more than a year without work). Finally, respondents were asked to assess the current financial situation of their household on a five-point scale (ranging from '1' large surplus to '5' large deficit). By using household income, financial resilience thus does not automatically refer to resilience resulting from economic activity, but rather to resilience of the individual or the household, even when this sometimes means that solo self-employed rely on their partner.

Social protection was operationalised by asking whether self-employed have a disability insurance for their work as a self-employed without employees ('1' yes, '0' no), whether they are entitled to supplementary pension from additional measures (e.g. savings, (life) insurance or (other) investments to generate more income in old age) ('1' yes, '0' no) and whether their 'pension savings and other sources of income are sufficient to live comfortably after retirement' (five-point Likert scale ranging from '1' completely disagree to '5' completely agree).

Autonomy and control was measured by asking to what extent self-employed can decide for themselves how much they work and when they work and to what extent they can determine their own day rate/hourly rate (five-point Likert scale ranging from '1' completely disagree to '5' completely agree).

The degree of work (un)certainty was operationalised by asking self-employed to what extent they experience strong competition in their work (five-point Likert scale ranging from '1' completely disagree to '5' completely agree) and the number of different clients or customers they had in the past 12 months, with a higher number indicating less dependency on a particular client or customer for future work (3 categories: '1' ≤ 3, '2' 4–19, '3' 20+).

---

summarises the measurement of the four dimensions in our survey data. Model selection was based on two criteria: formal model fit and substantial interpretability of the clusters. A hierarchical cluster analysis, using Ward's method and the squared Euclidean distance, produced five clusters. We chose Ward's method because it minimises the variation in each cluster and is considered to be the most robust method, performing well under a range of circumstances (see e.g. Aldenderfer and Blashfield, 1984; Overall et al., 1993).

To analyse the similarities and differences between Germany and the Netherlands on the various dimensions of precariousness, including attitudes and behaviour towards social risks, in more depth we used the interview data. Transcripts of interviews, field notes and desk research materials were imported into a software package for data storage, retrieval and analysis (NVivo). The analysis was carried out with the help of this program as interviews were re-read and coded according to the different dimensions of precariousness.

RESULTS

Identification of the Precariously Solo Self-employed

Based on the conditional probabilities of the clusters to their initial constituting dimensions of precariousness, substantive interpretation is given to the typology and clusters are given a name that refers to their main features (Table 7.3).

The first cluster comprises the group of 'precariously' solo self-employed (12.9 per cent). These self-employed are characterised by overall rather low scores on the four dimensions of precariousness. Respondents in this cluster have a high probability of having a yearly household income which is well below the average income, tend to have the financial means to bridge a period of less than a month without work and the financial situation of the household is often evaluated as having 'some deficit'. Respondents in this cluster hardly have disability insurances and tend to lack adequate pension provisions. Moreover, they generally experience relatively little control over their work processes, experience a relatively high competitive environment and relatively often have only a few clients or customers per year.

The second and largest cluster (40.6 per cent) is characterised by more 'moderate' scores on the following dimensions of precariousness: financial resilience, autonomy and control and degree of work (un)certainty. However, solo self-employed in this cluster have a rather low probability of having social protection. This may either indicate that (a part of) this group comprises self-employed who depend on this income and *should* have social security provisions but do not have it due to either a lack of financial means or because they do not think about these aspects related to self-employment (the 'unsustainables'), but it may also comprise self-employed who have, for instance, 'financial back-up' in the form of a spouse, a second job or as a result of 'financial windfalls' and therefore do not need additional social security provisions for their jobs in self-employment (still 'sustainables') (Taylor, 2001; Delmar et al., 2008, Conen et al., 2016). Therefore, this type of solo self-employed is labelled as 'moderate, potentially at risk'. The third cluster (11.5 per cent) resembles the second cluster in most respects, with the exception that solo self-employed in this cluster

Table 7.3 Distribution of cluster conditional probabilities over four dimensions of precariousness

	Overall distribution	Precarious (1)	Moderate, potentially at risk (2)	Moderate, sustainable (3)	Professionals, potentially at risk (4)	Professionals, sustainable (5)
Cluster size		0.129	0.406	0.115	0.191	0.159
Financial resilience						
*Gross yearly household income**						
Minimum income or below	0.051	0.160	0.064	0.035	0.000	0.000
Higher than minimum income, below average income	0.326	0.665	0.375	0.503	0.087	0.100
Average income	0.203	0.144	0.254	0.168	0.194	0.167
Higher than average income	0.419	0.031	0.308	0.295	0.719	0.732
Financial means to bridge period						
Up to a month	0.314	0.845	0.334	0.445	0.017	0.075
1–6 months	0.328	0.108	0.372	0.387	0.236	0.469
More than 6 months	0.359	0.046	0.295	0.168	0.747	0.456
Financial situation of household						
Deficit	0.221	0.732	0.200	0.335	0.003	0.025
Get by	0.286	0.232	0.437	0.382	0.045	0.167
Surplus	0.493	0.036	0.363	0.283	0.951	0.808
Social protection						
Disability insurance						
Yes	0.257	0.005	0.000	0.861	0.000	1.000
No	0.743	0.995	1.000	0.139	1.000	0.000
Supplementary pension						
Yes	0.650	0.227	0.519	0.653	0.965	0.954
No	0.350	0.773	0.481	0.347	0.035	0.046

	Col 1	Col 2	Col 3	Col 4	Col 5	Col 6
Sufficient income after retirement						
(completely) disagree	0.335	0.856	0.334	0.445	0.076	0.126
neither agree nor disagree	0.326	0.124	0.429	0.399	0.212	0.318
(completely) agree	0.339	0.021	0.237	0.156	0.712	0.556
Autonomy and control						
Autonomy in amount of work						
(completely) disagree	0.083	0.268	0.010	0.220	0.035	0.063
neither agree nor disagree	0.131	0.242	0.103	0.173	0.087	0.138
(completely) agree	0.787	0.490	0.887	0.607	0.878	0.799
Autonomy in working times						
(completely) disagree	0.081	0.258	0.020	0.231	0.042	0.029
neither agree nor disagree	0.140	0.180	0.110	0.185	0.118	0.180
(completely) agree	0.779	0.562	0.871	0.584	0.840	0.791
Control over day rate/hourly rate						
(completely) disagree	0.152	0.376	0.108	0.283	0.083	0.063
neither agree nor disagree	0.198	0.201	0.211	0.231	0.163	0.180
(completely) agree	0.650	0.423	0.681	0.486	0.753	0.757
Degree of work (un)certainty						
Competitive work environment						
(completely) disagree	0.174	0.088	0.142	0.168	0.285	0.197
neither agree nor disagree	0.291	0.175	0.264	0.225	0.392	0.381
(completely) agree	0.536	0.737	0.594	0.607	0.323	0.423
Number of clients/customers						
≤3	0.178	0.258	0.177	0.133	0.184	0.142
4–19	0.390	0.340	0.385	0.416	0.424	0.381
20+	0.431	0.402	0.439	0.451	0.392	0.477

Note: * Adjusted for household composition.

Source: Survey Solo Self-employment (SSE) (2014).

score relatively high on social security provisions. Therefore, this cluster is described as 'moderate, sustainable'.

Finally, the fourth and fifth cluster are characterised by relatively high scores on financial resilience, autonomy and control and degree of work (un)certainty. Again, one group scores relatively low on social protection and are therefore labelled 'professionals, potentially at risk' (19.1 per cent), whereas the other group scores relatively high on social protection ('professionals, sustainable') (15.9 per cent).

Figure 7.1 depicts the results of this cluster analysis for the two countries separately on the dimensions 'financial resilience' and 'social protection'. Cluster 1 represents the precariously self-employed with limited social security provisions and low financial resilience. Cluster 5 represents the professionals with good social security provisions and adequate financial resilience. The figure shows clear similarities between the two countries and cluster 2 (moderate, potentially at risk) is the largest cluster in both countries. In the Netherlands, fewer solo self-employed are categorised into cluster 1 (precarious) and 2 (moderate, potentially at risk), whereas cluster 4 (professionals, potentially at risk) is relatively large in the Netherlands.

Dimensions of Precarious Self-employment

In this section, the dimensions of precariousness will be investigated in more detail using the qualitative interviews from Germany and the Netherlands. The dimensions 'financial resilience', 'social protection', 'autonomy and control', and 'degree of work (un)certainty' are discussed separately.

Financial resilience – In both countries, the distribution of financial resilience is substantial among interviewees. The qualitative interviews provide on the one hand several examples of solo self-employed who can be considered precarious in terms of financial resilience. Some interviewees indicate, for instance, that every month they do not know how to get through the next month, that they are not able to earn a subsistence wage in their self-employment job and that their debts actually grow over the years. Their descriptions also show that these interviewees depend on this income from self-employment and there are no other sources in the form of for instance a spouse or financial reserves. On the other hand, some interviewees make a very decent living from their jobs in self-employment for themselves or their families. The importance of including 'other sources of income' as well as the household level in research on solo self-employment clearly emerges from the interviews. Various interviewees mention, for instance, that they live in a house or apartment owned by their parents, so they have low living costs, and financial back-up in the form of a spouse is also fre-

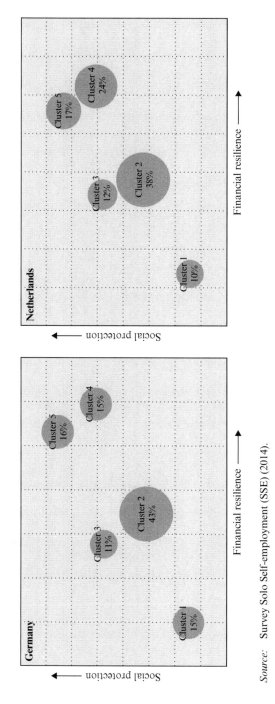

Source: Survey Solo Self-employment (SSE) (2014).

Figure 7.1   Cluster analysis of solo self-employed in Germany and the Netherlands

quently mentioned. In the following quote, Jack is talking about the birth of his second child and the job of his partner in relation to the financial resilience of their household:

> We just had our second [child], so starting as a self-employed was quite a challenge. But my partner also had a permanent job, a fairly good job, so financially I never worried too much. (Jack, 50–59 years)

Social protection – From the quantitative analyses we distinguished various groups of solo self-employed. First, there is the group of self-employed who are precarious on all four dimensions, including the social protection dimension which is mostly lacking from the general financial restrictions they face. Second, there are groups of 'moderate' and 'professional' solo self-employed who have adequate social protection in terms of both disability insurance and pension savings, rational and sensible in line with the 'traditional' view of the entrepreneur. But third, there are also two groups, moderate and professional, which are considered 'potentially at risk'. Perhaps they do not have social security provisions because they do not *need* it, which would still be in line with the 'traditional' view. However, from the interviews the picture emerges that often those solo self-employed in fact would need social protection provisions, but face restrictions in their decision-making.

First, the qualitative research provides examples of solo self-employed with 'conditions', facing severe barriers in entering social security schemes. A poignant example comes from a self-employed in construction, who – after obtaining information from various insurance companies – concludes that he cannot find a reasonable way to insure himself:

> I encountered various problems with my disability insurance at that time. I work in construction and construction already comes with a higher risk premium. Moreover, I had a chronic illness, making it virtually impossible for me to get insurance. The risk is considered too high according to the insurance companies, so 9 out of 10 refused to insure me at all at that time, and number 10 comes up with a premium which was way too high, especially for a starting entrepreneur. So, at that time I did not see any option to insure myself. (Thomas, 20–29 years)

But also for solo self-employed with moderate to good incomes and *without* conditions the interviews contain numerous examples of solo self-employed who indicate it is too costly to take up social insurance themselves – especially those who are in their start-up phase and when income flows are not stable. Although it is sometimes suggested that solo self-employed may not really think about insurance, this is not the picture that emerges from the interviews; most solo self-employed have given it serious thought. A representative narrative of a 40-year-old solo self-employed shows the level of stress her 'decision' involves:

> Insurances and everything, that is really coming between me and my sleep. From the fact that I do not have any disability insurance at all; that really scares me. Because: how am I going to do that? If I cannot work, what can I do . . . Then I receive nothing. And then what about my child? What choice do I really have then? Living on social security? That is a distressing problem; I really am losing sleep over this. (Sansa, 40–49 years)

Although a lack of adequate pension savings may not lead to such immediate stress, many solo self-employed also express their worries about their retirement saving adequacy. Some of them are certain that they save too little, but indicate that they do as much as they can; often via saving accounts. As with financial resilience, the interviews also point towards the importance of taking into account 'other sources of income' and the household level in solo self-employeds' assessments of retirement saving adequacy. Some of the interviewees in the 'moderate' or 'professional' group know they save too little for retirement, but have 'alternative' ideas on how they are going to make ends meet after retirement. Several interviewees, for instance, mention that they own a house, that they expect a substantial inheritance or mention other sources of income as their pension plan. Adam, for instance, combines various types of pension savings in his assessment:

> Back then, I got a departure bonus of about 100,000 – I think it was in euros. From this amount, I put aside as much money as possible for my retirement; I think I paid an amount equal to at least ten years of premium. And I already spent twenty-four years working at the bank, which had the best pension fund in the Netherlands. So, I think I have saved sufficiently by now. So, from the AOW [basic pension] and my own pension savings, and my wife also works three days a week. (Adam, 50–59 years)

Autonomy and control – From the existing literature as well as the interviews in our study the picture emerges that freedom and autonomy in working times, location, practices and content is often among the reasons to become self-employed and for a substantial part of self-employed also realised in practice – albeit to a varying extent and partly influenced by occupational restrictions. Technological developments seem to contribute:

> Owing to technical developments, still ongoing and advancing, more work can be taken home. So, nowadays, I can for instance cut at home; the costs are negligible. Ten years ago, at the beginning of the millennium, I would rent expensive equipment in a production house. (Anthony, 40–49 years)

Although precariousness on the dimension of autonomy in working conditions, practices and content did not come forward in our interviews, this may be due to selection effects, for instance related to the used method and/ or the sectors of industry and countries involved. For instance, 'new' self-employed in 'bogus' construction work or delivering packages are perhaps more likely to be precariously employed in terms of working conditions, times, location, practices and content.

The interviews indicate that control over the day rate or hourly rate is an issue many solo self-employed worry about. Sometimes in terms of the role *other* self-employed play in terms of 'destructive competition' (asking prices that do not cover costs) and the role of consumers or clients who lack knowledge on what a decent price involves. Sometimes in terms of their own responsibility, acknowledging that – especially at start-up and in services – it is hard to know what a fair price is.

> I see a lot of them when I go to wholesalers; I see people wearing tracksuits and sneakers ordering building materials . . . They probably get a substantial part of the work, going well below the prices and after a while you can repair all kind of things they 'made'. I do not think it is right and I do not believe that they have arranged anything in terms of pensions or disability. (Jack, 50–59 years)

> I think price setting is an issue among solo self-employed, at least in the creative sector. How much should I charge? What is reasonable? And how do I keep the sector healthy? I know we have to ask reasonable prices, otherwise the market gets spoiled . . . Related to that is that many consumers do not understand the pricing. (Ann, 40–49 years)

Degree of uncertainty – Although solo self-employed may enjoy many plus-sides on being their 'own boss', they also have a relatively high degree of work uncertainty – almost by the nature of their employment form:

> People always talk about the autonomy and the freedom. Then I think: yes, of course, you have the freedom in terms of deciding your own working times and work activities. But in a way it is also less freedom, because you are thinking about your work 24 hours a day. And you're always occupied with the question: when will the next job come along? (Rachel, 40–49 years)

Nevertheless, the level of uncertainty they experience may vary substantially and depend on both 'factual' uncertainty (like the size of the (potential) clientele base and level of competition) as well as on more personal traits. Either way, precariousness on this dimension seems to involve a clear straining effect:

> Sometimes people cancel a job, and you need to find something else. No work is no money . . . And if I do not find a new job for a week or two, I am thinking

like: "I need to earn a daily bread" and then I start to worry, I will sweat and be awake for a night, and I wake up early and think: "do I have a job today or not?" That is stressful. After ten years, I think I can conclude that I finally have some continuity in my company, which increasingly gives me the feeling that I will be fine. (Liam, 50–59 years)

It is strenuous not to know how to earn a living next week or next month; that is physically, mentally and emotionally strenuous. (Ella, 50–59 years)

Behaviour and Attitudes Towards Social Risks in Germany and the Netherlands

When comparing the interviews of solo self-employed from Germany and the Netherlands on the four dimensions of precariousness, we did not find marked differences between the two countries in types of answers on the dimensions of 'financial resilience', 'autonomy and control' and 'degree of uncertainty'. However, differences between the two countries in terms of their behaviour and attitudes towards 'social protection' seem substantial.

From the interviews the picture emerges that German solo self-employed have a more dismal view of the future when it comes to retirement than Dutch solo self-employed – especially among those who do not have financial means to save for their 'evening of life'. In more general terms, several of the German interviewees foresee a gloomy future, where many will live in poverty in old age. On a more individual level, German interviewees also seem to have adjusted their dreams about the future and they more regularly indicate that they will not need much in old-age:

My assessment is that my whole generation will typically not have a nice evening of life. I know, though, that I am someone who can be satisfied and happy with only a little. Satisfaction does not depend on materialistic possessions for me. I wish and hope that my evening of life will be, also without materialistic insurance, still a beautiful one. (Rob, 40–49 years)

That question [whether the interviewee thinks his savings and other sources of income will suffice to have a nice evening of life] can only be answered by suppression. Many, many people do not want to think about that . . . Will it suffice? No: it will not, it definitely will not. (Anthony, 40–49 years)

[After retirement] I would like to have a small site somewhere where the sun tends to shine – I have some places I like – and then read all the books I still want to read. I have many unread books at home. I think that is a pleasant outlook. And I found out that you do not need much money for that. (Benjamin, 40–49 years)

Although many Dutch solo self-employed also think they will not save enough to live very comfortably after retirement, such generalist views were not expressed by any of the Dutch respondents. Some think they will find a way to save later on, while others think they may have to adjust their wishes a bit to what they can afford. All in all, the future does not look nearly as bleak as with some German interviewees. There may be several reasons for this. First, whereas in the Netherlands all solo self-employed know they will be covered by the basic public pension scheme, in Germany the majority of solo self-employed is not covered by any kind of state pension insurance and even when they are, they are not assured of a poverty-avoiding coverage (see also 'Institutional context'). In addition, relatively many Dutch solo self-employed indicated that they had a working history in paid employment. Since second pillar occupational pension schemes play a dominant role in the Dutch pension system, with more than 90 per cent of employees being covered by some form of occupational pension, this means that a substantial amount of solo self-employed may have additional savings from earlier jobs via this second pillar. Responses about third pillar pension savings and 'alternative' pension provisions (like property and inheritance) do not seem to differ much between the two countries, although it attracts attention that in Germany relatively many interviewees put forward that they have or expect to inherit a house that will function one day as their retirement income:

> Well, that [house] is a very important element of my pension savings. When I would not have that, I would be seized by panic. (Anthony, 40–49 years)

In the Dutch interviews, on the other hand, the focus regarding social risk coverage is much more on the problems surrounding a free market for disability insurance. In the creative industries there seems to be a substantial divide between the two countries under study: whereas in the Netherlands interviewees tend to indicate that they cannot afford disability insurance and highly worry about it, many of the German solo self-employed indicate they had the possibility to participate in sector-specific disability insurance schemes, which they almost all participated in and seem relieved about (see also 'Institutional context'). But also in construction Dutch interviewees pay relatively more attention to the 'issue' of disability insurance as compared to German interviewees. A substantial part of the Dutch solo self-employed seems to be of the opinion that this risk should not be covered via the private insurance market. A Dutch solo self-employed in construction formulates it this way:

> Accidents happen. When you are not insured, you automatically fall back on society, one way or another. And it can happen when you are only 21 years old. You get into an accident and you lose two legs; then there is not much work for you anymore if you work in construction. So I think it would be to the benefit of society as a whole to make people insure themselves, or actually to make it a national insurance, in which everybody participates and we can take care of

those who strike so unlucky together . . . I think a government should take care of this; I am not a proponent of a free market for something that is so national insurance-like. (Liam, 50–59 years)

He also compares it to the situation regarding pension savings:

I think it is very different when it comes to pensions. I think that choice should be up to the self-employed or even more with 'workers' in general. Because one may want to spend more money now and after retirement has difficulties to hold it together, and another may want to save now and put all money aside saying 'I am not buying even an ice-cream' and wants to have plenty of money after retirement. That is his or her call. (Liam, 50–59 years)

This raises the question of whether this is a 'typical' Dutch point of view: although it seems at first that he is proposing two distinct systems for disability insurance and pension savings, in fact he may be proposing exactly the same system. Remember that underneath his remark on pension savings lies the assumption that Dutch solo self-employed already *have* a basic pension, so there is a first pillar plus 'additional' savings via the second or third pillar. Disability insurance could be organised in a similar vein: a first pillar (with universal coverage, organised as a national insurance) plus 'additional' insurance via the second or third pillar.

CONCLUSION AND DISCUSSION

In this chapter we examined the extent and dimensions of 'precariousness' (vis-à-vis 'self-sufficiency') among solo self-employed in Germany and the Netherlands. To that aim, we analysed survey data and qualitative interviews with solo self-employed in two growth sectors (construction and creative industries). Based on previous research we focused – in both the survey and the interviews – on four dimensions of precariousness: financial resilience, social protection, autonomy and control, and degree of work uncertainty. Using cluster analyses, we classified solo self-employed into five types:

1. 'precarious' (12.9 per cent): solo self-employed with low scores on all four dimensions of precariousness;
2. 'moderate, potentially at risk' (40.6 per cent): solo self-employed who have moderate scores on financial resilience, autonomy and control and degree of work uncertainty, but a low probability of having social protection;
3. 'moderate, sustainable' (11.5 per cent): solo self-employed who have moderate scores on financial resilience, autonomy and control and

degree of work uncertainty, but a high probability of having social protection;

4. 'professionals, potentially at risk' (19.1 per cent): solo self-employed who have high scores on financial resilience, autonomy and control and degree of work uncertainty, but a low probability of having social protection;
5. 'professionals, sustainable' (15.9 per cent): solo self-employed with high scores on all four dimensions.

Germany and the Netherlands show clear similarities in the structure of clusters and cluster 2 (moderate, potentially at risk) is the largest cluster in both countries. In Germany, relatively many solo self-employed are categorised into cluster 1 (precarious) and 2 (moderate, potentially at risk), whereas cluster 4 (professionals, potentially at risk) is relatively large in the Netherlands.

The in-depth interviews provide more detailed insight into the umbrella concepts used in the survey data. First, the interviews richly illustrate the importance of including both the household level and 'other sources of income' in research on precariousness among solo self-employed. Financial resilience, social protection and (perceived) work uncertainty are often largely influenced by extant other sources of income (such as property and financial back-up) or expected sources of income (such as inheritance), which solo self-employed take into account in their decision-making. Second, although some groups have adequately and 'traditionally' taken care of social risks and some have 'alternative' ways to deal with social risks, for a seemingly substantial group of solo self-employed social protection is actually a genuine sore point. This not only applies to those who are precarious on all dimensions: other groups also face difficulties in adequately directing this dimension of precariousness.

German and Dutch solo self-employed especially seem to differ on the social protection dimension. Whereas the sticking point for many German interviewees is the idea of poverty in old age and having inadequate facilities to deal with this, the Dutch self-employed mainly seem to worry about the low levels of disability insurance. Reasons for this different point of view may originate from the underlying institutional context: whereas in the Netherlands all solo self-employed know they are covered against poverty by the basic public pension schemes, in Germany the majority of solo self-employed is not covered by any kind of state pension insurance and even when they are, they are not assured of poverty-avoiding coverage. In addition, relatively many Dutch solo self-employed indicated that they had a working history in paid employment with supplementary second pillar savings. When it comes to disability insurance: in Germany, some of the relatively vulnerable self-employed individuals have insurance via sector-specific disability insurance schemes.

Overall, the group of solo self-employed is highly varied, but there certainly seem to be more 'general' issues for social policy makers to address. First, in terms of autonomy and control (but probably also fundamentally related to other dimensions like financial resilience and social protection), the interviews indicate that control over the day rate or hourly rate is an issue many solo self-employed worry about. Sometimes in terms of the role other self-employed play in terms of 'destructive competition' (asking prices that do not cover costs) and the role of consumers or clients who are considered to lack knowledge on what a decent price involves. Sometimes in terms of their individual responsibility, acknowledging that – especially at start-up and in services – it is hard to know what a fair price is. This raises the question whether there may be more awareness and information needed to support solo self-employed in 'asking the right price', or maybe more awareness is needed among customers and clients in terms of 'paying a decent price'?

However, maybe the most pressing dimension involves the social protection of solo self-employed. Underneath the surface this probably starts from a more fundamental question on what kind of welfare state a country wants to be. Do you consider solo self-employed – without exception – as independent entrepreneurs, in a more neoliberal way? Do you follow the path of corporatist countries, with a substantial divide in terms of which social protection rights apply to whom, also present in the employee-like self-employment discussion? Or do you consider principles of social security with universal coverage vital to all citizens, that is: in a more social democratic way? If none of these options seem appealing, perhaps a 'polder' solution could be a system combining basic universal coverage with supplementary insurance provisions, providing a certain level of poverty-avoiding basic security, while preserving the autonomy of self-employed with substantial degrees of freedom on how to deal with additional social risks.

NOTES

1. In Germany, self-employed persons who are compulsorily or voluntarily insured under statutory pension insurance are entitled to benefits in the event of incapacity for work.
2. Mandatory age insurance schemes apply to domestic workers, teachers, educators, nursing staff, midwives, coasters and coastal fishermen, tradesmen with entry into the craft roll and district chimney sweepers, artists and publicists, farmers as well as free professions such as lawyers, notaries or doctors and so-called worker-like persons.
3. This variation in the response rate is probably partly due to the fact that in Germany the

number of bounced emails was unknown. This means that in Germany the gross sample base could not be corrected for ineligible non-response, i.e. no contact with the selected self-employed individual was ever established.

REFERENCES

Aldenderfer, M.S. and Blashfield, R.K. (1984). *Cluster Analysis. Quantitative Applications in the Social Sciences Series*, no. 44. Newbury Park, CA: Sage.

Baruch, Y. and Holtom, B.C. (2008). Survey response levels and trends in organizational research. *Human Relations*, 61(8), 1139–60.

Baumann, F. and Brändle, T. (2012). Self-employment, educational attainment and employment protection legislation. *Labour Economics*, 19(6), 846–59.

Brenke, K. and Beznoska, M. (2016). *Solo-Selbstständige in Deutschland – Strukturen und Erwerbsverläufe*. Berlin: BMAS-Forschungsbericht Nr. 465.

Choi, J. (2009). Pension schemes for the self-employed in OECD countries. *OECD Social, Employment and Migration Working Papers*, No. 84. Paris: OECD Publishing.

Conen, W.S., Schippers, J.J. and Schulze Buschoff, K. (2016). *Self-Employed without Personnel – Between Freedom and Insecurity*. Düsseldorf: Hans Böckler Foundation.

Crettaz, E. (2013). A state-of-the-art review of working poverty in advanced economies: theoretical models, measurement issues and risk groups. *Journal of European Social Policy*, 23(4), 347–62.

D'Amours, M. and Crespo, S. (2004). Les dimensions de l'hétérogénéité de la catégorie de travailleur indépendant sans employé: Éléments pour une typologie. *Relations Industrielles*, 59(3), 459–89.

Delmar, F., Folta, T. and Wennberg, K. (2008). The dynamics of combining self-employment and employment. *Working Paper IFAU-Institute for Labour Market Policy Evaluation*, No. 2008, 23.

Dutch National Government [Rijksoverheid] (2015). *IBO Zelfstandigen zonder personeel*. The Hague: Dutch National Government.

ETUC (2016). *Towards new protection for self-employed workers in Europe*. https://www.etuc.org/sites/www.etuc.org/files/document/files/adopted-10-en-towards_new_protection_for_self-employed_workers_in_europe.pdf (accessed 25 August 2017).

European Commission (2010). *Self-employment in Europe 2010*. Luxembourg: Publications Office of the European Union.

Eurostat (2017). *Labour force survey*. Luxembourg: Eurostat Database. http://ec.europa.eu/eurostat/data/database (accessed 25 August 2017).

Haake, G. (2016). Digitalisierung und Gewerkschaften: Solo-Selbstständige integrieren. In: Schröder, L. and Urban, H.J. (eds), *Gute Arbeit. Digitale Arbeitswelt – Trends und Anforderungen*. Ausgabe 2016. Bund-Verlag. S. 310–325.

Kalleberg, A.L. (2011). *Good Jobs, Bad Jobs. The Rise of Polarised and Precarious Employment Systems in the United States, 1970s to 2000s*. New York: Russell Sage Foundation.

Overall, J.E., Gibson, J.M. and Novy, D.M. (1993). Population recovery capabilities of 35 cluster analysis methods. *Journal of Clinical Psychology*, 49(4), 459–70.

Parker, S.C. (2004). *The Economics of Self-Employment and Entrepreneurship.* Cambridge: Cambridge University Press.

Schulze Buschoff, K. (2007). *Neue Selbständige im europäischen Vergleich. Struktur, Dynamik und soziale Sicherheit.* Düsseldorf: Hans-Böckler-Stiftung.

Schulze Buschoff, K. (2016). Solo-Selbstständigkeit in Deutschland – Aktuelle Reformoptionen. *WSI Policy Brief*, Nr. 4. Düsseldorf 2016.

Schulze Buschoff, K. and Schmidt, C. (2009). Adapting labour law and social security to the needs of the 'new self-employed' – comparing the UK, Germany and the Netherlands. *Journal of European Social Policy*, 19(2), 147–59.

Scott-Marshall, H. and Tompa, E. (2011). The health consequences of precarious employment experiences. *Work: A Journal of Prevention Assessment & Rehabilitation*, 38(4), 369–82.

SSE (2014). *Survey Solo Self-employment.* Utrecht: Utrecht University School of Economics.

Statistics Netherlands (2017). *Dossier ZZP.* https://www.cbs.nl/nl-nl/dossier/dossier-zzp (accessed 31 October 2018).

Stone, K.V. (2006). Legal protections for atypical employees: employment law for workers without workplaces and employees without employers. *Berkeley Journal of Employment & Labour Law*, 27(2), 251–86.

Taylor, M.P. (2001). Self-employment and windfall gains in Britain: evidence from panel data. *Economica*, 68(272), 539–65.

Torrini, R. (2005). Cross-country differences in self-employment rates: the role of institutions. *Labour Economics*, 12(5), 661–83.

Vosko, L.F. (ed.) (2006). *Precarious Employment: Understanding Labour Market Insecurity in Canada.* Montreal: McGill-Queen's University Press.

Westerveld, M. (2012). The 'new' self-employed: an issue for social policy? *European Journal of Social Security*, 14(3), 156–73.

Westerveld, M. (2016). Social protection for the self-employed, a legal perspective. Conference on Solo self-employment, 1 July 2016, Utrecht, the Netherlands.

Ybema, J. F., Van der Torre, W., De Vroome, E., Van den Bossche, S., Lautenbach, H., Banning, R. and Dirven, H.-J. (2013). *Zelfstandigen Enquête Arbeid 2012. Methodologie en beschrijvende resultaten.* Hoofddorp/Heerlen: TNO/CBS.

Zandvliet, K., Gravesteijn, J., Tanis, O., Dekker, R., Skugor, D. and Meij, M. (2013). *ZZP tussen werknemer en ondernemer.* Rotterdam: SEOR BV.

8. Between precariousness and freedom: the ambivalent condition of independent professionals in Italy[1]

Paolo Borghi and Annalisa Murgia

INTRODUCTION

Self-employment is at the core of the current dominant discourses of productivity, profit, knowledge, and success (Fenwick, 2002), which all emphasise the role of entrepreneurs as autonomous, self-sufficient and strategic subjects for innovation, growth, and wealth. In the 1990s Paul du Gay (1996) argued that the 'enterprising self' has become the driving identity in the new economy. At the same time, awareness that self-employment is a very heterogeneous category composed of entrepreneurs but also of workers at risk of precariousness (Vosko et al., 2003; Buschoff and Schmidt, 2009) who are subject to 'constrained choices' (Gill, 2002; Smeaton, 2003) and have relatively low levels of social security (Spasova et al., 2017; Jessoula et al., 2017) has grown progressively in recent years. Within self-employment, in fact, very diverse individuals share the same work arrangement, despite having extremely different working conditions: from 'bogus' (Buschoff and Schmidt, 2009) and 'dependent' self-employed workers (Muehlberger, 2007a), who are completely or largely dependent on a single company, with low degrees of autonomy (Eichhorst et al., 2013), to freelancers and 'portfolio workers' (Cohen and Mallon, 1999; Fraser and Gold, 2001), who have high levels of freedom in managing their professional activity and their own time (Arum and Müller, 2004).

In its last report on self-employment in Europe, Eurofound (2017) tried to capture this heterogeneity in a more detailed way, by providing a nuanced understanding of self-employment based on an analysis of data from the sixth European Working Conditions Survey (EWCS). Five distinct clusters of self-employed workers have been identified: (1) entrepreneurs and (2) stable own-account workers, who tend to have more favourable characteristics and a high level of autonomy; (3) small traders and farmers, who have both good and bad working conditions; and the (4) vulnerable and (5) concealed self-employed, who are economically dependent and have low work autonomy.

In this chapter, the focus is on a category of self-employed workers that transversally crosses the clusters identified by Eurofound: independent professionals. Most independent professionals are included in the group of 'stable own-account workers' (32 per cent), but more than 20 per cent feed the ranks of 'vulnerable' and 'concealed' self-employed workers (Eurofound, 2017). Following the definition provided by Rapelli (2012, p. 4), independent professionals are "self-employed workers, without employees, who are engaged in an activity which does not belong to the farming, craft or retail sector. They engage in activities of an intellectual nature and/or which come under service sectors". The interest in this category of workers derives primarily from their constant increase in the last decade, despite a general decline in self-employment (Borghi et al., 2018). Moreover, they embody the ambivalence and contradiction typical of 'reflexive modernisation', which combines "first, the democratization of individualization processes and, second (and closely connected), the fact that basic conditions in society favour or enforce individualization (the job market, the need for mobility and training, labour and social legislation, pension provisions etc.)" (Beck and Beck-Gernsheim, 2002, p. 8). Therefore, independent professionals experience what Beck and Beck-Gernsheim (1996) defined as a 'precarious freedom', which basically means both emancipation and anomie at the same time: the increase in the margins of freedom and the simultaneous greater exposure to the risk of precariousness.

The chapter is structured as follows: first, we discuss how self-employment has evolved in Italy along with the legal framework; following from this, we provide a statistical overview of the main changes in self-employment, paying particular attention to the category of independent professionals. To further clarify our decision to restrict our analysis to this specific category of workers, we then offer a review of the key themes and debates connected to how, in the Italian context, 'precarious freedom' is experienced by independent professionals, often also defined as 'freelancers', and part of the broader group of 'knowledge workers'. This is a growing area of research, where the main topics under discussion are: the construction of a self-employed career between resources and capabilities; their degree of freedom; their limited access to social protection; and the issue of collective representation. In the conclusion, we discuss the main ambivalences and challenges of self-employment in Italy and the potential for further research in this area.

THE THREE GENERATIONS OF SELF-EMPLOYED WORKERS: A HISTORICAL OVERVIEW

Self-employment has always played an important role in the Italian labour market (Coletto, 2009). During the Fordist period, the 'first generation of self-employed' coincided essentially with craftsmen and small retailers along with a restricted group of liberal professionals who were the elite of self-employment. The number of small firms significantly increased, particularly in the 1970s and 1980s, while the traditional industries (e.g. metallurgy, chemicals, etc.) started losing their dynamism. This was mainly due to the phenomenon known as the 'Third Italy' (Bagnasco, 1977) consisting of specialised industrial districts in the north-eastern regions of the country. The growing number of small firms had specific traits. They were flexible in the introduction of new technologies and effective in the definition of cooperative agreements with other firms and with employees. Moreover, since the majority of the companies had fewer than fifteen employees, they could rely on less restrictive labour legislation (Amin, 1989). During this phase, therefore, in the Italian context the first generation of self-employed workers was functional to the organisational model, based on reticular networks of small enterprises (Fumagalli, 2015). At the same time, this emerging group of workers was also experiencing, albeit in contradictory ways, "the liberation from salaried work, overcoming a mind-set that appeared to be the only possibility in modern capitalist society, and a mentality that viewed subordinate labour as the natural form of work" (Bologna, 2018, p. 61).

During the 1980s, the de-industrialisation and tertiarisation processes – especially concentrated in the north-west of the country – reshaped what has been defined as the 'second generation of self-employed workers', who were not traders or farmers and did not belong to liberal professions (Bologna, 1997, 2014). Technological changes, together with re-organisation of production systems, generated a stronger connection between emerging self-employment and Italian enterprises. The new working environment was shaped by global trends that celebrated the figure of the self-entrepreneur (Foucault, 2004; Dardot and Laval, 2009). On the one hand, outsourcing processes generated new self-employed professionals in the multifaceted environment of small and medium-sized businesses. On the other, self-employment became more and more diffused, both in the context of material work (logistics, construction, retail sector) and in the growing service sector, where knowledge-based immaterial production was becoming prevalent. In such a context, self-employed workers were represented as the key drivers of innovation. They were supposed to bring new skills and knowledge, creatively reacting to rapid market changes, in order to remain always competitive in the labour market (Boltanski and Chiapello, 1999).

At the end of the 1990s, the composition of self-employed workers changed again, together with the socio-economic paradigm. On the one side, 'fake' or 'bogus' self-employment grew apace (Buschoff and Schmidt, 2009; Keune, 2013). On the other, the ideology of neoliberal post-Fordism further fostered the myth of the 'knowledge worker' (Bologna, 2014), based on a contradictory relationship between cooperative work and individual excellence. What distinguishes this group of workers – termed by some scholars as the 'third generation of self-employment' (Fumagalli, 2015) – is mainly their relationship with the traditional forms of employment and the level of social protection they are entitled to. Indeed, this new generation of self-employed – in which women are increasingly over-represented (Morini, 2007) – often enter in the labour market with vulnerable positions, experiencing insecurity, low levels of income and fragmented careers. Therefore, in the last decades – alongside a narrow elite of self-employed workers with good career opportunities – a different profile of self-employed has spread across the country, composed of workers with limited bargaining opportunities, low social protection, and little experience of struggles for social rights (Fumagalli, 2015). This category of workers includes not only bogus or dependent self-employed workers, but also workers who are self-employed out of choice, yet increasingly exposed to precariousness and poor working conditions.

In the following sections we introduce the legal framework within which self-employment has evolved in the Italian context. We then outline recent empirical research on independent professionals, in order to show the main characteristics of this category of self-employed workers and the main risks to which they are currently exposed.

LEGAL FRAMEWORK AND LABOUR MARKET REFORMS

In Italy, self-employment (*lavoro autonomo*) is regulated by the Civil Code (Book V, Title III, art. 2222–2238) introduced in March 1942. Article 2222 establishes that a self-employed worker is a worker who legally commits themselves to performing a service or work upon payment, without being subject to any form of subordination. When a self-employed worker signs a contract, they assume an 'obligation of result' agreed with the client and pursued independently through their own work tools. This general legal framework comprises an extremely heterogeneous group of workers: from small business persons, craftsmen, traders, farmers, with and without employees, to professionals (VAT-registered self-employed workers – *partita IVA* – the tax scheme for self-employed) without specific social security funds, and those belonging to liberal professions (such as lawyers, architects, journalists, and accountants). The latter group typically have their own private social security fund and need to pass a state examination and be enrolled on a register of a professional body, which controls access to the profession, deontology, and service quality.

Since the 1990s this already complex scenario has become even more scattered and fragmented. Indeed, Italy is one of the few countries among European member states that has created a hybrid employment contract between self-employment and dependent employment, the so-called 'collaborations' (Samek Lodovici, 2018). These contracts have existed in the Italian legislation since the 1970s, but they were only fully regulated by the labour reform approved in 1997 (the so called *Pacchetto Treu*. See Table 8.1). Collaborations were also created as an attempt to reduce bogus self-employment, but they have often been misused by the employers and used as a cheap opportunity to hire a flexible and scarcely protected workforce. During this period, the old generation of professionals were able to maintain (at least partially) their dominant position in the changing labour markets, while the younger professionals were experiencing more and more precarious and competitive working conditions. Since the end of the 1990s, many reforms have changed the regulation of self-employment and access to social protection.

As summarised in Table 8.1, in 1995, under the guise of a pension reform, a special fund for self-employed workers was created by the National Institute for Social Security (INPS). For the first time the self-employed of non-regulated professions were compulsorily included in a public pension scheme. Some years later, in 2003, a new labour reform (Act 30/2003) was approved with the aim to foster flexibility and, at the same time, limiting bogus self-employment. Nevertheless, in the 2000s, self-employment was extensively used by Italian companies, especially in the tertiary sector, so that it became increasingly difficult to distinguish between a genuine independent employment relation and bogus self-employment used as a low-cost alternative to fixed term and open-ended contracts (Muehlberger, 2007b).

Only in 2012, ten years after the Act 30/2003, the Fornero Reform (Act 92/2012) attempted to deal again with the issue of bogus self-employment, albeit through limited measures. The following year, the Italian Parliament approved Act 4/2013, addressing the new independent non-regulated professions (excluding health professions, crafts, commercial and public activities, since they already had specific regulations), mainly through the empowerment of professional associations. Finally, self-employment has

Table 8.1   Labour reforms on self-employment in Italy

Year	Reform	Description
1995	Act. 335/95 (Art. 2, c. 26) Pension Reform *Riforma Dini*	Compulsory public pension scheme for non-regulated self-employed and collaborators (co.co.co.).
1997	Act 196/1997 Labour Reform *Pacchetto Treu*	Fostered the growth of atypical flexible contracts reducing social protection and pension provisions. Private temporary agencies are allowed to operate in the market of placement services. Employers have more discretion in the use of part-time work. Collaborators are entitled to reduced social protection rights (maternity and sickness leave, pension schemes, and unemployment benefits) in comparison with employees.
2003	Act 30/2003 Labour Reform *Legge Biagi*	Increased the variety of non-standard contracts: job on-call, job-sharing, new temporary agency work contracts, and new forms of apprenticeship. With the declared aim of limiting the increase of bogus self-employment, collaborations ('co.co.co.') are partially replaced with the 'project contracts' (co.co.pro.), which have to relate explicitly to a specific project.
2012	Act 92/2012 Labour Reform *Riforma Fornero*	Solo self-employed (*partite IVA*) should be automatically employed with a collaboration contract if they meet two of the three following requirements: collaboration for more than eight months within a period of two consecutive years; pay amounting to more than 80% of the yearly total income from the same employer; a fixed work-space/station and the use of the client's working tools.
2013	Act 4/2013 Law on non-regulated professions *Disposizioni in materia di professioni non organizzate*	For the first time, non-regulated professions are regulated by national law. It assigns new responsibilities to professional organisations in relation to accreditation and certification procedures. Moreover, it introduced some measures aimed at consumer protection.
2015	Act 81/2015 Labour Reform *Jobs Act*	Eliminates 'project contracts' (co.co.pro.) introduced with Act 30/2003, bringing it back to a dependent employment relationship in case the workplace and schedules are decided by the employer. At the same time, collaborations (co.co.co.) are re-introduced, but only if it is the self-employed worker who decides how, where and when to work.

Table 8.1   (continued)

Year	Reform	Description
2017	Act 81/2017 *Jobs Act of self-employment*	Improves some crucial issues for self-employed workers: intellectual property, parental and maternity leave, sickness leave. It also provides tax relief for training and travel expenses and dedicated support for job orientation. Collaborators (co. co.co.) are entitled to unemployment benefit (even if limited compared to employees) whereas self-employed are still excluded.

been recently tackled by two labour reforms introduced in 2015 and 2017: the so-called 'Jobs Act' (Act 81/2015), which focused again on collaborations trying to limit their abuse. However, despite the main aim of the reform, it resulted in an increased flexibility of the workforce accompanied by the reduction of social protection for employees (Pini, 2015). Paradoxically, this trend has made the conditions of self-employed and employees more similar, because of the worsened conditions of the latter and the limited improved working conditions of the former. In 2017, after a long negotiation process, the 'Jobs Act of self-employment' (Act 81/2017) was introduced. For the first time a national act systematically addressed crucial aspects of social protection for self-employed workers, only partially granted in the past (Perulli, 2017). This reform represents a step forward, though once again it missed the opportunity to structurally address the gap between regulated and non-regulated professions, between economically dependent and independent self-employed workers, as well as between bogus and genuine self-employment, including the growing area of platform jobs.

STATISTICAL OVERVIEW

With almost 22 per cent of the entire employed population, self-employment in Italy represents the second largest group after Greece (with around 30 per cent), a percentage much higher than the European average (13.9 per cent; see Table 8.2). In particular, the solo self-employed (self-employed workers without employees), are the largest group among the self-employed, representing more than 15 per cent of the working population, against a Europe average of 10 per cent (Eurostat, 2017).

A brief overview of self-employment in Italy (Table 8.2) shows that, from 2008 to 2016, Italian self-employment decreased by more than

Table 8.2   Total employment (employment and self-employment), self-employed, solo self-employed and I-Pros (thousand and %) in EU-28 and Italy. Years 2008–2012–2016

	EU-28			Italy		
	2008	2012	2016	2008	2012	2016
Total employment (TE)	218,924.1	211,351.1	218,843.2	22,698.6	22,149.2	22,241.1
Self-employed (SE)	31,121.8	30,650.6	30,523.5	5,188.2	4,982.5	4,764.7
Self-employed / TE (%)	*14.2%*	*14.5%*	*13.9%*	*22.9%*	*22.5%*	*21.4%*
Solo self-employed	21,436.6	21,837	21,879.5	3,682.7	3,588.5	3,419.9
Solo self-employed / TE (%)	*9.8%*	*10.3%*	*10.0%*	*16.2%*	*16.2%*	*15.4%*
Solo self-employed / SE (%)	*68.9%*	*71.2%*	*71.7%*	*71.0%*	*72.0%*	*71.8%*
I-Pros	7,251.9	8,318.2	9,113.2	1,540.5	1,604.7	1,566.2
I-Pros / Solo SE (%)	*33.8%*	*38.1%*	*41.7%*	*41.8%*	*44.7%*	*45.8%*

Source: Our elaboration on Eurostat dataset (2017).

400,000 units (Eurostat, 2017). In the same period, solo self-employment also declined (around 262,000 units). This trend is in contrast to a moderate growth of solo self-employment in Europe, where this work arrangement has also increased in relation to total employment (from 9.8 per cent in 2008 to 10 per cent in 2016).

Despite the general reduction of self-employment in Europe, and of solo self-employment in Italy, the group of independent professionals[2] is substantially stable in Italy and is growing significantly in Europe. Moreover, the rate of independent professionals in Italy is constantly increasing in relation to the broader group of solo self-employed (from 41.8 per cent in 2008 to 45.8 per cent in 2016). This process might indicate a possible structural change in self-employment. In fact, it might be argued that the labour market reforms introduced between 1995 and 2017 substantially altered the configuration of self-employment, raising new questions about its potentiality and risks. According to the analysis of the Ministry of Labour (Ministero del lavoro et al., 2017), the financial crisis has fostered the trends towards staff reduction, transforming part of the self-employed with employees into solo self-employed workers. Moreover, the more valuable segments of self-employment (e.g. services to individuals) have better resisted the impact of the crisis, to the detriment of the more traditional service sectors. These changes have favoured mainly independent professionals, and especially those with high levels of education and high degree of autonomy. However, as shown by the analysis of administrative sources (Ministero del lavoro et al., 2017), almost 40 per cent of their income comes from a single client. These trends then suggest that independent professionals are characterised by relatively high degrees of freedom, but at the same time by economic dependence and financial risks. A research survey conducted at the national level, in fact, estimates that 45 per cent of independent professionals earn less than 15,000 euros per year (Di Nunzio and Toscano, 2015[3]).

Being aware of the difficulties of assessing the magnitude of such a phenomenon and its modalities by analysing available statistical data (Cieślik, 2015), in what follows we discuss the key elements addressed by both quantitative and qualitative studies focused on independent professionals in Italy. By integrating different perspectives on this object of study, we aim to provide an accurate picture to outline the ambivalences and contradictions of this kaleidoscopic category of workers.

INDEPENDENT PROFESSIONALS IN ITALY: BETWEEN PRECARIOUSNESS AND FREEDOM

The historical overview and changes in the legal framework described above provide the outlines of a changing landscape of self-employment in Italy. Over the past decade, there has been a decline in self-employment, but a significant increase among independent professionals, as shown in the previous section. Moreover, this growing group of workers is experiencing what has been defined as the 'paradox of individualisation' (Honneth, 2004): while on the one hand they enjoy autonomy and freedom, on the other, they are also exposed to multiple risks of precariousness and atomisation.

This ambivalence is at the centre of several studies in Italy that have dealt with framing the growing phenomenon of independent professionals, also called 'I-Pros'. The main issues addressed in the academic debate aim to understand: (1) the resources and capabilities that allow the self-employed to build a career; (2) the degree of freedom in managing their work; (3) social protection gaps; and (4) the emerging forms of collective representation. While referring to the same group of workers, the studies conducted in recent years in the Italian context do not all use the label of 'independent professionals', in some cases preferring other terms, such as freelancers, unregulated professions or knowledge workers. Most of this research does not exclusively focus on independent professionals, but on different groups of the solo self-employed. In this chapter, we decided to adopt

Rapelli's definition (2012) of I-Pros because it can be operationalised by using the European Labour Force Survey. This allows for the analysis of both quantitative and qualitative studies. Below we provide a review of the main empirical research recently carried out on independent professionals in Italy.

Building a Self-employed Career: Between Resources and Capabilities

In recent years, the last generation of independent professionals has faced new and unprecedented conditions, due to a combination of global and national factors. On the one hand, the re-organisation of productive systems, the digital revolution and the development of platform economies have redefined professional opportunities and increased competition among self-employed workers. On the other, the specific role played by self-employment in the national economy (Butera et al., 2008; Ranci, 2012), along with territorial inequalities, has concentrated the opportunities in northern Italy, especially in the tertiary sector (ISTAT, 2016), while making independent professionals' careers more difficult in the south of the country (Longo and Merico, 2016). Moreover, in similarity with other European countries, the effects of the international economic crisis have contributed to the deterioration of professional trajectories by further increasing the poverty risk rate for the solo self-employed, which is much higher than that of employees (Spasova et al., 2017).

A significant distinctive trait of the new generation of independent professionals, also those with significant professional experience, concerns the risk of prolonged entrapment in weak professional trajectories. Very often, in fact, they experience discontinuity in their working activity, and women's professional careers are significantly more discontinuous than those of men (ADEPP-CENSIS, 2015). Borghi et al. (2016) analysed the main factors affecting their career outcomes considering both resources and capabilities. Support from family members continues to represent a strategic resource, as well as involvement in professional networks, which are useful for career development. At the same time, the ability to select job offers and clients is crucial to avoid a condition of precariousness. In particular, the choice of accepting a low paid job, based on the hope of creating future opportunities, produces in many cases a work engagement that absorbs energy and leaves no room for the development of a professional strategy. To maintain a low, but apparently safe, level of remuneration has a significant effect on the risk of experiencing an entrapped career as well. On the contrary, an investment in self-promotion, by exploiting both online and traditional social networks, plays a relevant role in supporting career strategies. Reputation is an especially determinant element for career success, and independent professionals can leverage their reputational capital to expand their networks and increase their income (Gandini, 2016).

The differences between the risks of precariousness for salaried non-standard workers and independent professionals in building their careers are also discussed by Armano and Murgia (2013), who showed how I-Pros in Italy are characterised by two simultaneous dimensions: a continuous search for independence and freedom to express their creativity, and an experience of misalignment between their aspiration and their professional careers. Therefore, the precariousness of their trajectories is specific to this group of workers because they need to be part of a network, but they also must know how to make choices, because careers and biographies increasingly become a 'product of individual agency' (Rodrigues et al., 2016). For independent professionals, in fact, the risk of precariousness is correlated with the ability to realise projects successfully (Kalff, 2017). Moreover, they are constantly required to reconcile work resources and capabilities with their aspirations and self-identification, above all in the long term. In the next section we will discuss how the aspiration to enjoy greater autonomy, together with job self-identification, becomes inextricably bound up with the experience of precariousness (Murgia et al., 2017), which is incorporated in the risk of self-exploitation.

An Ambivalent Freedom

One of the main differences between independent professionals and employees concerns work organisation, and especially their autonomy in organising working activities in space and time (Bologna, 1997). For the independent professionals, the workplace disappears and is reterritorialised in an intermediate space that is neither public nor private. Mobile technology is used to carry out professional activities at home, on public transport, in libraries or cafés. What is important is not where workers are, but whether they are connected and how responsive they are, so that the freedom in terms of mobility is traded for a permanent availability, regardless of where the worker is physically located (Turrini and Chicchi, 2013; Borghi and Cavalca, 2016). As well as the spaces, even the times of life and work become more and more blurred. The 'working day', in fact, loses its meaning because the activities are mainly task-oriented, organised by projects, and paid by results (Armano, 2010). Structural traits of the service sector are common alongside the variety of contexts in which independent professionals are present, but in some specific professions such common trends are particularly evident. Especially in creative industries and digital work, the boundaries between work and life become more and more nuanced (Gandini, 2016).

To describe the assimilation of work within the set of rules of private life, even when the two spaces – home and work – are kept separate, Bologna (1997, 2018) coined the term 'domestication of work', a condition in which it is up to individuals "to use it to attain greater freedom or undergo greater slavery" (Bologna, 2018, p.109). A first consequence of this phenomenon is in fact the loss of work measurability (Turrini and Chicchi, 2013), and a second is that self-identification and the pleasure of being involved in a rewarding profession can lead to self-exploitation (Morini et al., 2014), beyond contractual obligations and fixed working hours (Chicchi et al., 2014; Armano et al., 2017). This is an ambivalent process in which independent professionals experience a particular form of 'free work', which is autonomous and unpaid at the same time, and is remunerated in terms of identity more than economically (Armano and Murgia, 2017).

These ambiguities might explain the apparent contradictory results of two recent Italian surveys conducted at national level with independent professionals. The large majority (more than 80 per cent) stated that they were satisfied with their professional activity (ADEPP-CENSIS, 2015; Di Nunzio and Toscano, 2015). However, at the same time, more than 50 per cent of the sample declared that they had endured excessive workloads, being consequently exposed to significant burnout risks. Therefore, despite work densification and high pressure, a high level of commitment and satisfaction seem to prevail among independent professionals.

Freedom and self-identification, therefore, are common traits of independent professionals across different professions and territories. They make independent professionals functional to both the contingent needs of markets and the ever-increasing need for innovation in production and work organisation. However, the constant pressure to balance different projects and to respect increasingly tight deadlines, on the one hand, and the request of being constantly available on the other, raise urgent issues concerning the quality of the job markets that independent professionals can access in Italy, and about their real opportunities to freely manage their everyday professional and personal lives, especially in a context of limited employment and lack of social protection.

Social Protection Gaps

One of the main factors that makes self-employed workers more exposed to precariousness in comparison to employees in Europe is the difference in access to social protection, both legally and de facto (Eurofound, 2017; Jessoula et al., 2017). In this frame, Italy is not an exception: the recent reform of self-employment (Act 81/2017) has not introduced substantial measures to include independent professionals and, more generally, self-employed workers in the social protection system.

Social protection systems mainly cover healthcare, accidents at work, sickness, family benefits, maternity, unemployment and pension. The Italian public health system, financed by the national tax system, guarantees healthcare for all citizens. The self-employed also have access to accident at work and occupational injury benefits. However, with regard to sickness benefits, there are significant differences between self-employed and employees. Indeed, self-employed are not compulsorily covered by sickness insurance, with the exception of some categories, such as 'collaborators', that are included in a specific scheme that also covers some categories of non-standard workers (Spasova et al., 2017). As for the family benefits, the self-employed have very limited access and there is no benefit for the liberal professions. Moreover, self-employed mothers have fewer benefits than employees and several qualitative studies have registered the difficulties for female self-employed workers to meet their desire of maternity, both because of the intense day-to-day demands of their job, and because of the lack of social protection (see Samek Lodovici and Semenza, 2012). The national survey that involved liberal professionals (ADEPP-CENSIS, 2015) pointed out that, in the period between 2010 and 2014, 24.7 per cent of respondents had to stop their activity for health problems, to take care of a family member dealing with health issues, or to manage the birth of a child. Similar results are also registered among independent professionals in non-liberal professions (Di Nunzio and Toscano, 2015).

Concerning unemployment protection, Italy is one of the countries where the self-employed are not entitled to unemployment benefits. As already mentioned in the section dedicated to the legal framework, only collaborators (co.co.co) have recently gained access to them, albeit in a limited way. Moreover, no specific forms of credit access for the self-employed are foreseen, and they are usually unable to build up sufficient entitlements for an old-age pension. As in most European countries, Italy also has a pay-as-you-go statutory public pension scheme (Spasova et al., 2017) that is not able to provide adequate pensions for the self-employed (ADEPP-CENSIS, 2015; Di Nunzio and Toscano, 2015), mainly because of their reduced earning capacity, and of the reduced capacity of public finance contributions aimed at supporting social security funds.

This situation requires an adaptation of the social protection system that has only recently, and only partially, addressed these issues. The inclusion of independent professionals proceeds slowly and still varies for different categories of self-employed: liberal professionals have their social security funds, each following a specific system of rules, while non-liberal professionals have their own public special fund, separate to that of employees. Moreover, the attempts of the last reform (Act 81/2017) to improve self-employed workers' rights in terms of sickness and maternity benefits risk being ineffective. In fact, the new reform allows suspension of the contract for a maximum of 150 days per year, *but only in cases where the client agrees.* This last specification clearly undermines the potential positive effects of the norm, since there is nothing that prevents the client from resolving the contract in case of absence. However, there are some improvements with respect to maternity, as it is now possible to replace a pregnant self-employed worker with another self-employed worker with the required professional skills (periods of job sharing are also possible).

Despite a lack of social protection, especially in comparison to salaried workers, it is worth pointing out that several qualitative studies (Samek Lodovici and Semenza, 2012; Mingione et al., 2014) have highlighted that independent professionals in Italy tend not to aspire to become employees, even if this would mean gaining full access to social protection provision. Independent professionals rather claim the right to extend universal social rights, such as maternity and family benefits, and social benefits, like unemployment benefits and pensions. Therefore, the key does not seem to be including independent professionals in traditional employment relations, but rather extending social protection to the emerging hybrid forms of work, hence also reframing the traditional employment relation system.

Collective Representations

There are differing views on the changing face of collective representation, and specifically on the future of collective bargaining for the solo self-employed (Keune, 2013). One of the main difficulties in organising workers in such a contractual position involves their complex commercial arrangements (Gallagher and Sverke, 2005; Leighton and Wynn, 2011), and the fact that they can either be closer to self-employment with multiple clients or be more similar to dependent employment (Wynn, 2015).

For decades, both trades unions and employer organisations almost ignored this category of workers. Starting from the mid-1990s, in the Italian context, some specific departments of the three main unions (NIdiL-CGIL,[4] UIL-Temp, FeLSA-CISL[5]) were focused on atypical workers, including the self-employed (Ambra, 2013). However, they only marginally intercepted the independent professionals. Symbolic events and isolated actions – aimed at raising awareness among the third generation of independent professionals – tended to prevail in this phase, where traditional trade unions were strongly and openly criticised because of their absence in dealing with the growing risks of precariousness among the self-employed. In this phase the spread of the internet opened new, direct and cheap examples of organising among independent professionals (Mingione et al., 2014), but claims-making activities and actions were still highly fragmented (Semenza et al., 2017) and showed some evident limits.

In the early 2000s, something began to slowly influence change, especially thanks to the effort of emerging independent professionals' associations. New organisations were created (such as ACTA, the national association of independent professionals,[6] and CoLAP, the national coordination of professional associations[7]), with the aim of bridging the existing representation gap between employees and independent professionals, especially those in non-liberal professions. In recent years, other organisations, cooperatives and collective movements have been created both from existing associations and from emerging initiatives such as 'Confassociazioni', 'SMart', 'DOC Servizi', 'Il Quinto Stato' or 'CLAP'. As a whole, new and old forms of organising are seeking to meet the needs of collective representation of independent professionals, but they are currently hardly able to reduce their fragmentation and mutual mistrust because cooperative and corporate efforts often hinder each other (Borghi and Cavalca, 2016).

The panorama of independent professionals' representation has proved to be rather lively in the last decade (Fulton, 2018). Nowadays, also in the Italian context trade unions are finally developing an internal discussion, which is rather intense but mostly not yet visible and known from the outside (Borghi, 2018). The attempt to adapt their strategy of representation through new initiatives is also fostering a change of the organisational culture (for example 'Consulta delle Professioni – CGIL'[8] and 'vIVAce! – CISL'[9]). At the same time, the rivalry between unions and alternative organisations has also decreased, leaving room for dialogue and common actions. During recent years, in fact, temporary coalitions of trades unions, professional organisations and new forms of organising have been created in order to improve social protection for the self-employed. The representation of independent professionals is still very limited, but its ability to influence the political decision-makers is progressively increasing, so its evolution calls for constant attention in the near future.

CONCLUSION: FUTURE CHALLENGES FOR THE I-PROS

Independent professionals show a variety of characteristics, needs and working conditions with respect to professional sectors, territories, and local labour markets. Nonetheless, an accurate review of the most recent empirical research conducted in Italy on this specific group of workers has allowed us to describe transversal conditions and common traits.

Both quantitative and qualitative research identify elements of freedom and precariousness as the two contradictory features embodied in their professional experience. On the one side, independent professionals tend to appreciate the flexibility of being self-employed, thereby working autonomously and being able to manage the balance between work and private life. On the other, however, the freedom under which they work as self-employed workers can become deleterious. In fact, apart from a minority of independent professionals that can be considered the elite in their specific professional context, a significant number are exposed to precariousness and encounter obstacles that can seriously threaten the sustainability of their careers.

In this chapter we have shown how career outcomes are connected to available resources, such as family support and professional networks, and to the capability of creating reputational capital and selecting clients and projects. However, this type of career creates subjectivities that emphasise proactivity and self-identification. Therefore, independent professionals can enjoy high degrees of autonomy and can escape from traditional work arrangements, but they are simultaneously forced to take charge of their own career and the connected risks. Very often they can decide where to work and freely manage their working time, but the blurred boundaries between working, social and private lives in many cases generate dynamics of self-exploitation, justified by the need to obtain new jobs, maintain a position in the market and pursue their own aspirations.

These ambivalences and contradictions make independent professionals an emblematic category for understanding the double face of the process of individualisation, defined by Beck and Beck-Gernsheim (1996) as 'precarious freedom'. In the 1990s, in their pioneering work on individualisation, the two German authors described the combination of emancipation and anomie as an 'explosive mixture', especially in a context of limited social protection.

As highlighted by the studies reviewed in our contribution, the limited access to social protection for independent professionals fosters the perception of insecurity with serious negative impacts on life projects, particularly for the weaker segments of this group of workers. Such insecurity worsens when the lack of social protection cannot be compensated, at least partially, by family and informal welfare mechanisms. The recent legislative changes (Act 81/2017, Jobs Act of self-employment) have been conceived to tackle some unresolved issues concerning the inclusion of independent professionals in the social protection system. Nevertheless, with the exception of collaborators (who are a very small part of the self-employed), they are still excluded from unemployment benefits and only partially entitled to sickness leave. In addition, pension levels are largely insufficient to ensure an acceptable livelihood threshold (especially if we consider the purely contributory calculation method used to determine Italian pensions). Moreover, the absence of an effective labour market regulation that tackles both the emerging economies based on digital platforms and a professional environment that is rapidly evolving (with respect to liberal professions and, in general, to self-employment in the tertiary sector) expose a significant number of self-employed, especially women and young workers, to precarious conditions.

The combination of a growing number of independent professionals experiencing precarious working conditions and the structural change in the internal composition of self-employment is a stimulus for both traditional and emerging organisations that aim to mobilise and represent the self-employed. The public debate on the role, potentialities and fragilities of the self-employed has been fostered since the creation of new organisations and grassroots groups. More recently, trade unions and some professional associations have also developed new strategies of representation.

In such a frame, the question "How then are processes of individualisation transformed into their opposite, into a quest for new social identities and ties and the development of new ways of living?" (Beck and Beck-Gernsheim, 2002, p. 36) is as relevant as ever. Independent professionals are at the centre of the process of individualisation within a post-traditional society of employees. The answer will be different depending on the new social relations and collective identities that this growing group of workers will be able to create, as well as on the capacity of social protection systems and collective representation to cope with the new risks of precariousness to which unprotected areas of the workforce are exposed.

NOTES

1. The following analysis is based on the research project SHARE – Seizing the Hybrid Areas of work by Representing self-Employment, which has been funded by the European Research Council (ERC) under the European Union's Horizon 2020 research and innovation programme (grant agreement N. 715950).
2. According to Rapelli's definition, independent professionals are self-employed workers without employees engaging in a service activity and/or intellectual service not in the farming, craft or retail sectors. From a statistical point of view, the author analyses the data of the European Labour Force Survey selecting solo self-employed workers included in the following NACE categories: Information and communication (NACE key J); Financial and insurance activity (key K); Real estate activities (key L); Professional, scientific and technical activities (key M); Administrative and support services (key N); Education (key P); Human health and social work (key Q); Arts, entertainment and recreation (key R); and Other service activities (key S).
3. The survey was conducted by means of an online questionnaire to which 2,210 professionals responded. The sample design used was non-probabilistic (snowball sampling).

The sample was weighted in relation to the reference universe indicated by ISFOL (Institute for the Development of Vocational Training of Workers – National Research Institute supervised by the Ministry of Labour and Social Policies).

4. NIdiL (New Work Identities) is part of CGIL, and since 1998 has been the reference structure for workers managed by private agencies for temporary work and atypical workers.

5. FeLSA-CISL (Federation of Self-Employed and Atypical Employees) was created in 2009 within the union CISL to merge ALAI and CLACS, two previous structures devoted to atypical workers, small businesses and shopkeepers.

6. Created in 2004, ACTA is mainly focused on independent professionals without employees in the advanced tertiary sector. It is part of the European network EFIP (European Forum of Independent Professionals).

7. Created in 1999, it gathers more than 200 liberal professional associations, with more than 300,000 members.

8. Created in 2009, the Board of Professions is promoted by the largest Italian trade union, CGIL (thanks to the impulse of Davide Imola), historically linked to the Italian Communist Party and then to the left-wing parties that have taken over its legacy. The Board is composed of organisations dealing with independent professionals, umbrella organisations, and individual professional activists in order to develop confrontation on the most relevant issues for independent professionals and lobbying activities in their favour.

9. Created in 2016 by the second largest trade union in Italy, CISL, traditionally tied to Catholic parties, vIVAce! is an online community that aims to support the identity of independent professionals by creating networks, delivering services, and lobbying.

REFERENCES

ADEPP-CENSIS (2015). *Le Professioni in Italia: Una Ricchezza per l'Europa.* Roma.

Ambra, M.C. (2013). Modelli di rappresentanza sindacale nella società post-industriale. Come i sindacati si stanno riorganizzando. *Quaderni rassegna sindacale*, 4, 75–94.

Amin, A. (1989). Flexible specialisation and small firms in Italy: myths and realities. *Antipode*, 21(1), 13–34.

Armano, A. (2010). *Precarietà e innovazione nel postfordismo. Una ricerca qualitativa sui lavoratori della conoscenza a Torino.* Bologna: Odoya.

Armano, E. and Murgia, A. (2013). The precariousnesses of young knowledge workers. A subject-oriented approach. *Global Discourse*, 3 (3–4), 486–501.

Armano, A. and Murgia, A. (2017). Hybrid areas of work in Italy. Hypotheses to interpret the transformations of precariousness and subjectivity. In: Armano, E., Bove, A. and Murgia, A. (eds), *Mapping Precariousness, Labour Insecurity and Uncertain Livelihoods: Subjectivities and Resistance.* London: Routledge, pp. 47–59.

Armano, E., Briziarelli, M., Chicchi, F. and Risi, E. (eds) (2017). Il lavoro delle relazioni: commitment e processi di soggettivazione nel free work. *Sociologia del lavoro*, 145, 1.

Arum, R. and Müller, W. (eds) (2004). *The Reemergence of Self-Employment: A Comparative Study of Self-Employment Dynamics and Social Inequality.* New Haven: Princeton University Press.

Bagnasco, A. (1977). *Tre Italie: La problematica territoriale dello sviluppo italiano.* Bologna: Il Mulino.

Beck, U. and Beck-Gernsheim, E. (1996). Individualization and 'precarious freedoms': perspectives and controversies of a subject-oriented sociology. In: Helas, P., Lash, S. and Morris, P. (eds), *Detraditionalisation. Critical Reflections on Authority and Identity*. Cambridge: Blackwell, pp. 23–48.

Beck, U. and Beck-Gernsheim, E. (2002). *Individualization: Institutionalized Individualism and its Social and Political Consequences*. London: Sage.

Bologna, S. (1997). Dieci tesi per la definizione di uno statuto del lavoro autonomo. In: Bologna, S. and Fumagalli, A. (eds), *Il lavoro autonomo di seconda generazione*. Milano: Feltrinelli, pp. 13–42.

Bologna, S. (2014). Workerism: an inside view. from the mass-worker to self-employed labour. In: Van der Linden, M. and Heinz Roth, K. (eds), *Beyond Marx: Theorising the Global Labour Relations of the Twenty-First Century*. Leiden and Boston: Brill, pp. 121–44.

Bologna, S. (2018). *The Rise of the European Self-employed Workforce*. Milan-Udine: Mimesis International.

Boltanski, L. and Chiapello, E. (1999). *Le nouvel esprit du capitalism*. Paris: Gallimard.

Borghi, P. (2018). *Self-employed Collective Representation. Strategies in Emerging Fields: A Comparative Perspective on Italy and Germany*. PhD Thesis. Milan: University of Milano Bicocca, Berlin: Humboldt-Universität.

Borghi, P. and Cavalca, G. (2016). Identità collettive tra i professionals. Esplorare le tentazioni corporative e le sperimentazioni di contro-soggettivazione a Milano. In: Armano, E. and Murgia, A. (eds), *Le reti del lavoro gratuito. Spazi urbani e nuove soggettività*. Verona: Ombre Corte, pp. 43–58.

Borghi, P., Cavalca, G. and Fellini, I. (2016). Dimensions of precariousness: independent professionals between market risks and entrapment in poor occupational careers. *Work Organisation, Labour & Globalisation*, 10(2), 50–67.

Borghi, P., Mori, A. and Semenza, R. (2018). Self-employed professionals in the European labour market. A comparison between Italy, Germany and the UK. *Transfer: European Review of Labour and Research*, 1024258918761564.

Buschoff, K.S. and Schmidt, C. (2009). Adapting labour law and social security to the needs of the 'new self-employed': comparing the UK, Germany and the Netherlands. *Journal of European Social Policy*, 19(2), 147–59.

Butera, F., Bagnara, S., Cesaria, R. and Di Guardo, S. (2008). *Knowledge Working. Lavoro, lavoratori, società della conoscenza*. Milano: Mondadori.

Chicchi, F., Risi, E., Fisher, E. and Armano, E. (eds) (2014). *Free and unpaid work, gratuity, collaborative activity and precariousness. Processes of subjectivity in the age of digital production*. Special Issue of *Sociologia del lavoro*, 133.

Cieślik, J. (2015). Capturing statistically the intermediate zone. Between the employee and employer firm owner. *International Review of Entrepreneurship*, 13(3), 205–14.

Cohen, L., and Mallon, M. (1999). The transition from organisational employment to portfolio working: perceptions of 'boundarylessness'. *Work, Employment and Society*, 13(2), 329–52.

Coletto, D. (2009). Italy: self-employed workers. *European industrial relations observatory online*. http://www.eurofound.europa.eu/comparative/tn0801018s/it0801019q.htm (accessed 28 September 2017).

Dardot, P. and Laval, C. (2009). *La Nouvelle Raison du monde. Essai sur la société néolibérale*. Paris: La Découverte.

Di Nunzio, D. and Toscano, E. (2015). *Vita Da Professionisti*. Roma: Associazione Bruno Trentin.

du Gay, P. (1996). *Consumption and Identity at Work*. Thousand Oaks, CA: Sage.

Eichhorst, W., Braga, M., Famira-Mühlberger, U., Gerard, M., Horvath, T., Kahancová, M., Kendzia, M.J., Martišková, M., Monti, P., Pedersen, J.L., Stanley, J., Vandeweghe, B., Wehner, C. and White, C. (2013). *Social Protection Rights of Economically Dependent Self-employed Workers*. Brussels: Study for European Parliament's Committee on Employment and Social Affairs.

Eurofound (2017). *Exploring Self-employment in the European Union*. Luxembourg: Publications Office of the European Union.

Eurostat (2017). *Labour Force Survey*. *Luxembourg: Eurostat Database*. http://ec.europa.eu/eurostat/data/database (accessed 28 September 2017).

Fenwick, T.J. (2002). Transgressive desires: new enterprising selves in the new capitalism. *Work, Employment and Society*, 16(4), 703–23.

Foucault, M. (2004). *Naissance de la biopolitique. Cours de 1978–1979*. Paris: Gallimard-Seuil.

Fraser, J. and Gold, M. (2001). 'Portfolio workers': autonomy and control amongst freelance translators. *Work, Employment and Society*, 15(4), 679–97.

Fulton, L. (2018). *Les syndicats s'engagent pour la protection des travailleurs indépendants*. Brussels: ETUC.

Fumagalli, A. (2015). Le trasformazioni del lavoro autonomo tra crisi e precarietà: il lavoro autonomo di III generazione. *Quaderni di ricerca sull'artigianato*, 3(2), 225–54.

Gallagher, D.G. and Sverke, M. (2005). Contingent employment contracts: are existing employment theories still relevant? *Economic and Industrial Democracy*, 26(2), 181–203.

Gandini, A. (2016). *The Reputation Economy: Understanding Knowledge Work in Digital Society*. New York: Springer.

Gill, R. (2002). Cool, creative and egalitarian? Exploring gender in project-based new media work in Europe. *Information, Communication & Society*, 5, 70–89.

Honneth, A. (2004). Organized self-realization: some paradoxes of individualization. *European Journal of Social Theory*, 7(4), 463–78.

ISTAT (2016). *Rapporto annuale. La situazione del Paese nel 2015*. Roma: ISTAT.

Jessoula, M., Pavolini, E. and Strati, F. (2017). *ESPN Thematic Report on Access to social protection of people working as self-employed or on non-standard contracts – Italy*. Brussels: European Commission.

Kalff, Y. (2017). The knowledge worker and the projectified self: domesticating and disciplining creativity. *Work Organisation Labour & Globalisation*, 11(1), 10–27.

Keune, M. (2013). Trade union responses to precarious work in seven European countries. *International Journal of Labour Research*, 5(1), 59–78.

Leighton, P. and Wynn, M. (2011). Classifying employment relationships: more sliding doors or a better regulatory framework? *Industrial Law Journal*, 40(1), 5–44.

Longo, M. and Merico, M. (2016). Educational and professional trajectories of knowledge workers. Special Issue of the *Italian Journal of Sociology of Education*, 8(3).

Mingione, E., Andreotti, A., Benassi, D., Borghi, P., Cavalca, G. and Fellini, I. (2014). Le organizzazioni sociali e i giovani professionisti nell'area Milanese. *Quaderni di Rassegna Sindacale*, 1, 123–40.

Ministero del lavoro, ISTAT, INPS, INAIL, ANPAL (2017). *Il mercato del lavoro, verso una lettura integrata*. Roma: ISTAT.

Morini, C. (2007). The feminization of labour in cognitive capitalism. *Feminist Review*, 87(1), 40–59.

Morini, C., Carls, K. and Armano, E. (2014). Precarious passion or passionate precariousness? Narratives from co-research in journalism and editing. *Recherches sociologiques et anthropologiques*, 45(2), 61–83.

Muehlberger, U. (2007a). *Dependent Self-employment: Workers on the Border between Employment and Self-employment*. Dordrecht: Springer.

Muehlberger, U. (2007b). Hierarchical forms of outsourcing and the creation of dependency. *Organization Studies*, 28(5), 709–27.

Murgia, A., Maestripieri, L. and Armano, E. (2017). The precariousness of knowledge workers (Part 2): forms and critiques of autonomy and self-representation. *Work Organisation Labour & Globalisation*, 11(1), 1–9.

Perulli, A. (2017). Il Jobs Act Degli Autonomi: Nuove (E Vecchie) Tutele per Il Lavoro Autonomo Non Imprenditoriale. *Rivista Italiana Di Diritto Del Lavoro*, 2, 173–201.

Pini, P. (2015). Il Jobs Act tra surrealismo e mistificazione: una lettura critica. *Economia & lavoro*, 49(2), 177–216.

Ranci, C. (2012). *Partite Iva. Il lavoro autonomo nella crisi italiana*. Bologna: Il Mulino.

Rapelli, S. (2012). *European I-Pros: A Study*. London: Professional Contractors Group (PCG).

Rodrigues, R., Guest, D. and Budjanovcanin, A. (2016). Bounded or boundaryless? An empirical investigation of career boundaries and boundary crossing. *Work, Employment and Society*, 30(4), 669–86.

Samek Lodovici, M. (2018). Self-employment and temporary work in Italy: five years of labour reforms. Peer Review on *The rise of precarious work (including some forms of solo self-employment) – causes, challenges and policy options* – Peer Country Comments Paper.

Samek Lodovici, M. and Semenza, R. (2012). *Precarious Work and High-Skilled Youth in Europe*. Milano: Franco Angeli.

Semenza, R., Mori, A. and Borghi, P. (2017). Rappresentare i professionisti indipendenti. Paesi europei a confront. *Quaderni di Rassegna Sindacale*, 2, 41–59.

Smeaton, D. (2003). Self-employed workers: calling the shots or hesitant independents? A consideration of the trends. *Work Employment and Society*, 17(2), 379–91.

Spasova S., Bouget D., Ghailani, D. and Vanhercke B. (2017). *Access to Social Protection for People Working on Non-Standard Contracts and as Self-Employed in Europe. A Study of National Policies*. Brussels: European Commission.

Turrini, M. and Chicchi F. (2013). Precarious subjectivities are not for sale: the loss of the measurability of labour for performing arts workers. *Global Discourse*, 3(3–4), 507–21.

Vosko, L.F., Zukewich, N. and Cranford, C. (2003). Precarious jobs: a new typology of employment. *Perspectives on Labour and Income*, 15(4), 16–26.

Wynn, M. (2015). Organising freelancers: a hard case or a new opportunity? *International Review of Entrepreneurship*, 13(2), 93–102.

9. Bogus self-employment in Sweden

Dominique Anxo and Thomas Ericson

INTRODUCTION

Like many modern economies, Sweden has experienced an increase in flexible and precarious forms of employment during the last three decades. Successive reforms of the employment protection system in Sweden – especially the introduction of fixed-term contracts not requiring justification and the deregulation of employment intermediation in the early 1990s – contributed to a significant increase in employment instability and fuelled duality in the labour market. In the aftermath of the 1990s crisis, Swedish companies have to a larger extent than before made use of external numerical flexibility in order to cope with variations of demand across the business cycle (see Anxo, 2011). Against this background, fixed-term contracts and agency work have increased significantly, by almost 70 per cent between 1990 and 2016, and correspond to around 16 per cent of dependent employees in 2016. While this development has been well documented (see Holmlund and Storrie 2002; Anxo, 2011; Anxo, 2015), to our best knowledge very few studies have analysed false/bogus self-employment[1] as an instrument of companies' external numerical flexibility. The main objective of this chapter is to fill this gap and analyse the extent to which bogus/false self-employment is present in Sweden and try to identify the institutional and economic factors that may explain its magnitude and development.

Since the last decade, successive Swedish governments have taken initiatives to promote entrepreneurship and favour the development of self-employment. These measures include: public and educational campaigns to encourage positive attitudes towards entrepreneurship among Swedish citizens, in particular young people; measures aimed at reducing administrative burdens arising from government regulations; reduction of taxes; measures aimed at easing the participation of small and medium enterprises (SME) in public procurement; policies intended to increase the diversity of providers (in particular SMEs) in previously sheltered sectors of welfare services (healthcare, elderly care, social services and education);

measures facilitating access to capital; and, last but not least, active labour market policy programmes (start-up programmes). Furthermore, in order to facilitate the transition from dependent employment to self-employment, the government has during the last decade launched several reforms of the social security system aimed at harmonizing social protection entitlements of wage earners and the self-employed. It is likely that some of these measures have increased the risk of bogus self-employment. In particular, since 2009 legislation allows self-employed persons to have only one client, including their former employer. While this reform may encourage start-ups of new firms and favour entrepreneurship it may also effectively allow employers to transfer costs, risks and responsibilities to workers by contracting out work that previously was performed in house by employees.

The chapter is structured as follows. The next section analyses the legal framework and explores the extent to which bogus self-employment is legally defined. Then, we describe the main characteristics and the development of self-employment in Sweden. In the next section, we estimate the prevalence of bogus self-employed in the Nordic countries and analyse the main disparities between self- and bogus self-employment drawing on the last wave of the European Working Condition Survey conducted by Eurofound in 2015 (EWCS, 2016). The final section provides some concluding remarks.

LEGAL FRAMEWORK: EMPLOYMENT STATUS, SOCIAL PROTECTION AND LEGAL DEFINITION OF BOGUS SELF-EMPLOYMENT

There is no legal, statutory definition of a dependent employee in Swedish labour law, but it is defined in case law.[2] Similarly, there is no legal definition of self-employment and therefore, to our best knowledge no legal definition of bogus self-employment in Sweden. Swedish contract law governs the relationship between the self-employed and their clients where the two parties formally are regarded as equal parties. Even though the distinction between wage employment and self-employment is not explicitly regulated by the law, according to the Act on Co-determination in Working life (MBL 1976:580), however, "(S)elf-employed workers who are legally deemed to be 'dependent contractors' should be considered as employees and covered by labour laws and collective agreements" (Thörnquist, 2015a, p. 414). "When there is uncertainty about the employment status, the true employment status of a worker should be assessed on a case-by-case basis with regards to all relevant circumstances. Ultimately, it is up to the courts to decide if a person should be regarded as employed or self-employed. In practice, however, relatively few cases are taken to court" (Thörnquist, 2015a, p. 414).

In general, bogus self-employment can be regarded as a means for employers to escape their responsibilities and obligations stipulated by labour law and collective agreements by contracting out and outsourcing work to independent self-employed persons, thereby transferring costs, risks and responsibilities to the independent workers. This 'hidden behaviour' in the grey area of the labour market is often accompanied by tax evasion and violations of other regulations on working hours and working conditions (Skatteverket, 2015). Employers may find bogus self-employment as an attractive way of reducing labour costs and increasing flexibility, while employees may find it hard to obtain a regular open-ended employment contract. It should be noted that in Sweden access to social protection is independent of employment status. Social security systems in Sweden (health insurance, parental leave, old age pension, occupational injury insurance, and unemployment benefits) are mostly financed via payroll and social contribution taxes. Self-employed workers in Sweden pay their own income tax and social contributions and benefit from the same social protection system as dependent employees (see Anxo and Ericson, 2015).

As previously mentioned, since the last decade, successive Swedish governments have taken initiatives to promote entrepreneurship and favour the development of self-employment. Some of these measures may have increased the risk of bogus self-employment. In particular, in 2009, the liberalizations of the regulations on corporate taxation of self-employed (F-tax) allowed self-employed persons to have only one client, including their former employer (Swedish Government, Bill 2008/09 No. 1). While this reform may encourage start-ups of new firms and entrepreneurship it may also effectively allow employers to transfer costs, risks and responsibilities to workers by contracting out work that previously was performed by employees. Other measures intended to stimulate self-employment and decrease undeclared work in domestic services were also introduced in 2007 by the former Swedish government. The so called RUT-reform (2007:346) made household expenditures on household-related services deductible from income-taxation, thereby significantly lowering the households' costs of these services. Although this reform reduced undeclared work and increased the number of small cleaning companies among in particular foreign-born women, it may also have increased the risk of bogus self-employment. Self-employed cleaners can be working for a single private cleaning company that uses the RUT-reform to lower the prices on cleaning services supplied to households. The self-employed cleaner thus becomes a subcontractor but is in practice dependent on the cleaning company's customers (Thörnquist, 2015b).

There are several institutional conditions on the Swedish labour market that should be considered when discussing and analysing the incidence of bogus self-employment. First, like many other EU Member States, Swedish production of goods and services are highly export-oriented and exposed to continuous structural changes due to international competition from countries where the labour costs are substantially lower. There is a significant trend of increasing outsourcing and specialization of production in both private and public Swedish companies and organizations. Against this background bogus self-employment can be an attractive strategy to reduce labour costs and a component of firms' external numerical flexibility. On the other hand, some idiosyncratic institutional features may limit the development of bogus self-employment in Sweden. First the Employment Protection Act (SFS (1982:80), *Lag om anställningsskydd*) is a legal instrument restricting employers' use of external numerical flexibility. International comparisons of employment protection indicate that Sweden has fairly restrictive legislation, although it does not stand out as extreme by European standards. The law presumes that, unless otherwise stipulated, an employment contract is open-ended. When terminating the contract, the employer must provide a valid reason and advance notice. In other words, the Swedish legislation on employment protection can be an efficient legal barrier to the development of bogus self-employment and limiting the transition from dependent employment towards bogus self-employment. Secondly, the Swedish industrial relations system is characterized by a high union density and a high coverage rate of collective agreements[3] (Anxo, 2017, 2018) which restricts de jure and de facto employers' possibilities to substitute employees with self-employed workers that perform the same tasks as the former employees. Such a substitution would provoke major conflicts between the two sides of industry.

As a consequence, bogus self-employment may be more prevalent in a limited number of industries where labour law and collective agreements do not constitute an effective barrier against the replacement of wage employment by self-employed workers. It should also be stressed that the increasing labour migration within the European Union has opened the door for the development of bogus self-employment in certain sectors. One such sector is the construction sector where workers from the newer Member States in the former Eastern Bloc have been recruited as self-employed (Thörnquist, 2015a, p. 419). A major cause of this recent development is the frequent use of long subcontracting chain where self-employed migrant workers' employment status can be concealed at the end-point of the supply-chain. Also in the road haulage industry the transnational road freight transport market within the EU has become increasingly deregulated, allowing non-resident hauliers to carry out three transport journeys in the host country within seven days of the delivery of the international consignment (the EU regulation on cabotage traffic, EC 1072/09, see Thörnquist, 2013). However, many foreign trucks stay for longer periods and carry out illegal transport at low prices. The downward pressure on transport prices has caused hauliers to seek various ways to reduce labour costs including using foreign self-employed drivers (Thörnquist, 2015a, p. 422).

In both the construction sector and the road haulage industry, the low-wage competition and intense price pressure in the procurement of services have caused an increased use of self-employed Swedish workers instead of employed personnel paid in accordance with the collective agreement. This form of 'involuntary' self-employment constitutes an obvious risk of bogus self-employment also among native workers in Sweden. The employers may require workers to be registered for corporate taxation (F-tax) when recruiting them, in order to evade the Employment Protection Act (SFS (1982:80), *Lag om anställningsskydd*) and to reduce other labour costs and production risks. Consequently, there is an obvious risk of market failure in the labour markets of construction workers and the road haulage industry, where firms that comply with labour laws and collective agreements are unable to compete in a market subject to unfair competition (Thörnquist, 2015a, p. 425).

The Swedish cleaning industry is another example where low-cost competition has resulted in a precarious situation for many workers (Thörnquist, 2015a, 2015b). This industry is highly segregated by gender and ethnicity, where the vast majority of the workforce consists of female workers and around 50 per cent are foreign born. In contrast to the construction and road haulage industries, the precarious situation for the workers is mainly created by conditions within the Swedish labour market. First, cleaning in the domestic sector has a low union density compared to other sectors, where in many small companies neither workers nor employers are organized in union and employer organizations. Second, the customer choice system (LOV) in home-based elderly care uses a procurement system where municipalities offer the providing company a fixed amount per hour intended to cover wage costs and all other production costs. Consequently, the suppliers compete for services that often are underfunded leading to the workers having to pay for transportation between clients and even cleaning equipment and cleaning materials. The aim is thus to transfer costs, risks and liabilities to the workers (Thörnquist, 2015a, p. 426).

TRENDS AND EVOLUTION OF SELF-EMPLOYMENT

Main Features of Self-employment in Sweden: Common Traits and Heterogeneity

From an international perspective the incidence of self-employment in Sweden is relatively low. According to Eurostat (2018), the rate of self-employment in Sweden in 2016 was 9 per cent compared to 14 per cent for the EU as a whole. Since the mid-1980s, the share of self-employed men as a percentage of the total adult working population has oscillated around 14 per cent, the corresponding figure for women being 5 per cent (see Figure 9.1).

As in many other modern economies, self-employment is less frequent among women. The incidence of self-employment increased significantly during the severe recession in the early 1990s, indicating that the rate of self-employed workers in Sweden is counter-cyclical to the business cycle. Looking at the economic downturn in 2008, it seems that the share of self-employment in total employment has slightly increased but to a much lesser extent than during the last severe recession of the early 1990s.

Compared to wage earners, self-employed workers in Sweden are on average older and have lower educational attainment. The share of self-employed persons is also slightly higher among natives compared to foreign-born (10.2 and 9.2 per cent respectively). Self-employment is also higher in industries such as retail, business and personal services (SCB, 2017). Another stylized fact is that the majority of self-employed workers

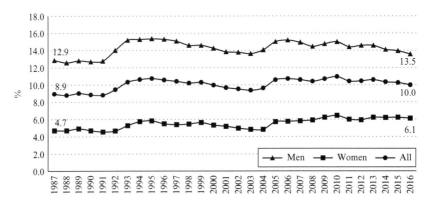

Source: Labour Force Survey (SCB, 2017).

Figure 9.1   Trends for self-employment in Sweden, 1987–2016, in per cent of the employed population 16–64 years old

in Sweden do not have any employees, 60 per cent in 2016; this share of solo-entrepreneurs has remained stable during the last two decades.

Regarding working conditions, self-employed persons work significantly more hours per week than wage-earners.[4] A recent study (see Anxo and Ericson, 2015), shows that the self-employed in Sweden have a higher frequency of irregular working time patterns, working to a larger extent during evening and night-time as well as during weekends. As far as earnings are concerned, the self-employed have on average lower annual incomes and the earnings dispersion is larger than among dependent employees.

Nevertheless, several empirical studies have shown that the self-employed in Sweden are more satisfied with their jobs than dependent employees[5] and that this is not a result of a self-selection of happier people into self-employment (Andersson, 2008). Recurring factors explaining higher levels of job satisfaction among the self-employed include: enjoying greater independence and autonomy, absence of hierarchy, larger opportunities for flexible working time arrangements and higher control over work effort. On the other hand, the self-employed perceive their jobs as more stressful and mentally straining.

As illustrated by Figure 9.2, the Swedish occupational structure of wage earners is heavily weighted towards professionals (ICSO-08: 2), technicians and associated professionals (3) and service and sales workers (5), with around 64 per cent of total wage employment (the lower panel of Figure 9.2). The occupational structure of the self-employed (the upper panel of Figure 9.2) is heavily skewed towards skilled agriculture (6), managers (1) and craft and related trades workers (7) where the share of the self-employed workers exceeds the share of the wage earners.

As developed in the previous section, there are strong reasons to suspect that workers that run the risk of bogus self-employment can to a larger extent be found within the occupational groups (ICSO-08) 7–9. These occupational groups contain 22.6 per cent of the wage employment, while their share of all self-employed amounts to 24.9 per cent. This implies that roughly one in four Swedish self-employed could run the risk of being exposed as bogus self-employment. Considering that around 10 per cent of the Swedish workforce are self-employed, it leads to the conclusion that an upper limit of 2.5 per cent of the workforce might be *potentially* in bogus self-employment. This indicates that bogus self-employment is not a central problem on the Swedish labour market in quantitative terms, although it may be a significant issue in a few number of specific industries and/or occupations.

We have seen that for foreign workers and occupations where the share of foreign workers is particularly high, the risk of bogus self-employment

Source: Labour Force Survey (SCB, 2017).

Figure 9.2   *Distribution of employment by occupational group, self-employed (upper panel) and wage-earners (lower panel) 2015*

could be relatively higher. As described in the previous section, the combination of labour migration within the EU and low-cost competition in certain industries (construction, road haulage, cleaning) has resulted in cases of bogus self-employment or employment in the grey area of the labour market where workers are subject to poor working conditions, temporary employment and low pay.

According to Statistics Sweden, during the period 2001–2013, there was a relatively larger increase of foreign born employees across all occupations compared to the increasing employment of natives. In particular, the occupational groups (ISCO-08) 7–9 demonstrate an increase of foreign born employees while the number of native workers in these occupations have decreased in group 8 or essentially remained constant in group 7 and 9. It should be noticed that this increase of foreign born workers took place during a period where several liberalizing reforms on self-employment were implemented (RUT; LOV; liberalization of the F-tax, see the second section) at the same time as migration of workers from the new candidate countries in the EU increased significantly. A resulting question is how much of the increased employment in the occupational groups (ISCO-08) 7–9 may have resulted in bogus self-employment.

Magnitude and Main Characteristics of Bogus Self-employment in the Nordic Countries

The prevalence of bogus self-employment in Sweden can mainly be explained by a combination of two conditions: (1) There is a 'low-price' competition of standardized services where a worker is relatively easy to replace by another worker. In other words, there is a demand for workers' general skills but a very limited demand for firm-specific skills or skills that would lead to significant recruitment costs for the employer and hence strengthen the bargaining position of the workers. (2) Employers are unable to locate the production of these services outside the Swedish labour market, as in the case of construction, transport and cleaning. As a consequence, the production cannot be outsourced to other countries. Under such circumstances, bogus self-employment becomes an effective way of lowering employment costs through tax evasion and pay below the wage-levels that are set by collective agreements on the Swedish labour market. The bogus self-employed workers are often migrant workers with a weak attachment to the Swedish labour market (Thörnquist, 2015a). This makes it also persistently difficult to assess the extent of bogus self-employment.

Nevertheless, in order to try to identify and assess the incidence of bogus self-employment in Sweden we draw on the last wave of the European Working Condition Survey conducted in 2015 (EWCS, 2016). Since the early 1990s, the European Foundation for the Improvement of Living and Working Conditions has conducted every five years a survey focusing on working conditions across Europe. The current sixth wave of the European Working Condition Survey (EWCS) provides data for 35 European countries: 28 EU Member States, the five EU candidate countries as well as Norway and Switzerland. The EWCS sample contains working women and men, self-employed or wage earners. In the present study, we restrict our analysis of bogus self-employment to the Nordic countries (Denmark, Finland, Norway and Sweden). All these countries present some common institutional features that justify their clustering (see Esping-Andersen, 1990; Amable, 2003; Anxo et al., 2017). We exclude also individuals working in the Agriculture, Forestry, and Fishery sector. After the imposition of these restrictions, our sample contains 3,545 valid observations.

Our empirical definition of bogus self-employment is the following: to be a solo-entrepreneur (self-employed person with no employee) and having no more than one client or customer.[6] Since freelancers[7] can hardly be considered as genuine bogus self-employed persons[8] we exclude them from the analysis of bogus self-employed.

Table 9.1 presents some descriptive statistics regarding the proportion of self-employed and the estimated share of bogus self-employed in our four Nordic countries and the EU-28 as a whole.

As shown by the table, self-employment is less frequent in the Nordic countries, less than 8 per cent compared to 13 per cent for the EU as a whole. Among the Nordic countries, the proportion of self-employed in the employed population ranges from 13 per cent (Finland) to less than 5 per cent (Denmark). A large majority of self-employed persons in the Nordic countries are solo-entrepreneurs, the share of self-employed without employees reaching 69 per cent. The proportion of solo-entrepreneurs varies also slightly among our Nordic countries ranging from 78 per cent in Sweden to 67 per cent in Finland.

Regarding bogus self-employment, our estimations show that the

Table 9.1   *Proportion of self-employed and bogus self-employed persons in Denmark, Finland, Norway and Sweden, and the EU as a whole in per cent of employed persons, 2015, agriculture fishery and forestry not included*

Countries	Share of self-employed in total employment (%)	Share of self-employed without employees in total employment (%), and among self-employed within parenthesis	Share of bogus self-employed among self-employed	Estimated share of bogus self-employed in total employment (%)
Denmark	4.7	3.3 (70%)	5.9	0.3
Finland	13.3	8.9 (67%)	11.9	1.6
Norway	7.2	4.9 (68%)	6.2	0.5
Sweden	6.3	4.9 (78%)	2.3	0.2
Nordic	7.8	5.4 (69%)	7.7	0.6
EU-28	13.1	9.3 (71%)	9.8	1.3

Source: EWCS (2016) and own calculations.

proportion of bogus self-employed among the employed population is significantly lower in the Nordic countries compared to the EU (0.6 per cent in the Nordic countries compared to 1.3 per cent in the EU-28 as a whole). Among self-employed persons, Sweden has the lowest share of bogus self-employment with around 2 per cent, followed by Norway, around 6 per cent and Finland, 12 per cent. All in all, the incidence of bogus self-employment appears therefore limited in the Nordic countries, particularly in Sweden where only 0.2 per cent of the employed population (around 9,000 individuals) can be considered as bogus self-employed in 2015.

Table 9.2 displays some descriptive statistics comparing wage earners, self-employed and bogus self-employed in the Nordic countries.

Table 9.2   Descriptive statistics: mean values of variables, wage earners, self-employed persons and bogus self-employed in the Nordic countries, 2015

Variables	Wage earners	Self-employed workers	Bogus self-employed
Age, in years	42.5	49.7	48.6
Women	51.1	33.3	15.5
Foreign born	14.7	12.9	5.8
Self-employed without employees	–	67.8	–
Bogus self-employed	–	7.7	–
Freelance	–	8.7	–
Manufacturing	13.4	8.0	6.9
Construction	5.2	14.3	11.0
Wholesale and retail	15.9	16.9	6.7
Transport	5.7	6.3	4.9
Financial services	3.7	2.7	–
Administration	6.5	–	–
Education	10.9	2.7	–
Health	19.4	9.4	4.3
Personal services	19.5	39.8	66.3
Public sector	39.0	–	–
Working time, in hours	35.5	38.5	35.4
Part-time	25.3	28.7	25.1
Weekend work	34.5	53.1	47.8
Night work	21.6	35.5	27.3
Low-skilled	13.8	11.0	34.3
Medium-skilled	57.4	57.7	36.1
High-skilled	28.8	31.3	29.6
Number of observations	3545	334	27

Source: EWCS (2016) and own calculations.

Confirming previous empirical research, the self-employed compared to wage earners are slightly older, more prevalent among natives and less feminized in the four Nordic countries. Regarding skill level, the share of high-skilled workers is slightly higher among self-employed, but overall the distribution of skill is rather similar. Part-time, and atypical working time arrangements such as night and weekend work are also relatively more prevalent among self-employed. Regarding industries, self-employment is more prevalent in construction and other/personal services. Concerning the disparities between self- and bogus self-employed, men, low-skilled workers as well as individuals working in personal services appear to be over-represented among bogus self-employed.

In order to control for potential structural differences and compositional effects we report in the following two tables some estimations using regression analysis. Since our two dependent variables are dichotomous – to be self-employed or to be bogus self-employed – we use standard logit models controlling for a set of usual socio-economic variables, such as age, gender, skill level, industries and some job characteristics. Tables 9.3 and 9.4 report the results of our estimations for the EU as a whole and Nordic countries respectively.

Starting with the results for the EU as a whole, our estimations show that individuals living in the Nordic countries, except Finland, are ceteris paribus less prone to be self-employed compared to their counterparts in other EU Member States. As show by Table 9.3, younger workers, women and foreign born are less likely to be self-employed. Confirming previous research (Anxo and Ericson, 2015), self-employed are more likely to work part-time (mainly female self-employed) but also to work long hours (mainly male self-employed). They are also more likely to work during the weekend but less prone to work at night. They also to a larger extent work in industries such as construction, retail and personal services compared to their employees' counterparts. Among the self-employed and compared to other Member States, the likelihood of being bogus self-employed is ceteris paribus lower in Sweden but does not differ significantly in the remaining Nordic countries. While overall to be highly-skilled increases the probability of being self-employed, low-skilled self-employed workers are more prone to be bogus self-employed. Bogus self-employed are also more prone to work part-time compared to their self-employed counterparts. Worth noting also is that bogus self-employed workers differ from their self-employed counterparts only in two industries: They are more likely to work within the educational sector and personal services.

Restricting the sample to the Nordic countries (see Table 9.4) some interesting differences should be noted. Starting with the likelihood of being self-employed, high-skilled workers are no longer more likely to be

Table 9.3   Logit. Dependent variable to be self-employed (first column), EU-28, to be bogus self-employed conditional to being self-employed (second column), marginal effect estimated at sample mean

Variables	Self-employed EU-28	Bogus self-employed EU-28
Age	0.00272***	0.000713**
Women	−0.0263***	−0.0101
Foreign born	−0.00774*	0.0161
Low-skilled	−0.0488***	0.0825***
High-skilled	0.0372***	−0.0485***
Construction	0.0683***	−0.0174
Wholesale and retail	0.0427***	−0.0146
Transport	0.00526	−0.0205
Financial services	0.0124	−0.0381
Education	−0.159***	0.0720***
Health	−0.0886***	0.0383
Personal services	−0.0294***	0.0264*
Part-time	0.0644***	0.0401***
Long working time	0.0698***	−0.0165
Weekend work	0.0301***	−0.00952
Night work	−0.00824**	−0.00996
Denmark	−0.0824***	−0.0973
Finland	0.000151	−0.00193
Norway	−0.0522***	−0.0260
Sweden	−0.0650***	−0.0979**
Predicted probability	*0.1225*	*0.0898*
Number of observations	*32,702*	*3,753*

Notes:
*, ** and *** statistically significant at 10 %, 5 % and 1 % level.
Interpretation of the table: The figures in the table show how the probability of being self-employed (first column) and the probability of bogus self-employment conditional to being self-employed (second column) changes when the variables changes from their reference categories. The reference categories are thus men, natives, medium-skilled, working in manufacturing and standard working hours and working outside the Nordic countries.

Source: EWCS (2016) and own calculations.

self-employed compared to their wage-earner counterparts. Confirming the descriptive statistics, individuals living in Finland are more prone to be self-employed compared to individuals living in other Nordic countries.

Regarding bogus self-employed, we found no statistically significant differences between Nordic countries in the incidence of bogus

*Table 9.4   Logit. Dependent variable to be self-employed (first column),
              Nordic countries, to be bogus self-employed conditional to being
              self-employed (second column), marginal effect estimated at
              sample mean*

Variables	Self-employed Nordic countries	Bogus self-employed Nordic countries
Age	0.00213***	0.000217
Women	−0.0170**	−0.0678**
Foreign born	0.00239	−0.0463
Low-skilled	−0.0208**	0.0937**
High-skilled	0.00692	0.0234
Construction	0.0675***	−0.0150
Wholesale and retail	0.0390***	0.0117
Transport	0.0193	−0.0674
Financial services	0.0103	−
Education	−0.0470**	−
Health	−0.0111	0.0188
Personal services	0.0532***	0.0565
Part-time	0.0323***	−0.0168
Long working time	0.0443***	−0.0476
Weekend work	0.0272***	−0.0165
Night work	0.0197***	−0.0291
Denmark	−0.0102	−0.0153
Finland	0.0390***	0.0514
Norway	0.0114	0.0255
Predicted probability	*0.0806*	*0.0845*
Number of observations	*3,542*	*239*

Note: *, ** and *** statistically significant at 10 %, 5 % and 1 % level.

Source: EWCS (2916) and own calculation.

self-employment. Women living in the Nordic countries are ceteris paribus
less likely to be bogus self-employed compared to their male counterparts. The stronger effect regards skill levels where low-skilled workers
are significantly more likely to be bogus self-employed in the Nordic
countries (doubled so high likelihood). We did not find other statistically
significant differences between self- and bogus self-employed regarding
other characteristics such as age, industries or working time arrangements.
In other words, bogus self-employed in the Nordic countries do not differ
significantly from other self-employed individuals, except for gender and
skill level.

CONCLUDING REMARKS

The aim of this chapter was to analyse the extent to which bogus self-employment is widespread in Sweden and to identify the institutional and economic factors that may explain its magnitude and development. Bogus self-employment indeed appears to be prevalent in certain segments of the Swedish labour market. The trend of organizing production by subcontracting chains where self-employed workers' employment status can be concealed at the end-point of the supply chain, has stimulated conditions that open the door for the development of bogus self-employment. In general, we think that the combination of a growing supply of low-cost services that mainly require workers' general skills and the fact that production in certain industries (construction, transport and cleaning/ personal services) cannot be located in other countries has created strong incentives for some employers to lower the production costs by employing workers that are prepared to work under precarious employment conditions, with less employment security, poor working conditions and lower pay. The economic integration in the EU has resulted in an increase of mobile workers from the former Eastern bloc, often in sectors with weak regulation and low coverage rate of collective agreements. However, because in Sweden there is high union density and extensive coverage of collective agreements in all sectors of the economy, this has probably limited the development of bogus self-employment and explains why it is relatively less prevalent than in other Member States. Another explanation is the importance of the public sector in providing a large range of services (in particular for personal services, such as child care, home care, etc.).

According to our estimates less than 8 per cent of the self-employed persons or 0.2 per cent of total employment in Sweden could be, according to our definition (solo-entrepreneurs having no more than one client or customer, freelancers excluded), considered as bogus self-employed, which corresponds to around 9,000 individuals. However, this number of individuals excludes migrant workers without a permanent residence in Sweden, and should therefore be regarded as a lower bound estimate of the number of bogus self-employed on the Swedish labour market.

While this is a relatively small proportion, our findings indicate that there is a need for policy interventions. In November 2017, the Swedish government launched a public enquiry and appointed a special investigator (see Swedish Government, 2017) for assessing the importance of bogus self-employment, the extent to which the F-tax system is fraudulently used by companies for tax evasion, and examining the possibility of revising the regulation concerning the current 'one client' clause for business registration. The special investigator will present its conclusions and recommendations in 2018.

NOTES

1. Following Thörnquist (2015a) we define bogus/false self-employed persons as: "self-employed persons having only one client, and working under similar conditions as employees, but without the rights and protection that employees are entitled to under labour law and collective agreements . . . In other words, this notion refers to employment disguised as self-employment in order to circumvent collective agreements, labour laws, payroll taxes and social security contributions . . . False and dependent forms of self-employment can thus be described as phenomena in the 'grey area' between subordinate/dependent employment and genuine/independent self-employment" (Thörnquist, 2015a, pp. 411–12).
2. According to Inghammar (2015, p. 198) "The primary or decisive features determining whether a person is an employee are: Contractual arrangement (for employment), Personal liability to perform the duties agreed in the contract, the duties agreed in the contract are performed on behalf of someone else (the employer), The person is guided and/or supervised by the other party to the contract (the employer), In return for remuneration".
3. Despite a recent decline, the average union density in Sweden remains one of the highest among modern economies – at around 70 per cent in 2016. In the same year, the coverage rate of collective agreements stood at around 90 per cent. It is important to note that the high coverage rate of collective bargaining in Sweden does not relate to the existence of legal provisions for the mandatory extension of collective agreements but rather to the high-density rate of employers' associations and the strong presence of trade unions at the firm/organization level.
4. In 2016, the average actual weekly working time for male self-employed (20–64 years) was 40.5 compared to 33.1 hours for wage earners, the corresponding figure for women was at the same date 31.3 hours and 27.6 hours respectively. Looking only at self-employed persons without employees, the actual weekly working time was 37.3 hours for males and 30.5 hours for female solo-entrepreneurs (SCB, 2017).
5. Controlling for a set of socio-economic variables, the number of self-employed stating that they are very satisfied with their job is about 15 percentage points higher compared to dependent employees.
6. The three questions from the EWCS questionnaire are: Q7 Are you working as an employee or are you self-employed?, Q16b How many employees in total work in your business? and Q9 Regarding your business, do you: Generally, have more than one client or customer?
7. We identify freelancers by the question Q8b Please select the category which applies to your main paid-job? 5). Doing freelance work.
8. The share of freelancers in the Nordic countries among self-employed amounted to around 10 per cent (see Table 9.1). Among dependent self-employed around 19 percent were freelance. If we exclude freelancers the share of bogus employed amount to around 0.6 per cent of the employed population in the Nordic countries and 0.2 per cent (around 9,000 individuals) in Sweden (as compared to 1.3 per cent in the EU as a whole).

REFERENCES

Amable, B. (2003). *The Diversity of Modern Capitalism*. New York: Oxford University Press.

Andersson, P. (2008). Happiness and health: well-being among the self-employed. *The Journal of Socio-Economics*, 37, 213–36.

Anxo, D. (2011). Negotiated flexibility in Sweden: a more egalitarian response to the crisis? In: Vaughan-Whitehead, D. (ed.), *Inequalities in the World of Work:*

The Effects of the Crisis. Cheltenham, UK and Northampton, MA, USA: Edward Elgar Publishing, 445–76.

Anxo, D. (2015). The Swedish social model: resilience and success in turbulent times. In: Vaughan-Whitehead, D. (ed.), *The European Social Model in Crisis. Is Europe Losing its Soul?* Cheltenham, UK and Northampton, MA, USA: Edward Elgar Publishing, 507–52.

Anxo, D. (2017). Turbulent time and beyond: the Swedish experience. In: Guardianchic, I. and Molina, O. (eds), *Talking Through the Crisis: Social Dialogue and Industrial Relations Trends in Selected EU Countries*. Geneva: International Labour Office, 281–97.

Anxo, D. (2018). Shaping the future of work in Sweden: the crucial role of social partnership. In: Vaughan-Whitehead, D. (ed.), *Reducing Inequalities in Europe. How Industrial Relations and Labour Policies Can Close the Gap*. Cheltenham, UK and Northampton, MA, USA: Edward Elgar Publishing, 519–54.

Anxo D. and Ericson T. (2015). Self-employment and parental leave. *Small Business Economics*, 45(4), 751–70. doi 10.1007/s11187-015-9669-6.

Anxo, D., Boulin, J.-Y. and Cabreta, J. (2017). *Working Time Patterns for Sustainable Work*, https://www.eurofound.europa.eu/publications/report/2017/working-time-patterns-for-sustainable-work.

Esping-Andersen, G. (1990). *The Three Worlds of Welfare Capitalism*. Cambridge: Polity Press.

Eurostat (2018). *Statistics Database*. http://ec.europa.eu/eurostat/data/database (accessed May 2018).

EWCS (2016). *European Working Condition Survey, 6th Wave*. Dublin: European Foundation for the Improvement of Living and Working Conditions.

Holmlund, B. and Storrie, D. (2002). Temporary work in turbulent times: the Swedish experience. *The Economic Journal*, 112(480), F245–F269.

Inghammar, A. (2015). Information request 25 November 2015, European Labour Law network, 197–200.

SCB (2017). *Labour Force Survey*. Statistics Sweden.

Skatteverket (2015). Svartarbete och social dumpning (Black work and social dumping), Bilaga till dnr. 1 31 575009-15/113, https://www.skatteverket.se/download/18.3810a01c150939e893f20dc/1446042898232/Regleringsbrevsuppdrag_+svartarbete+och+social+dumpning.pdf (accessed February 2018).

Swedish Government (2017). Översyn av F-Skattesystemet (Review of ther F-tax system), dir:2017:108, https://www.regeringen.se/4aba88/contentassets/80b9795a30b5475aa399c0f94e6bba33/oversyn-av-f-skattesystemet-dir.2017108.pdf (accessed February 2018).

Thörnquist, A. (2013). False (bogus) self-employment in east-west labour migration: recent trends in the Swedish construction and road haulage industries. *TheMes* 41 (RESMO, Linköping: Linköping University), 7–9.

Thörnquist, A. (2015a). False self-employment and other precarious forms of employment in the 'grey area' of the labour market. *The International Journal of Comparative Labour Law and Industrial Relations*, 31(4), 411–30.

Thörnquist, A. (2015b). East–west labour migration and the Swedish cleaning industry: a matter of immigrant competition? *TheMes* 42 (RESMO, Linköping: Linköping University), 25–6.

10. Precariousness among older self-employed workers in Europe

Wieteke Conen

INTRODUCTION

Studies generally find a positive relation between age and self-employment (Blanchflower, 2004; Giandrea et al., 2008). The positive effect of age has been attributed to a larger stock of human capital, financial capital and social capital (such as a more diversified and dense network) (Zissimopoulos and Karoly, 2007; Cahill et al., 2013; Van Solinge, 2014), a desire for more flexible employment (e.g. due to health-related issues) (Giandrea et al., 2008) and senior self-employment as a bridge to retirement or to extend working lives (either necessity or opportunity driven) (Kerr and Armstrong-Stassen, 2011; Van Solinge, 2014; Been and Knoef, 2015; Wahrendorf et al., 2017). A negative relation between age and self-employment may arise from higher risk aversion levels among elderly and a shorter time horizon to recover costs on initial investments.

Self-employment among older workers (50 years of age and older) is diverse. Some of these individuals have been self-employed much or all of their working lives, while many older workers make the transition into self-employment after age 50 and, for some, as part of a transition into retirement (Giandrea et al., 2008; Zissimopoulos and Karoly, 2009; Kerr and Armstrong-Stassen, 2011; Cahill et al., 2013). This chapter examines considerations for different groups of older workers to enter self-employment and studies precariousness among older self-employed workers between 50 and 80 years in Europe. The question is addressed of who works beyond state pension age and why. Earlier studies on working beyond state pension age have typically focused on attitudes and behaviour of employees (e.g. Dingemans, 2016) or the employers' perspective towards working after retirement age (e.g. Oude Mulders, 2016). Generally, this research finds that two groups of retirees exist (albeit to a higher or lesser extent in various countries): those who experience little constraint in their decisions with respect to retirement, and those who feel severely restricted and feel forced to participate for financial reasons; the 'haves' and the 'have-nots' (Flynn,

2010; Dingemans, 2016). Although research in this field has started to develop for employees, studies explicitly focusing on self-employed are lagging behind. This explorative chapter aims to present some initial findings in this area and studies whether and how precariousness and behaviour differs between older self-employed workers and employees.

AGEING AND THE LABOUR MARKET IN EUROPE

Current demographic developments due to the ageing of the population have significant consequences for labour markets and welfare states in Europe. Important parameters underlying the ageing process are the sharp drop in fertility rates since the early 1960s (in many countries towards a state below replacement levels) and increasing life expectancy at birth. Population ageing affects all regions of the world, but is relatively advanced in Europe.

Demographic developments will have significant consequences for the development of the (potential) workforce as well as the share of people beyond state pension age. In the coming years, an increasing number of seniors will depend on old-age pensions, while the share of people that contribute in terms of taxes and social security premiums is falling. These developments will affect the old age dependency ratio, that is, the ratio of those typically not in the labour force (dependent) and those typically in the labour force (productive), measuring the pressure on the productive population. Figure 10.1 presents the old age dependency ratio for five case countries that were examined in other chapters of this book. In the 1960s, Italy had the lowest old age dependency ratio (14 persons aged 65 and older per 100 persons aged 15–64) and the United Kingdom the highest (18 per 100). After a steady increase of the old age dependency ratio the consequences of the ageing population will be felt particularly in the coming decades: in 2020 the number of old aged as a percentage of the potential labour force in Europe will be approximately 33 per cent; that is, every pensioner is potentially supported by three workers. The old age dependency ratio will increase further and in 2060 every pensioner will probably be supported by two workers. This old age dependency ratio increases particularly strongly in Germany and Italy.

Enlarging the pool of productive workers, including raising participation levels of older workers and extending people's working life, has frequently been proposed by both experts and policy makers as a key element in facing the consequences of this ageing population and the rising welfare state expenditures. Since the mid-1990s, European governments have been using various sets of policy instruments to achieve extension of

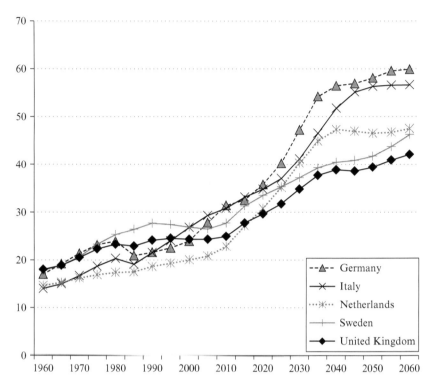

Note: Statistics for the period 1960–2010 were retrieved from Eurostat's Demography
database (2012); projections for the period 2015–2060 were retrieved from EUROPOP2010
(2012). Any missing figures for the period 1960–1985 were inserted from United Nations
Statistics Division (2012).

Source: Based on Conen (2013), p. 15.

*Figure 10.1   Old age dependency ratio (1960–2010) and projected old age
dependency ratio (2015–2060) in five European countries,
ratio of the persons aged 65 and more over the number of
persons of working age (15–64)*

working lives (for an overview, see Conen, 2013). However, organisations
have only too often been found to be reluctant in promoting the recruitment and retention of older workers (Van Dalen et al., 2009; Conen et al.,
2012, 2014; Karpinska et al., 2013). Therefore, the question arises whether
the combination of extension of working lives and restrictions faced by
older workers may lead to particular risks to end up in precarious forms
of employment and self-employment. Self-employment is indeed rising

among older age groups, but do we need to worry about these older self-employed workers?

THEORETICAL CONSIDERATIONS

From the literature we know that individuals are attracted to self-employment because of distinctive features such as independence, more autonomy and higher expected earnings relative to employment (Taylor, 1996; Dawson et al., 2009). However, individuals may also make the transition into self-employment out of necessity, motivated by an 'unemployment push' or employers forcing employees to become self-employed subcontractors (Kautonen et al., 2010; Amorós and Bosma, 2014).

In this study, three career phases among older workers will be distinguished to test whether considerations to become self-employed differ between various transition moments. The first group consists of individuals who make the transition while in their fifties. On the one hand, this group may be opportunity-driven. Perhaps workers in this career phase consider their stock of human, financial and/or social capital large enough to (finally) take the risk and pursue a career in self-employment; perhaps even a career they have always dreamed of, but did not dare to follow before. Or perhaps individuals have waited for their children to have left the household, as family responsibilities may increase parents' degree of risk aversion and child-rearing is sometimes considered to be difficult to reconcile with a flexible or high-demanding self-employment job. On the other hand, when workers (have to) leave the labour market after age 50 this is often translated into inactivity or long-term unemployment; unemployed older workers are disproportionately represented among the long-term unemployed in most industrial economies (Daniel and Heywood, 2007). Therefore, some individuals who make the transition into self-employment while in their fifties may have a relatively high probability of being driven by the lack of employment opportunities in the primary labour market. Motives from older workers who make the transition while in their fifties may differ from those who have been self-employed from well before their fifties, for instance due to different compositions of human, financial and social capital and other household compositions. Motives may also differ from individuals who make the transition in late-career, for instance in the form of bridge employment. In other words, the group of workers often aggregated under the heading of 'older workers' may in fact cover a variety of employment types, differing in their motives to make the transition into self-employment.

Considerations to continue working beyond state pension age are often attributed to opportunity-based or intrinsic motivations rather than to necessity-based or extrinsic motivations. One image is that of an independent entrepreneur, who enjoys his or her work so much that prolongation of working life is aspired to, and intrinsic rather than extrinsic motivations affect the decision to work beyond state pension age. Another is for instance the image of the passionate winegrower or artist, or more in general those working in the liberal professions, people who 'are' their work and they wish to do this work until the end of time. Several studies find that self-employed who work beyond state pension age seem more privileged in terms of financial and human capital, health and entrepreneurial attitudes (e.g. Van Solinge, 2014; Wahrendorf et al., 2017), while others find some evidence for necessity-driven self-employment (e.g. Been and Knoef, 2015). In this study, necessity-driven self-employment will be addressed explicitly and the question will be addressed whether self-employed in more precarious positions have a propensity for working beyond state pension age, and whether this differs from the situation among employees.

Underlying assumptions on how workers motivate choices in the areas of work and retirement vary along disciplinary lines. Economists tend to principally emphasise the impact on labour market and retirement behaviour from both financial incentives and non-financial constraints such as time and health (e.g. Blundell et al., 2002; Kalwij and Vermeulen, 2008). Sociologists consider labour market behaviour to be more socially set, for instance by family life spheres, employing organisations and earlier experiences in both work and family life (e.g. Damman et al., 2011; Raymo et al., 2011). Psychological research pays particular attention to the part played by role identities, personal values and goals in work and retirement decisions (e.g. Brougham and Walsh, 2007; Wang and Shi, 2014). In this chapter I assume, in line with, for instance, Maslow's hierarchy of needs, that older workers need basic physiological and security needs to be fulfilled and that 'higher' motives (such as personal values) start playing a more dominant role once fundamental needs are fulfilled. I also assume that older workers' decisions regarding work and retirement are made within a household context.

METHODS

Data

For the analyses regarding motives in relation to career phases, data was used from the Survey Solo Self-Employment. The survey contains data on behaviour and attitudes among solo self-employed in Germany and the Netherlands in 2014. More details about SSE and its methods are described elsewhere (Conen et al., 2016). The sample was restricted to older workers, defined in this chapter as workers aged 50 years or older. This results in a total sample of 333 women and 643 men ($n = 976$).

For the analyses regarding precariousness and working beyond state pension age, data was used from the Survey of Health, Ageing and Retirement in Europe (SHARE, release 6.1.1) collected in 2013. SHARE is a cross-national and multidisciplinary research project periodically collecting data on a variety of social, economic and health-related topics among nationally representative samples of individuals aged 50 or older. The countries included are: Austria, Belgium, Denmark, France, Germany, Italy, Luxembourg, the Netherlands, Spain, Sweden and Switzerland. The included countries are relatively similar in terms of their statutory retirement age. The retirement ages are among the highest in Europe (65 years of age for men and in most cases also for women). More details about SHARE and its methods are available online (www.share-project.org) and described elsewhere (e.g. Börsch-Supan et al., 2013; Malter and Börsch-Supan, 2015). The sample was restricted to older workers who described their current job situation as 'employed or self-employed'. In the analyses explaining working beyond state pension age, workers were compared to those who declared themselves 'retired'. We excluded individuals older than 80 years, because they may have particular work situations (e.g. working in a family run business). This results in a total sample of 8,207 women and 9,129 men ($n = 17,336$).

Measuring Precariousness

As has also been shown in other chapters of this volume, the operationalisation of precariousness is a complex task. Considering precarious work as an employment situation in which individuals or households are unable to fulfil fundamental physiological and security needs while working, this chapter emphasises two indicators of precariousness which seem particularly relevant in the context of older self-employed: indicators measuring in-work financial precariousness and indicators measuring poor health and well-being.

Financial precariousness is measured at the household level, as a substantial share of older workers who have a job in self-employment are – perhaps more often than is the case with employees or younger self-employed – not or not completely dependent on this income. In line with the concept of in-work poverty, the measurement of 'low income' is based on the idea of working individuals at risk of poverty, that is, their annual equivalised household disposable income is below 60 per cent of the national median. Household incomes have been equivalised because while the needs of a household grow with each additional member, they do not increase proportionally (due to economies of scale in consumption). For instance needs for housing and electricity will not be three times as high for a household with three members than for a single person. Self-employed are considered to be in low-income households when their annual equivalised household net income is below 60 per cent of the national median (using the OECD modified equivalence-scale).

As wealth measures are not based on direct income but on accumulated savings, they are sometimes considered to constitute an important additional indicator of financial circumstances for older populations (e.g. Wahrendorf et al., 2017). Wealth is measured based on both household net financial assets (e.g. savings, net stock value, mutual funds and bonds) and household real assets (e.g. value of primary residence, other real estates and cars). Individuals are considered to live in households with low financial assets and low real assets measures if they belong to the households in the lowest decile of the final sample in the respective country.

Financial precariousness of self-employed was not compared to the situation of employees, because of the particular problems that arise from measuring and comparing income from self-employment. These difficulties stem for instance from a lack of clear distinction between the (incorporated) business income and the personal or household consumption and because self-employed have large variation in their income flows.

Three indicators were used to measure precariousness in terms of different aspects of health and well-being: poor self-rated health, activity limitations and poor quality of life. These indicators were applied to the situation of both self-employed and employees. Health and well-being indicators are particularly interesting in the case of older self-employed, as it touches on the social security aspect of precariousness. European social security frameworks are partly designed to protect individuals in poor health from the necessity to earn an income from paid labour. Therefore, despite some groups who may *want* to continue working albeit in poor health conditions, those who work while in poor health are perhaps more likely to be workers to whom the safety nets do not apply (i.e. precarity-driven in-work).

Poor self-perceived health was assessed by a question with five possible answer categories, ranging from '1' excellent to '5' poor; only individuals indicating to be in 'poor' health were included. The Global Activity Limitation Index (GALI) is a single-item instrument measuring long-standing activity limitations (six months or more) (answer categories '1' limited, '0' not limited). To measure poor quality of life we use the theoretically grounded measure of quality of life in older age (CASP-12) (see Mehrbrodt et al., 2017 for more information on these measures). For both self-employed workers and employees precariousness in terms of poor physical conditions is related to labour market participation.

Analyses

Multivariate logistic regression analyses were used to estimate the impact of income, wealth, health and various control variables on the probability of working beyond pension age. Control variables include gender, country of birth, educational attainment level, sector of industry and country dummies. We test whether those who are working beyond state pension age are relatively privileged or precarious in terms of income, wealth and health. The analyses were performed for self-employed and employees separately. The odds ratio presents the ratio of the probability that workers work beyond state pension age to the probability they do not.

RESULTS

Motives

Table 10.1 shows considerations for making the transition into self-employment for the group of older workers as a whole and for older workers by moment of transition into self-employment (before age 50, in their fifties or in late-career). The importance of motives to become solo self-employed was operationalised by asking respondents: 'To what extent did the following reasons or motivations play a role in making the transition into solo self-employment?' (answer categories: '1' did not play a role, '2' low extent, '3' some extent, '4' high extent).

The results show that for the group of older workers as a whole, the majority of respondents mentioned that 'pull' factors played a role 'to a high extent': a desire for more autonomy, taking advantage of a business opportunity and looking for a new challenge. Nevertheless, the table also shows several noteworthy results with respect to necessity-based motives. Around one-fifth of older workers indicate self-employment was the only possibility to earn an income and they could not find a job as an employee. A small minority of self-employed indicated their employer wanted them to work as self-employed. For 10 per cent of respondents, income from self-employment had the function of an additional income.

The results also show some differences between older workers in terms of when the transition into self-employment was made. Opportunity-driven self-employment seems to be relatively high among workers who

Table 10.1 *Motives to become self-employed by moment of transition,* self-employed aged 50 to 80 years, percentage played a role 'to a high extent'*

	Total older workers	Before age 50	Fifties	Late-career
More autonomy in how much and when I work	46	49	40	34
Business opportunity	30	29	31	26
Looking for new challenge	29	30	30	26
Could earn more in self-employment	13	15	11	9
Only possibility to earn an income	20	15	32	31
Could not find a suitable job as an employee	20	16	33	15
My employer wanted me to work as a self-employed	2	2	2	1
Additional income	10	8	9	26

Note: * 'Before age 50' when the transition into self-employment was made before the respondent turned 50, 'Fifties' when the transition was made between age 50 and 59, 'Late-career' when the transition into self-employment was made at age 59 or later.

Source: Survey Solo Self employment (SSE), 2014

make the transition before age 50, whereas necessity-based motives are especially prevalent among older workers who make the transition in their fifties. Older workers who make the transition in late-career relatively often indicate that the income from self-employment functions as an additional income.

Dimensions of Precariousness

Despite individual and subjective differences, there are certain objective characteristics that most people would agree are necessary for a job to be considered 'a good job' (Kalleberg, 2011). "A basic requirement is that the job should pay a wage that is high enough to satisfy a person's basic needs" (Kalleberg, 2011, p. 9). Panel *a* in Figure 10.2 presents indicators of financial precariousness among self-employed workers in the age groups 50 to 64 years and 65 to 80 years. In the European countries included in the analyses, statutory retirement age is 65 years for males and in most cases also for women. That is, at age 65 in principle all residents have reached statutory retirement age. The figure shows that 8 per cent of self-employed aged 50 to 64 years live in low-income households and 10 per cent of

Panel *a*

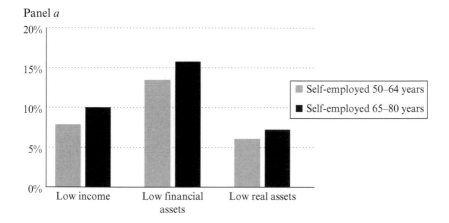

Panel *b*

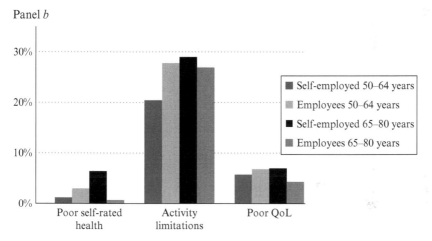

Source: Survey of Health, Ageing and Retirement in Europe, 2013 (Börsch-Supan, 2018).

Figure 10.2   Financial precariousness (panel a) and health and well-being (panel b) among workers aged 50 to 80 years, percentage

self-employed aged 65 to 80 years. The same pattern applies to wealth measures: the share of self-employed with low household net financial assets and household real assets is lower within the group before pension age.

When self-employed who work beyond state pension age are considered to be the ones who are relatively privileged in terms of financial capital rather than necessity-driven, one would expect a lower share of financially precarious self-employed working beyond pension age. In that light, the higher share of self-employed in low-income and low-wealth households after state pension age may provide some support for precarity-based motives to continue working beyond state pension age. Nevertheless, the figure does not provide any information about what causal relations underlie these findings; perhaps cohort- or period-effects play a role (e.g. younger cohorts may have higher levels of human capital) or specific countries have a relatively large impact on the findings (e.g. in the Netherlands self-employed are entitled to a basic pension after retirement age, which is likely to reduce their propensity to be in low-income households after retirement age).

A similar pattern can be found in panel *b* of Figure 10.2. Among European self-employed the share of respondents with poor health, with long-standing activity limitations and poor quality of life is lower in the group of older workers before than beyond state pension age. Contrarily, among European employees, the share of respondents in poor health, with long-standing activity limitations and poor quality of life is higher in the age group before than beyond state pension age. Compared to employees, self-employed seem relatively privileged in terms of health and well-being before state pension age, but relatively disadvantaged beyond state pension age.

Working Beyond State Pension Age

Table 10.2 presents the results of multivariate logistic regression analyses that were used to estimate the impact of income, wealth, health and various control variables on the probability to work beyond pension age. The analyses were performed for self-employed and employees separately. The odds ratio presents the ratio of the probability that workers work beyond state pension age to the probability they do not.

Column 1 of Table 10.2 shows that self-employed with higher total household net incomes are more likely to work beyond state pension age; the significance of the squared term indicates a non-linear income relation. Column 3 of Table 10.2 shows the same pattern among employees. Self-employed with low household net incomes and low household net financial assets also have a higher probability to continue working beyond state pension age; both indicators do not predict extension of working lives beyond state pension age among employees. These findings seem to indicate that among both self-employed workers and employees relatively privileged workers work beyond state pension age and that especially among self-employed necessity-based motivations also play a role in continuing working.

Table 10.2   *Working beyond state pension age (logistic regression analyses)*

	Self-employed		Employees	
	OR	z-value	OR	z-value
Total household net income	1.06**	7.80	1.04**	4.34
Total household net income^2	0.99**	−4.72	0.99**	−2.78
Low household net income (dummy)	3.13**	3.08	0.86	−0.40
Low household net financial assets (dummy)	2.27**	3.00	1.17	0.59
Low household real assets (dummy)	0.73	−0.83	1.76	1.89
Self-rated health	1.37**	3.53	1.40**	4.01
Poor self-rated health (dummy)	1.35	0.59	0.13**	−2.61
Gender (0 = female)	1.64*	2.38	1.41*	1.98
Country of birth (1 = native)	0.97	−0.10	0.99	−0.04
Educational attainment level				
Low (ref.)				
Medium	1.39	1.20	1.22	0.84
High	2.10**	2.61	1.66*	2.12
Sector of industry				
Public sector (ref.)				
Goods-producing industries	1.30	0.84	0.60	−1.54
Service industries	1.91*	2.10	0.93	−0.21
Countries				
Austria (ref.)				
Belgium	0.91	−0.23	1.26	0.56
Denmark	3.16**	3.06	8.50**	5.95
France	1.56	1.04	1.50	0.94
Germany	2.95**	2.75	3.39**	3.14
Italy	3.23**	2.66	2.42*	1.99
Luxembourg	0.16**	−2.62	0.54	−0.84
Netherlands	2.80**	2.72	2.20	1.87
Spain	4.09**	2.98	5.56**	3.85
Sweden	2.82**	2.81	5.46**	4.57
Switzerland	2.48*	2.42	3.56**	3.21
Pseudo R^2	0.15		0.11	
Observations	17,292		17,308	

Note: *Significant at p < .05; ** significant at p < .01. OR = odds ratio.

Source: Survey of Health, Ageing and Retirement in Europe, 2013 (Börsch-Supan, 2018).

In terms of self-rated health, column 1 shows that self-employed with better self-rated health are more likely to work beyond state pension age, whereas the effect of poor self-rated health is not significant. Column 3 of Table 10.2 shows that employees with better self-perceived health are also more likely to work beyond state pension age, but among employees poor self-rated health has a strong negative effect upon working beyond state pension age. This finding may indicate that employees are better protected against social risks around retirement age and are relatively less constrained in their decision to continue working. The presented results furthermore suggest that working beyond state pension age is patterned along lines of gender and endowment of human capital.

CONCLUSION AND DISCUSSION

With the ageing of European societies, governments have been using various sets of policy instruments to achieve extension of working lives among their citizens. Self-employment among older workers (50 years of age and older) is diverse. Some of these individuals have been self-employed much or all of their working lives, while many older workers make the transition into self-employment after age 50 and, for some, as part of a transition to retirement.

This chapter has examined motives and transition moments for older workers to become self-employed and has examined factors that contribute to the propensity to engage in paid work after retirement among older self-employed and employees aged 50 to 80 years in Europe. Focus was placed on the question whether and for what type of workers working beyond state pension age holds an opportunity-improvement driven or precarity-driven prolongation.

The results show that for the group of older workers as a whole, the majority of self-employed mention opportunity-driven motives to enter self-employment. Especially older workers who make the transition in their fifties mention necessity-based motives and those who make the transition in late-career relatively often indicate the income from self-employment functions as an additional income.

Indicators of financial precariousness among self-employed workers show a higher share of self-employed in low-income and low-wealth households after state pension age. Indicators of health and well-being show that among employees, the share of respondents in poor health, with long-standing activity limitations and poor quality of life is higher before than beyond state pension age. In other words, employees who work beyond state pension age seem to be the ones who are relatively advantaged in terms of health and well-being. Contrarily, among self-employed the share of respondents with poor health, with long-standing activity limitations and poor quality of life is lower in the group of older workers before than beyond state pension age. As compared to employees, self-employed seem relatively privileged in terms of health and well-being before state pension age, but relatively disadvantaged beyond state pension age.

The findings in this chapter provide further empirical evidence to support the suggestion put forward in earlier research that on the one hand relatively privileged workers tend to work beyond state pension age (Kerr and Armstrong-Stassen, 2011; Van Solinge, 2014; Been and Knoef, 2015; Wahrendorf et al, 2017); this is similar to findings among employees. However, the findings also seem to support the necessity-based hypotheses among European self-employed workers. From the self-employment as precarious work perspective, it seems likely that whereas on the one hand *employees* are for the most part relatively protected against the necessity to extend working life beyond state pension age, on the other hand *self-employed* may more often have to continue working because of financial precariousness and despite poor physical conditions. As this chapter has been exploratory in nature, relevant directions for future research include a closer examination of causal relations such as the impact of cohort- or period-effects (e.g. younger cohorts may have higher levels of human capital) and country-effects on precariousness and working beyond state pension age. Furthermore, it would be relevant to gain more insight into whether and how precariousness and extension of working lives among older self-employed has been *changing* over time.

ACKNOWLEDGEMENTS

This chapter uses data from SHARE Wave 5 (DOI: 10.6103/SHARE.w5.611). The SHARE data collection has been primarily funded by the European Commission through FP5 (QLK6-CT-2001-00360), FP6 (SHARE-I3: RII-CT-2006-062193, COMPARE: CIT5-CT-2005-028857, SHARELIFE: CIT4-CT-2006-028812) and FP7 (SHARE-PREP: N°211909, SHARE-LEAP: N°227822, SHARE M4: N°261982). Additional funding from the German Ministry of Education and Research, the Max Planck Society for the Advancement of Science, the U.S. National Institute on Aging (U01_AG09740-13S2, P01_AG005842, P01_AG08291, P30_AG12815, R21_AG025169, Y1-AG-4553-01, IAG_BSR06-11, OGHA_04-064, HHSN271201300071C) and from various national funding sources is gratefully acknowledged (see www.share-project.org).

REFERENCES

Amorós, J.E. and Bosma, N.S. (2014). *Global Entrepreneurship Monitor 2013 Global Report*. Babson Park, MA: Babson College, Santiago, Chile: Universidad del Desarollo, Kuala Lumpur, Malaysia: Universiti Tun Abdul Razak.

Been, J. and Knoef, M. (2015). The necessity of self-employment towards retirement: evidence from labor market dynamics and search requirements for unemployment benefits. *Netspar Discussion Paper*, 04/2015-009, Tilburg: Network for Studies on Pensions, Aging and Retirement.

Blanchflower, D.G. (2004). Self-employment: more may not be better. *Swedish Economic Policy Review*, 11(2), 15–74.

Blundell, R., Meghir, C. and Smith, S. (2002). Pension incentives and the pattern of early retirement. *Economic Journal*, 112(478), C153–C170.

Börsch-Supan, A. (2018). *Survey of Health, Ageing and Retirement in Europe (SHARE) Wave 5*. Release version: 6.1.0. SHARE-ERIC. Data set. DOI: 10.6103/SHARE.w5.611.

Börsch-Supan, A., Brandt, M., Hunkler, C., Kneip, T., Korbmacher, J., Malter, F., Schaan, B., Stuck, S. and Zuber, S. (2013). Data resource profile: the Survey of Health, Ageing and Retirement in Europe (SHARE). *International Journal of Epidemiology*, 42(4), 992–1001. doi: 10.1093/ije/dyt088.

Brougham, R.R. and Walsh, D.A. (2007). Image theory, goal incompatibility, and retirement intent. *The International Journal of Aging and Human Development*, 65(3), 203–29.

Cahill, K., Giandrea, M. and Quinn, J. (2013). New evidence on self-employment transitions among older Americans with career jobs. *U.S. Bureau of Labor Statistics Working Paper*, 463. Washington, DC: U.S. Department of Labor.

Conen, W.S. (2013). *Older Workers: the View of Dutch Employers in a European Perspective*. Amsterdam: Amsterdam University Press.

Conen, W.S., Henkens, K. and Schippers, J.J. (2012). Employers' attitudes and actions towards the extension of working lives in Europe. *International Journal of Manpower*, 33(6), 648–65.

Conen, W.S., Henkens, K. and Schippers, J.J. (2014). Ageing organisations and the extension of working lives: a case study approach. *Journal of Social Policy*, 43(4), 773–92.

Conen, W.S., Schippers, J.J. and Schulze Buschoff, K. (2016). *Self-Employed without Personnel – Between Freedom and Insecurity*. Düsseldorf: Hans Böckler Foundation.

Damman, M., Henkens, K. and Kalmijn, M. (2011). The impact of midlife educational, work, health and family experiences on men's early retirement. *Journal of Gerontology: Psychological Sciences*, 66(5), 617–27.

Daniel, K. and Heywood, J.S. (2007). The determinants of hiring older workers: UK evidence. *Labour Economics*, 14(1), 35–51.

Dawson, C., Henley, A. and Latreille, P.L. (2009). Why do individuals choose self-employment? *IZA Discussion Paper*, No. 3974.

Dingemans, E. (2016). *Working after retirement; determinants and consequences of bridge employment*. Doctoral dissertation. University of Groningen.

Flynn, M. (2010). Who would delay retirement? Typologies of older workers. *Personnel Review*, 39(3), 308–24.

Giandrea, M.D., Cahill, K.E. and Quinn, J.F. (2008). Self-employment transitions among older American workers with career jobs. *BLS Working Papers*, 418.

Kalleberg, A.L. (2011). *Good Jobs, Bad Jobs. The Rise of Polarised and Precarious Employment Systems in the United States, 1970s to 2000s*. New York: Russell Sage Foundation.

Kalwij, A. and Vermeulen, F. (2008). Health and labour force participation of older people in Europe: what do objective health indicators add to the analysis? *Health Economics*, 17(5), 619–38.

Karpinska, K., Henkens, K. and Schippers, J.J. (2013). Retention of older workers: impact of managers' age norms and stereotypes. *European Sociological Review*, 29(6), 1323–35.

Kautonen, T., Down, S., Welter, F., Vainio, P., Palmroos, J., Althoff, K. and Kolb, S. (2010). 'Involuntary self-employment' as a public policy issue: a cross-country European review. *International Journal of Entrepreneurial Behaviour & Research*, 16(2), 112–29.

Kerr, G. and Armstrong-Stassen, M. (2011). The bridge to retirement: older workers' engagement in post-career entrepreneurship and wage-and-salary employment. *The Journal of Entrepreneurship*, 20(1), 55–76.

Malter, F. and Börsch-Supan, A. (eds) (2015). *SHARE Wave 5: Innovations & Methodology*. Munich: MEA, Max Planck Institute for Social Law and Social Policy.

Mehrbrodt, T., Gruber, S. and Wagner, M. (2017). *Scales and Multi-Item Indicators*. Munich: MEA, Max Planck Institute for Social Law and Social Policy.

Oude Mulders, J. (2016). *Organizations, managers, and the employment of older workers after retirement*. Tjalling C. Koopmans Dissertation Series, USE 032. Utrecht University, School of Economics.

Raymo, J.M., Warren, J.R., Sweeney, M.M., Hauser, R.M. and Ho, J.-H. (2011). Precarious employment, bad jobs, labor unions, and early retirement. *The Journals of Gerontology*. Series B: Psychological Sciences and Social Sciences, 66(2), 249–59.

SSE (2014). *Survey Solo Self-employment*. Utrecht: Utrecht University School of Economics.

Taylor, M.P. (1996). Earnings, independence or unemployment: why become self-employed? *Oxford Bulletin of Economics and Statistics*, 58(2), 253–66.

Van Dalen, H.P., Henkens, K. and Schippers, J. (2009). Dealing with older workers in Europe: a comparative survey of employers' attitudes and actions. *Journal of European Social Policy*, 19(1), 47–60.

Van Solinge, H. (2014). Who opts for self-employment after retirement? A longitudinal study in the Netherlands. *European Journal of Ageing*, 11(3), 261–72.

Wahrendorf, M., Akinwale, B., Landy, R., Matthews, K. and Blane, D. (2017). Who in Europe works beyond the state pension age and under which conditions? Results from SHARE. *Journal of Population Ageing*, 10(3), 269–85.

Wang, M. and Shi, J. (2014). Psychological research on retirement. *Annual Review of Psychology*, 65, 209–33.

Zissimopoulos, J.M. and Karoly, L.A. (2007). Transitions to self-employment at older ages: the role of wealth, health, health insurance and other factors. *Labour Economics*, 14(2), 269–95.

Zissimopoulos, J.M. and Karoly, L.A. (2009). Labor-force dynamics at older ages: movements into self-employment for workers and nonworkers. *Research on Aging*, 31(1), 89–111.

11. Migrant self-employment in Germany: on the risks, characteristics and determinants of precarious work

Stefan Berwing, Andrew Isaak and René Leicht

INTRODUCTION

The increased significance of (solo) self-employment in the German labour market during the last two decades raised the suspicion that this goes hand in hand with a loss of autonomy, economic substance and social security of the self-employed (Bührmann and Pongratz, 2010; Bögenhold and Fachinger, 2016; Brenke and Beznoska, 2016; Conen et al., 2016; see also the contributions of other authors in this book). Regarding the central role of education for successful entrepreneurship (Brüderl et al., 1996) this may be surprising since people who start a business are generally better educated than ever before (Arum and Müller, 2004; Fritsch et al., 2015). Therefore, it can be assumed that post-Fordism and flexible work arrangements, in particular subcontracting and marginal, involuntary or pseudo self-employment, have captured a large portion of the high-skilled professions in the service sector – a process which ultimately leads to low income levels and poor working conditions (Bögenhold and Fachinger, 2016).

At the same time, another trend in Germany becomes clear: while self-employment among non-migrants decreased by 4 per cent between 2005 and 2016, there has been a 24 per cent growth of self-employment among those with a migrant background during the same period (Leicht and Berwing, 2017). Therefore migrant self-employment is becoming a focal issue for self-employment overall. This raises the question to what extent migrant self-employment is precarious. After all, in the portrayal of the mainstream media, immigrant businesses are often associated with fast food (e.g. doner kebab, pizza) and greengrocers. In the scientific debate, migrant self-employment is seen as niche economy with a high risk of precarious work (Apitzsch, 2006, p. 741; Lehmann et al., 2009, p. 32).

At first glance, there seem to be signs that precarious and migrant self-employment correspond to one another: Precarious self-employment typically refers to business activities that entail not only lower incomes but also excessive working hours and self-exploitation (Vosko et al., 2003; Bögenhold and Fachinger, 2007; Schulze Buschoff, 2007). Many scholars see such working conditions as characteristics of migrant entrepreneurship – at least regarding the debate around the formation and strategies of ethnic economies in the Anglo-American literature (Bonacich and Modell, 1980; Waldinger et al., 1990; Light and Gold, 2000). Researchers often assume that discrimination and (the threat of) unemployment forces immigrants into self-employment in sectors with low qualification requirements and low entry barriers. Following this narrative, immigrants are condemned to survive in highly competitive markets and sweatshops leaving them with low earnings, unpaid family work and in a vulnerable market position. In Germany however, the labour market is thriving and the share of migrant business owners that run restaurants or retail stores is decreasing, whereas more and more start businesses in knowledge-intensive services and other industries that require higher qualifications (Leicht and Berwing, 2017). This is mainly due to changes in the social structure of immigrants, in particular among those groups that arrived recently.

Against the backdrop of this debate, we address three questions: First, we ask how widespread the phenomenon of precarious self-employment is among migrants and non-migrants. Second, to shed further light on the topic, we ask in which industries and in which fields of occupation precarious migrant self-employment is prevalent. Third, using multivariate analysis, we seek to answer the question, which are the most important drivers of precarious migrant self-employment.

So far, to our knowledge, there has been no attempt to measure the extent of precarious work among self-employed migrants in Germany. For this, we create a composite indicator variable from three different key figures (income, working hours and underemployment). The indicator allows us to address different aspects of precarious self-employment in different social and economic contexts. In so doing, we contribute to research on migrant self-employment as well as to research on precarious work. To our knowledge, no study in Germany (except for the qualitative studies by Schmiz, 2013 and Yildiz, 2017) addresses the question of precariousness amongst self-employed with foreign roots.

PREVIOUS RESEARCH

Different Fields of Research With Different Views on Self-employment

It is remarkable that classical approaches to entrepreneurship research are not suitable for understanding precarious self-employment. Scholars are less interested in by what means business owners organize their livelihood, but rather in how they organize their enterprise strategically and influence the overall economy. Thus, economists rarely deal with social risks on the individual level or even with precariousness (Bührmann and Pongratz, 2010). This may be partially explained by the fact that self-employment is not seen as an entrepreneurial activity – even less so when dealing with people who are not employers. After all, in the eyes of economists a 'real' entrepreneur is commonly considered a protagonist who provides innovation and additional jobs (e.g. Henrekson and Sanandaji, 2014). By contrast, sociological research on immigrant or ethnic entrepreneurship is much closer to the life world of the self-employed. However, in this context the question of the extent of precariousness does not acutely arise since it is commonly assumed that "immigrant businesses are usually unprofitable" (Light, 2005, p. 655) and based on instability, uncertainty and "scanty returns for their owners" (Waldinger et al., 1990, p. 23).

Precarious work has mainly been discussed in the research on industrial relations, labour markets and social inequality. In these fields, the self-employed were not often considered an interesting subject of study. This turned however, by the end of the last century when the debate on neo-liberal policies and flexible work arrangements like subcontracting and outsourcing was in full swing (McManus, 2000; Vosko et al., 2003). At the same time, in many advanced economies, the historic decline of non-agricultural self-employment has been reversed (Luber and Leicht, 2000; OECD, 2000; Arum and Müller, 2004). Such findings, but also the contemporary increase of self-employment in certain countries, raised the suspicion that this goes hand in hand with the spread of precarious work – especially in the case of Germany where, until recently, the number of solo self-employed increased in large steps (Brenke and Beznoska, 2016; Conen et al., 2016).

However, migrants have played little role in the discourse on post-Fordism and self-employment. After all, the main focus was on native academics, whose investments into education were lost, having been forced out of the hitherto secure salaried employment into unstable and insecure jobs in the growing service sector (i.e. the 'grey area' between wage and self-employment). Likewise, this was long the case for less educated migrants in Germany, with the difference that they were forced from the shrinking manufacturing sector into unemployment, from where many of them fled into self-employment. Regarding the extent of precarious work, the implications for both groups (natives and migrants) have been assessed quite differently.

On the Role of Self-employed Migrants in the German Debate

So far, research on post-Fordism arrangements among immigrants focused mainly on those in wage- and salary-employment, who were the first victims of rationalization, globalization and flexibilization of work in the industrial sector (Sassen, 1990; Marcuse, 1997; Kloosterman, 2010). For decades, the unemployment rate among migrants has been about twice that of the native population. In addition, the earlier immigration cohorts, especially the former *Gastarbeiter* ('guest workers') and their offspring, are on average poorly qualified. They have also been reported to work more frequently in sectors that are characterized by bad working conditions, few or no chances for upward mobility and lower incomes vis-à-vis natives (Brinkmann et al., 2006).

These are just a few of the conditions under which an increasing number of German migrants have decided to pursue self-employment endeavours. However, in past research, the focus has been on the social position migrants have taken by entering self-employment, largely overlooking the precarious conditions they have left behind. In the mainstream discussion, the self-employment activities of migrants are seen as distress-originating ventures thought to occur in ethnic and economic niches with low incomes under exploitative circumstances out of survival motives (Wilpert, 2000; Lehmann et al., 2009; Schmiz, 2013). A large portion of the often qualitative studies in Germany hereby focus on 'ethnic economies' in socially weak quarters, where migrants operate in limited (and allegedly ethnic) markets and quickly reach upper limits of profitability. That topos of stunted migrant livelihoods dominated the public and scientific debate.

In the meantime, the development of migrant self-employment in Germany reveals a very different picture. The enlargement of the European Union at the beginning of the twenty-first century led to increasing immigration to Germany along with a considerable number of well-educated people as well as of lower qualified immigrants – who often (in)voluntarily entered self-employment directly after crossing the border. The overall growth in self-employment can be traced back mainly to the expansion of self-employed migrants in knowledge-intensive service industries and in the construction sector. As one of the results, the proportion of innovative start-ups among people from certain regions of origin (e.g. North America, South-East Asia or the Middle East) is higher than in the native population. In contrast, the prevalence of self-employed migrants in food services, catering and retail trade decreased considerably (Leicht and Berwing, 2017). Even though there is still a big stock of low-skilled immigrants in Germany stemming from earlier migration cohorts, this development gradually modified the social composition of migrant self-employment in terms of qualifications, occupations and industry affiliation and led to a greater heterogeneity (Leicht et al., 2017).

Influence of Resources, Opportunity Structures and the Institutional Environment

Existing research suggests that the absence of certain individual resources, mainly the lack of adequate qualifications, language skills or work experience, raises the risk of precarity or failure (Brüderl et al., 1996). The degree of new venture success is also determined by gender, age and social origin (Arum and Müller, 2004). However, influencing factors which are closely linked to the particular situation of migrants are of special interest. In this regard, substantial disadvantages also derive from unequal opportunity structures. Such opportunities may differ, for instance, because people with foreign roots have fewer chances of inheriting or taking over a well-established company and obtaining financing (Leicht and Berwing, 2017).

Further, the individual chances of entrepreneurial stability should be specified in view of inequality and social placement and thereby also on the basis of occupational differences. The unequal access to certain markets, economic sectors and occupations presents a major disparity in the opportunity structure of migrants (Ram et al., 2017). This could even be the case when the qualifications of migrants improve since they can only work with the resources made available to them by their environments (Waldinger et al., 1990). That means that the quality of self-employment is also shaped by rules and regulations and by how migrants are embedded into institutional environments (Kloosterman and Rath, 2001). Especially in Germany, access into certain areas of self-employment, namely the liberal professions ('Freie Berufe') or craft trades ('Handwerk'), is strictly regulated and reserved for those with German educational certificates. Corresponding foreign certificates are often not recognized by German institutions. Thus, self-employed migrants run the risk of exclusion from the zone of integration and participation.

Scenarios in the Face of Markets, Flexibility and Educational Differences

However, as the debate focuses on the influence of post-Fordism arrangements, the question arises to what extent specific forms of labour market flexibilization, such as outsourcing and subcontracting, are responsible for the growing number of migrant-led businesses. What are additional drivers on the macro level (e.g. opportunity structures) and how do they correspond with individual factors (e.g. educational attainment)? A look at the fields of self-employment that have most clearly increased and could have led to low incomes and bad working conditions provides us with a clearer picture. Against the backdrop of institutional settings and changing markets in Germany there are a number of scenarios in which less educated migrants are either forced or misled into precarious work: Due to low barriers to market entry, sweatshops in the food services and retail trade are still a breeding ground for migrant businesses since these sectors are increasingly favoured by demographic changes and an ongoing fast food trend. Further, it seems highly probable that the more recent amendment of the crafts code in Germany flooded the hairdressing sector with low skilled business founders. Regarding the construction boom in Germany, scenarios can be different: First, the strong demand for cheap labour tempted thousands of craftsmen from Eastern European countries to work on their own account beyond the borders of their respective country. Here, the great majority works freely and independently (Leicht and Langhauser, 2014). This group is in direct contact with private clients. By contrast, another portion of the 'newcomers' are often hired by big construction companies as 'quasi self-employed' subcontractors (Leicht and Langhauser, 2014). The latter is an example in which manner post-Fordist work arrangements appear in migrant self-employment.

Taken together these scenarios alone demonstrate the plurality of factors that may lead to precarious work. Since most self-employed migrants are additionally confronted with the same challenges as natives it is quite understandable why self-employed migrants – despite the described catching-up process – are still overrepresented in sectors with low qualification requirements, and why they earn less than self-employed natives on average (Leicht et al., 2015). Further, their volume of working hours is slightly higher, in particular regarding certain groups of origin. This is, however, much more an effect of qualifications and the related economic sector (Leicht and Langhauser, 2014).

But what about the highly skilled migrants? Until now there are hardly any examples in the debate which give us reasons to believe that better educated migrants are overrepresented in professions that run the risk of precarious work. In fact, empirical studies on the income of self-employed migrants in Germany conclude that income differentials vis-à-vis natives disappear as education levels increase (Leicht et al., 2015; Block et al., 2011). However, this positive relationship between education and income does not necessarily hold for all groups. We assume that native Germans, who are more likely to work in the shelter of highly regulated liberal professions, are protected against 'outside' competitors. This presumably largely prevents a race to the bottom for natives. Since migrants frequently experience difficultly getting their degrees or professional accreditations recognized in Germany and may face discrimination, they have a harder time accessing liberal professions. Due to this restricted market access, migrants can therefore hardly fall back on this kind of protection. This leads them to utilize their qualifications in other and often less profitable fields. Cultural professions present an exception to this rule and are among the fields in which both highly qualified migrants and natives are more strongly exposed to the risks of the market, since (in Germany) these are neither subject to the institutionally secured self-regulation of the professions nor do they have access to a corporatist regulation mode (Gottschall and Betzelt, 2001). Therefore, a question of increasing importance becomes not only whether the foreign qualifications of migrants are recognized in Germany, but also in which markets they can (best) utilize them.

Indicators of Precarious Work in Self-employment

Indicators to measure precariousness among the self-employed are limited. There are theoretical and empirical challenges with this as well, since success in self-employment is dependent not only on personal and firm resources, but also on markets (Pongratz and Simon, 2010). In the mainstream literature, the *solo* self-employed are generally suspected of working under precarious conditions. Own account workers are seen as a product of the de-limitation of work, in particular the dissolution of the boundaries between dependent labour and self-employment. Here, a grey area of atypical forms of employment has evolved, among them subcontractors, freelancers, false or involuntary self-employed, temporary workers and job nomads. The extent to which the 'Brasilianization' (Beck, 2000) of Western society includes self-employment cannot be proven alone by the fact that there are fewer and fewer employers. The expansion of the knowledge-intensive services sector and the spread of information technology increases the demand for those professional activities which are usually conducted alone (Bögenhold and Leicht, 2000).

Therefore, the suspected precariousness requires solid evidence of social risks and inequality. Since subjective perceptions like the '(in)voluntariness' of self-employment are difficult to measure (Kautonen et al., 2015) and such measures are not included in existing datasets, the majority of empirical research in Germany concentrates on existing 'hard' indicators. Therefore, researchers have investigated which income levels the self-employed reach and to which degree these are covered by social security in terms of insurance coverage, retirement preparations and living conditions (Betzelt and Fachinger, 2004; Schulze Buschoff, 2007; Wingerter, 2009; Koch et al., 2011; Fritsch et al., 2015; Brenke and Beznoska, 2016; Conen et al., 2016). Interpretations vary according to different statistical parameters (median, mean value, hourly rate, pre-tax etc.). Since other authors in this book contribute to these issues, we here forego the details of this particular debate. The structures that are investigated shed light on how precarious (solo) self-employment is in regard to individual characteristics (e.g. income, working hours and conditions). But certain indicators of precarious work overlap when observed at the individual level. Due to this interference it is difficult to assess the total numbers of self-employed that are actually affected by precariousness. Further, since no single database includes all indicators of precariousness, a complete indicator that encompasses all forms of precariousness is methodically very difficult to conceive.

OPERATIONALIZATION AND DATA

While there are well-established indicators to describe poverty, operationalizing precariousness empirically is a rather complex task. In contrast to poverty, precariousness is a much wider concept that, besides income levels, includes economic insecurity and economic vulnerability. Scholars utilize different measures to describe insecurity and vulnerability, but four dimensions seem to be crucial: (1) income, (2) job security, (3) access to professional development and (4) social security (Keller and Seifert, 2011). In order to answer the question how precarious the self-employment of migrants is, we need to draw comparison with other groups of the working population along these dimensions. However, since the regulatory framework of dependent employment differs strongly from that of self-employment, such a comparison becomes especially difficult.

For dependent employment, the employment law and collective agreements define standards for income, job or social security and for advanced vocational training. These standards can be used to construct the concept of a standard employment relationship (Bosch, 2013) as a possible benchmark to evaluate, whether or not dependent employment is precarious. Yet those standards do not apply to self-employment: for example, there are no working time regulations for the self-employed. In self-employment there is also no comparable equivalent to the working contract. In addition, in Germany there are no mandatory pension contributions for the self-employed. These legal differences make it difficult to find a multidimensional operationalization of precariousness that can be used across the total pool of employment.

Despite these obstacles, the German Microcensus presents a dataset (Federal Statistical Office of Germany, 2011) which includes a set of indicators that can be used to examine the extent of precarious work. The Microcensus is based on an annual 1 per cent sample survey of all German households and is conducted by the Federal Statistical Office of Germany. For our analysis, we use the dataset from the scientific use file of the 2011 Microcensus, which includes about 230,000 employed people (Destatis, 2017). Among migrants, 33,000 are in dependent employment and 3,700 are self-employed with their principal activities.

To define migrants, we used the standard definition of migration background by the Federal Statistical Office of Germany: ". . . all persons who have immigrated into the territory of today's Federal Republic of Germany after 1949, and of all foreigners born in Germany and all persons born in Germany who have at least one parent who immigrated into the country or was born as a foreigner in Germany". Occupation is an important dimension to describe the different fields of self-employment. To classify occupation we used the classification of Blossfeld (Blossfeld, 1985; Schimpl-Neimanns, 2003). Since this classification is very detailed we summarized some categories, for example, all skilled workers and clerks into one category. On the other hand we split the class 'professions' up into 'professions', 'liberal professions' and 'liberal professions in culture and education', using a classification of the liberal professions (Suprinovič et al., 2011). We did this for different reasons: First, the professions class is very heterogeneous regarding self-employment. Professions include the liberal professions, which have high qualifying conditions that control access to these professions. Second, the markets of some of the liberal professions, for example, lawyers, engineers or physicians, are protected by institutional regulations and therefore allow for higher incomes. Third, the liberal professions in culture and education are largely representative of cultural professions in general, which scholars assume are prone to precarious work (Gottschall and Betzelt, 2001; Gill and Pratt, 2008; Manske and Merkel, 2009).

In order to operationalize precariousness, we focused on three different indicators: income, working hours and underemployment. As a threshold value for income we use the minimum wage. The minimum wage was introduced in 2015, but the target of 8.50 € per working hour was already on the political agenda in 2011 (the year of our dataset). Since the Microcensus only includes net incomes, we had to estimate the net minimum wage. The minimum wage is about 6.50 € per hour after taxes and social security contributions, which makes about 1060 € per month when employed full-time (working 39.5 hours per week). As a first step, these two values are our central thresholds to operationalize precariousness. We thus include individuals who earn higher monthly incomes by working longer hours. We also cover individuals with higher hourly incomes but lower monthly incomes. Additionally, we include extreme working hours as a further indicator, which we defined as working more than 60 hours per week. This threshold is 25 per cent higher than the maximum working hours of the German working hours law, which allows working 48 hours per week (§3 ArbZG/German Labour Time Law). Thereby, we are able to distinguish two subtypes of precarious work: first, individuals with extreme working hours and second, individuals who earn sufficient hourly incomes, but state that they are underemployed. Therefore, for our analysis, we define precarious employment as income of less than 6.50 € per hour or less than 1060 € per month in a fulltime job or less than 1060 € per month working part-time, when the respondent states that he or she is underemployed.

We use this indicator to describe the extent of precarious work for self-employed migrants and natives. Employing logit regression analysis, we estimate the probabilities of precariousness for four different types of precarious working conditions: (1) low hourly income, (2) low monthly income, (3) extreme working hours and (4) underemployment.

RESULTS

Extent of Precarious Work in Migrant and Native Self-employment

Beginning with our overall indicator for precariousness, our results show that, in Germany, migrants work more frequently in precarious self-employment than natives (25.1 per cent, 19.2 per cent, Figure 11.1). The most important component indicator of this is low hourly incomes. Second place are low monthly incomes. The difference between these two components shows that many self-employed can only increase their income by working extreme overtime hours. This is the case for 3.4 per cent of the migrants and 2.1 per cent of the natives. Underemployment also contributes to the overall indicator, where 6 per cent of the migrants and 3.7 per cent of the natives are underemployed. As in the case of the overall indicator, migrants always show higher values in the components of the indicator. There is also great variation across different groups. For example, 39.7 per cent of the self-employed of Asian origin work under precarious conditions, while this is only the case for 23.8 per cent of those from the former guest-worker recruitment countries and only for 19.7 per cent of the self-employed from Western industrial nations.

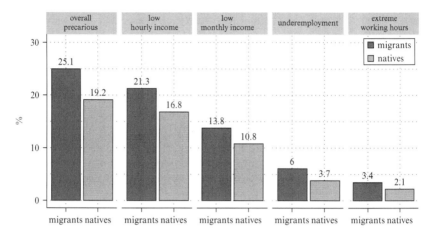

Source: Federal Statistical Office of Germany (2011), own calculations.

Figure 11.1   Precarious self-employment of natives and migrants

Due to our multidimensional definition of precariousness, the components of our precariousness indicator overlap and we therefore have different subsets, which constitute different groups (Figure 11.2). The first group is composed of self-employed with low monthly incomes, representing 63 per cent of precarious migrants and natives. The second group are self-employed with low hourly incomes, which account for up to about 98 per cent of migrants as well as natives. The overlap between the former two groups – people who earn low hourly and monthly incomes – sums up to about 50 per cent of the self-employed migrants and natives. The third group consists of the underemployed and the fourth group of those with extreme working hours. Both of these groups are also subsets of the two income groups, since we excluded all persons either without low hourly income or without low monthly income. The size of groups three and four ranges between 9.8 per cent and 15.4 per cent. It should also be noted, that the share of underemployed and persons with extreme working hours is slightly higher for migrants (12.3 per cent versus 9.8 per cent and 15.4 per cent versus 12.0 per cent).

The size of two subsets is especially interesting. The first comprises self-employed with hourly incomes above 6.50 € but low monthly incomes, who at the same time state that they are underemployed. However, this group is quite small, comprising about 0.5 per cent of the total. The majority of the underemployed earn less or equal to 6.50 € per hour. A numerically more important group are those who earn more than 1060 € per month, but can

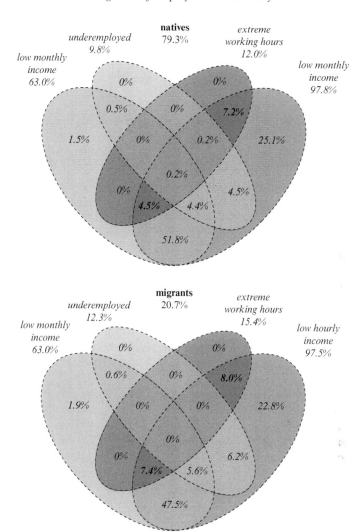

Source: Federal Statistical Office of Germany, Microcensus 2011, own calculations.

Figure 11.2   *Venn diagram of precarious self-employment of natives and*
              migrants

only do so by working more than 35 hours per week. Most of them work
between 35 and 60 hours, but more than a quarter of them work more than
60 hours per week. The share of the latter is slightly smaller for migrants.
A tiny but exceptional group are self-employed natives (0.2 per cent) who

work more than 60 hours per week, but still say they are underemployed. A possible explanation for this strange combination is that there is a small group of self-employed who earn such low hourly incomes that they are forced to work more than 60 hours a week to make a living.

Fields of Precarious Work in Migrant Self-employment

The branch of economic activity plays a major role in the literature about migrant self-employment. Many scholars see especially wholesale and retail trade as well as hotels and restaurants as the typical industries where migrant businesses emerge. In contrast to this, the analysis of the branches of economic activity in our analysis exhibits a more diverse picture. Our visualization as a tree map (Figure 11.3, panel *a*), shows that for both migrants and for natives, services are the most important sectors. In the case of migrants, knowledge intensive services are less relevant (25.4 per cent) than in the case of natives (38.9 per cent). Instead migrants are more often in non-knowledge intensive services (26.8 per cent versus 21.0 per cent). The most obvious difference between migrants and natives is nevertheless the branch of hotel and restaurants. About 14 per cent of self-employed migrants are working in this branch, while only 3.8 per cent of native self-employed earn their living there. However, in wholesale and retail trade, a branch that many also see as typical for migrant self-employment, there is almost no difference between migrants and natives.

The comparison of the extent of precariousness in the different branches makes two phenomena visible. On the one hand, we can see that the branches of economic activity are important drivers of precarity and as such, their impact seems to be relatively homogenous for migrants and natives. When we sort the branches of economic activity by the proportion of precarious work, the ranking is very similar for the two groups. On the other hand, the extent of precarious work is predominantly bigger in the case of migrants. Interestingly, the probability of precarity is lower for (self-employed) migrants in the hotel and restaurant industries – though on a very high level (35.2 per cent versus 39.4 per cent).

In addition, we plotted a similar map for the distribution across occupations (Figure 3, panel *b*). Here we can see a very similar pattern. When we order the occupation by the proportion of precarious work the sequence is almost the same for migrants and natives. Only workers and clerks are at a higher position in the case of migrants. At the top and the low ends of the list, we can find occupations with high levels of education. At the low end are the semi-professionals and the cultural professions; at the top end are the professions and the liberal professions, which in Germany include, for example, engineers, architects, lawyers and

Panel *a*

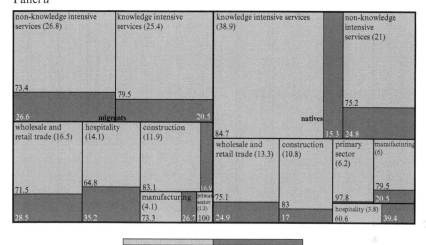

not precarious   precarious

Panel *b*

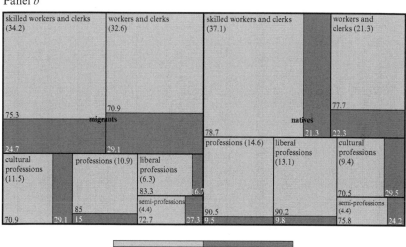

not precarious   precarious

Source: Federal Statistical Office of Germany, Microcensus 2011, own calculations.

Figure 11.3   Precarious work in self-employment by branch of economic activity (panel a) and by occupation (panel b)

tax consultants. Similar to the branch of economic activity, in almost all occupations, migrants exhibit a higher probability of being engaged in precarious work. Further, migrants are less likely to be self-employed in the professions, in the group of semi-professionals or the liberal professions (33.2 per cent versus 41.6 per cent).

Determinants of Precarious Work

Which groups of self-employed are characterized by precariousness? This is not only a question of a person's labour market position. It is also determined by gender, age, education and occupation, as well as social and ethnic origin. There has been little research in this direction. No empirical study addressed the risk of precarity among certain subgroups of self-employed in Germany along socio-demographic characteristics (Schmiz, 2013).

Research on the success of entrepreneurship activities emphasizes the importance of education (Brüderl et al., 1996; Arum and Müller, 2004; Fritsch et al., 2015). These findings are in line with the classic assumption of human capital theory (e.g. Mincer and Polachek 1974; Becker, 1985), that education reduces the risk of working under precarious conditions. Descriptive results of our education variable also confirm this standard argument (figure available upon request).

To see whether this assumption holds when considering the additional influence of the branch of economic activity and occupation, we calculated different logit regression models for the four different components of our overall precariousness indicator (Figure 11.1). This seemed sensible because we want to control for contradictory influences of the components of the overall precariousness indicator. Additionally, we controlled for age, gender, education, years in the current job of the self-employed, whether the entrepreneur is self-employed or an employer and whether the establishment is based in East or West Germany (Table 11.1). To address whether migrant self-employment is more precarious than the self-employment of natives, our central independent variable was initially migration background (analyses not shown). However, when we included this variable into our models, it was almost never statistically significant. The reason for this is the heterogeneity of the group 'migrants', for example, the precariousness value for Asians is at 39.7 per cent, while it is only 23.8 per cent for the former 'guest worker' countries (Spain, Greece, Turkey, Morocco, Portugal, Tunisia and former Yugoslavia). Therefore, we switched to the variable 'country of origin', which better reflects this heterogeneity. To crosscheck for differences between migrants and natives we also calculated two separate models for low monthly incomes for both groups (Table 11.2).

Table 11.1 Regression models for different components of the precariousness indicator

		Low monthly income			Low hourly income			Extreme working hours			Underemployment		
		Odds	l. 95%	h. 95%	Odds	l. 95%	h. 95%	Odds	l. 95%	h. 95%	Odds	l. 95%	h. 95%
Intercept		0,074 ***	0,053	0,105	0,14 ***	0,105	0,186	0,017 ***	0,008	0,032	0,088 ***	0,05	0,153
Branch of economic activity	Non-knowledge intensive services (ref.)												
	Knowledge intensive services	0,92	0,812	1,043	0,904 .	0,815	1,003	0,754 .	0,553	1,03	0,82 *	0,689	0,976
	Hospitality ↑	2,162 ***	1,791	2,608	2,74 *** ↑	2,337	3,212	4,933 ***	3,635	6,729	0,838	0,561	1,219
	Wholesale and retail trade ↑	1,616 ***	1,406	1,857	1,709 *** ↑	1,521	1,921	1,866 ***	1,403	2,494	0,645 ***	0,496	0,833
	Construction ↑	1,022	0,865	1,207	0,975	0,846	1,124	0,799	0,544	1,161	0,475 ***	0,336	0,66
	Manufacturing ↑	1,418 ***	1,165	1,719	1,556 *** ↑	1,323	1,826	1,516 *	1,018	2,219	0,751	0,513	1,07
	Primary sector	0,098 ***	0,055	0,16	0,089 ***	0,057	0,133	0,061 ***	0,01	0,197	0,037 ***	0,006	0,116
Occupation	Professions (ref.)												
	Workers and clerks ↑	2,3 ***	1,903	2,791	2,184 *** ↑	1,875	2,549	1,954 ***	1,416	2,732	1,492 * ↑	1,049	2,162
	Skilled workers and clerks ↑	2,071 ***	1,742	2,477	1,978 *** ↑	1,724	2,277	1,448 *	1,073	1,979	1,418 * ↑	1,026	2,002
	Semiprofessions ↑	1,669 ***	1,271	2,183	1,855 *** ↑	1,5	2,293	1,411	0,704	2,611	1,158 ↑	0,768	1,759
	Cultural professions ↑	2,601 ***	2,105	3,226	2,43 *** ↑	2,046	2,891	1,416	0,867	2,266	2,155 *** ↑	1,533	3,094
	Liberal professions ↑	1,255 .	0,998	1,577	1,074 ↑	0,89	1,293	0,716	0,423	1,172	0,997	0,67	1,495
Education	Low (ref.)												
	Medium	0,787 **	0,661	0,941	0,908	0,782	1,057	0,966	0,702	1,347	0,84	0,639	1,12
	High	0,689 ***	0,573	0,833	0,727 ***	0,621	0,854	0,916	0,645	1,316	0,677 **	0,506	0,917
Type of self-employment	Self-employed (ref.)												
	Employer	0,572 ***	0,517	0,632	0,605 *** ↑	0,556	0,657	1,634 ***	1,343	1,993	0,154 ***	0,118	0,198
Gender	Male (ref.)												
	Female ↑	1,344 ***	1,223	1,476	1,557 ***	1,44	1,683	0,734 **	0,597	0,9	1,721 *** ↑	1,484	1,999

Table 11.1   (continued)

	Intercept		Low monthly income				Low hourly income				Extreme working hours				Underemployment		
			Odds	l. 95%	h. 95%		Odds	l. 95%	h. 95%		Odds	l. 95%	h. 95%		Odds	l. 95%	h. 95%
			0,074 ***	0,053	0,105		0,14 ***	0,105	0,186		0,017 ***	0,008	0,032		0,088 ***	0,05	0,153
Age			0,995 *	0,991	0,999		0,992 ***	0,989	0,996		0,991 *	0,982	1		0,984 ***	0,978	0,991
Age of establishment	> 5 years (ref.)																
	3–5 years	↑	1,14 .	0,99	1,311	↑	1,116 .	0,991	1,255	↑	1,042	0,768	1,391	↑	1,252 *	0,996	1,564
	1–3 years	↑	1,124 .	0,982	1,286	↑	1,134 *	1,013	1,269	↑	1,163	0,876	1,526	↑	1,631 ***	1,339	1,979
	1 year	↑	1,381 ***	1,181	1,612	↑	1,247 ***	1,09	1,425	↑	1,034	0,72	1,451	↑	2,016 ***	1,623	2,491
East/West	West (ref.)																
	East	↑	4,08 ***	3,702	4,496	↑	3,307 ***	3,03	3,605	↑	1,384 **	1,102	1,727	↑	1,339 **	1,107	1,611
Country of origin	Natives (ref.)																
	Former recruitment countries	↑	1,059	0,83	1,338		0,998	0,817	1,214	↑	1,183	0,806	1,7		0,578 *	0,336	0,928
	Central and Eastern Europe	↑	1,314 *	1,019	1,675	↑	1,2 .	0,967	1,48	↑	1,103	0,606	1,847	↑	1,554 **	1,099	2,148
	Former USSR	↑	1,094	0,768	1,522	↑	1,065	0,795	1,408		0,267 .	0,044	0,842	↑	1,645 *	1,073	2,436
	Near and Middle East	↑	1,171	0,707	1,848		0,985	0,639	1,472	↑	1,958 *	0,963	3,608	↑	1,692	0,813	3,156
	Asia	↑	2,004 ***	1,342	2,937	↑	1,896 ***	1,324	2,695	↑	1,141	0,544	2,152		0,988	0,379	2,126
	Western industrial nations		0,886	0,645	1,192		0,932	0,727	1,184		0,762	0,428	1,268	↑	1,009	0,62	1,558
	Rest of the world		0,845	0,523	1,296	↑	1,021	0,715	1,425	↑	2,044 *	0,993	3,744	↑	1,014	0,528	1,773
llh			−7225				−9570				−2303				−3168		
llhNull			−9092				−11994				−2792				−4314		
McFadden			0,205				0,202				0,175				0,266		

Notes: . = 0.100, * = 0.005, ** = 0.990, *** = 0.999.

Source: Federal Statistical Office of Germany, Microcensus 2011, own calculations.

Starting with the models for low monthly and hourly incomes, we can see that the most important drivers for low incomes are the branch of economic activity and the occupation. As already noticeable in the descriptive results, working in retail trade and hospitality particularly raises the probability of earning less. Surprisingly, the separate models for migrants and natives show that, for migrants, the risk of precariousness is much lower in hospitality. It is also interesting to observe that working in knowledge intensive services does not statistically significantly lower the risk of precarity, although this sector has a high concentration of self-employed with high education levels. The reason for this becomes clear when we account for the impact of occupations: Namely, the self-employed in this kind of service are trained in the professions, liberal professions and semi-professions. While working in the professions or liberal professions lowers the probability of low income, working in the semi-professions and especially in the cultural professions raises this probability. There is also a strong negative effect of being a worker or a clerk.

The effects of the region of origin are very interesting. Overall, only a few regions of origin are statistically significant. For instance, only those self-employed with an Asian migration background or from Central and Eastern Europe are significantly more likely to earn less than natives. Strikingly, the coefficient for self-employed from the former guest worker recruitment countries (Anwerbeländer, e.g. Turkey, Yugoslavia, Italy, Spain, Portugal) is not significant and they were not likely to earn much worse than natives.

Moving on to the models for the underemployed and for the self-employed with extreme working hours, we can see how these models shed light on each other. We have already shown that working in wholesale and restaurants raises the risk of low incomes. Our model consistently shows that working in those sectors also leads to a higher probability of working extreme hours. Inverting the argument, underemployment is not common in these branches. Comparing the other branches of economic activity, we notice that compared to non-knowledge intensive services, all branches have a lower risk of underemployment. Turning to the occupations, the table depicts that underemployment is more likely in all occupations than in the professions, with the exception of the liberal professions. But, underemployment seems to be a very common phenomenon particularly in the cultural professions. Also, for these two models there is no clear pattern for migration background. People from the former recruitment countries are less likely to be underemployed, while self-employed from Central and Eastern Europe and the former USSR are often underemployed. Regarding working extreme hours, only people from the Near and Middle East and the class 'rest of the world' are likely to work extreme hours.

Table 11.2 Comparison of regressions models for low monthly incomes for migrants and natives

		Migrants				Natives		
		Odds	conf. 5%	conf. 95%		Odds	conf. 5%	conf. 95%
Intercept		0,051 ***	0,023	0,111		0,084 ***	0,057	0,123
Branch of economic activity	Non-knowledge intensive services (ref.)							
	Knowledge intensive services	1,004	0,716	1,405	↑	0,917	0,803	1,048
	Hospitality	1,713 **	1,191	2,463	↑	2,326 ***	1,874	2,881
	Wholesale and retail trade	1,772 ***	1,278	2,456	↑	1,598 ***	1,374	1,86
	Construction	0,914	0,588	1,395	↑	1,043	0,872	1,245
	Manufacturing	1,052	0,552	1,878	↑	1,454 ***	1,182	1,78
	Primary sector	0	0	0,093	↑	0,103 ***	0,058	0,168
Occupation	Professions (ref.)							
	Workers and clerks	2,829 ***	1,747	4,776	↑	2,214 ***	1,807	2,727
	Skilled workers and clerks	2,243 ***	1,406	3,733	↑	2,05 ***	1,706	2,478
	Semiprofessions	1,294	0,621	2,638	↑	1,726 ***	1,292	2,298
	Cultural professions	2,077 *	1,196	3,703	↑	2,694 ***	2,151	3,382
	Liberal professions	1,723	0,882	3,343	↑	1,21	0,951	1,54
Education	Low (ref.)							
	Medium	0,744 *	0,566	0,981		0,773 *	0,62	0,973
	High	0,783	0,569	1,078		0,667 ***	0,53	0,846
Type of self-employment	Self-employed (ref.)							
	Employer	0,648 ***	0,504	0,829		0,567 ***	0,509	0,631
Gender	Male (ref.)							
	Female	1,644 ***	1,302	2,073	↑	1,29 ***	1,166	1,428

Age	↑	1,001	0,99	1,012		0,994 **	0,989	0,998	
Age of establishment									
> 5 years (ref.)									
3–5 years	↑	1,264	0,92	1,721	↑	1,133	0,969	1,321	
1–3 years	↑	1,309 .	0,969	1,757	↑	1,067	0,918	1,238	
1 year	↑	1,481 *	1,062	2,051	↑	1,387 ***	1,164	1,646	
East/West									
West (ref.)									
East	↑	3,706 ***	2,552	5,328	↑	4,121 ***	3,726	4,556	
llh		−1183,258				−6234,02			
llhNull		−1440,436				−7644,159			
McFadden		0,179				0,184			

Notes: . = 0.100, * = 0.005, ** = 0.990, *** = 0.999.

Source: Federal Statistical Office of Germany, Microcensus 2011, own calculations.

Looking at our control variables, we observe different effects. First, we see that gender has a strong influence. Women are of higher risk of underemployment and are more likely to earn low incomes, whereas they have a lower risk of working extreme hours. The variable 'age of establishment' shows that the younger an establishment is, the more likely it is for its owners to work precariously. Additionally, having employees makes it much less likely to work precariously, while it clearly raises the chances of working long hours. In the case of Germany it is important to control for regional effects given the history of reunification (as of 1989). Being self-employed in East Germany raises the risk of low monthly incomes four times. This result has to be taken with a pinch of salt since we did not control for purchasing power parity. Nevertheless, taking the labour market situation in eastern Germany into account, the result seems to be plausible, although the size of the effect should be controlled by more sophisticated analyses (e.g. in a multilevel model).

Coming back to the effect of education, the starting point of this section, our results confirm the results of existing research. As could have been expected, we indeed observe a strong negative effect of education on the probability of low monthly incomes (i.e. additional education is likely to raise income). This is also true for the risk of low hourly incomes, although the effect is not as strong. However, higher educational levels are no panacea for precarity. While working in the liberal professions is not statistically significant for precariousness and is thus similar to the professions, the risk for precarity is clearly higher in the cultural professions and in the semi-professions. Both of the latter occupational classes are characterized by relatively high educational levels. Nevertheless, self-employed working in the cultural professions are much more likely to work precariously than skilled and unskilled workers and clerks. It is also noteworthy that the separate models (Table 11.2) show that high educational levels have no significant effect in the case of migrants. This is a stunning result, since existent research suggests that it should have a significant positive effect.

DISCUSSION

In the introduction, we posed three research questions: First, to what extent is migrant self-employment precarious? Second, in which industries and in which fields of occupation is precarious migrant self-employment prevalent? Third, is it possible to trace the precariousness of migrant self-employment back to certain determinants? In the following, we discuss these three questions against the backdrop of our results and then point out the limitations of our approach and directions for future research.

Extent of Precarious Work and Fields of Precarious Work

Regarding the extent of precarious work, the analysis of our overall indicator shows that approximately every fourth self-employed migrant is precarious, while this is only the case for every fifth native. The most important components of our indicator are low monthly and low hourly incomes. For the dataset under study (the 2011 German Microcensus), in both of these components, migrants fare worse than natives. Extreme working hours and underemployment are less important components of the overall indicator in their extent. Nevertheless, in these components, the values of migrants have higher values by a third and are thus especially prone for underemployment and extreme working hours. Taken together, our results regarding the extent of precarious migrant self-employment clearly show that migrants are more likely to work precariously.

Coming to our second question, a cursory glance at the data seems to confirm the common narrative of the typical migrant business. According to this narrative, migrants work to a much higher degree in hospitality and retail trade, which results in economically marginal migrant self-employment. Within this narrative, this is the reason why self-employment of migrants is more precarious than that of natives. However, our results show that the picture is much more complex in reality.

Summarizing our descriptive results, there are two major observations. First, it is true that about 30 per cent of migrants are working in retail trade and hospitality compared to about 17 per cent of their native counterparts. Still, 70 per cent of migrants work outside of these sectors. Second, if we compare the risk of precarity between migrants and natives our results show a higher risk for migrants across different economic sectors and occupations. Comparing the branches of economic activity, we see that migrants are at higher risk of precarity in all economic branches, except for construction where the risk level is comparable to that of natives, and the hospitality sector, where the risk is interestingly lower for migrants. The same pattern applies to professions: Here we can see that the risk of precarity is higher for migrants in all professions, except for the cultural professions, where migrants lie on par with natives.

Determinants of Precarious Work

In answer to our third research question, we interpret our multivariate results against the backdrop of our descriptive results. The overall model is consistent with the typical narrative about migrant self-employment and the other models show that migrants have a higher risk of low monthly and hourly incomes as well as a higher risk of extreme working hours in the retail trade and the restaurant business. However, the separate models reveal cracks in the narrative, since the risk of precarity in hospitality is actually lower for migrants. Although this is a surprising result it is nevertheless plausible. Migrants have a long tradition in the German hospitality sector. They often own old establishments and also have a lot of expertise on how to make a living in this sector. Ownership and sector-specific expertise are both important factors to lower the risk of precarity.

Taking the other independent variables into account, we see that with rising age of an establishment the risk of working precariously is lowered. Also, whether a self-employed person works alone or with other employees has an impact – the owners of businesses with employees are less often in precarity compared to those working alone. In the case of education and age of the self-employed, the overall models for low monthly and hourly incomes show the expected effects: Higher levels of education and rising age lower the risk of precarious work, since both variables are good proxies for expertise and work experience.

However, our separate results for migrants and natives reveal that these effects cannot be confirmed in the case of migrants, since high education levels and age are not statistically significant. If they were, high levels of education would lower the risk, but to a much lower degree than in the case of natives and rising age would have no effect since it would not lower or raise the risk of precarity. A possible explanation for the missing effect of high educational levels could be the German practice of recognizing foreign certificates. Until 2012 when legislation was changed, the recognition of certificates was very difficult. For this reason, migrants were often forced to find (self-)employment in jobs and sectors that did not fit their education, a possible explanation for the weak effect of education in the case of migrants. Recognition of certificates is a general (and global) problem for migrants but it seems reasonable to assume that the distribution of these restrictions across nationalities and occupations is diverse. Two points should be considered as relevant for these differences in distribution: First, German authorities evaluate the quality of certificates differently; second, it happens that qualifications are predominant in certain immigration cohorts.

An example of such selection effects is our result regarding under-employment. Overall, it proves the assumption of existent research that migrants are, despite high educational levels, especially prone to precari-ousness. Our results suggest that a major driver behind their higher risk is underemployment. Considering migration background, we can see a selection effect for immigrants from the former Soviet Union and Eastern Europe, who often work in artistic and musical occupations (Leicht et al., 2004, p. 139). In the contrary case of extreme working hours there is no

Table 11.3   *Results decomposition*

	value	prop.	s.e.	z value	P	ci l	ci u
char	0,018	50,03	0,006	2,929	0,002	0,006	0,03
coeff	0,018	49,97	0,008	2,286	0,011	0,002	0,033
diff tot	0,036	100	0,008	5,529	0	0,023	0,048

Source: Microcensus 2011 Federal Statistical Office of Germany, own calculations.

obvious explanation for the effect of the groups 'Rest of the world' and 'Near and Middle East'. As expected, extreme working hours are common in hospitality and retail trade.

When we try to understand the drivers of precarious work against the backdrop of the descriptive results, we can see cracks in the narrative about the migrant business as a typical example of precarious self-employment. Our multivariate results show that the overall effect of country of origin is very small. Certain countries of origin have an effect in different models, but these effects do not seem to be systematic but rather idiosyncratic. For example, self-employed of Asian origin, a rather small group in Germany so far, have a very high risk of low income, while self-employed from the former guest worker recruitment countries, a very large group known to be dominant in the retail trade and hospitality, are not significantly different in income level from natives. Taking this into account, it seems plausible to assume that a major driver of the higher precariousness of migrants are endowment effects due to different distribution across occupations and branches of economic activity. Nevertheless, our descriptive results show that migrants almost always have a higher risk of precarity in almost all occupations and branches of economic activity. This descriptive result should indicate a group effect, which we are not able to prove with our regression models. To cross check whether the differences can be attributed to endowment or group effects we conducted a decomposition analysis (Table 11.3). The results thereof suggest a mixture of endowment (50 per cent) and group effects (40 per cent). Keeping the missing effect of education and age in the case of migrants in mind this is a sound result, although we see no clear effect of migration background.

Limitations and Further Research

This leads us to the limitations of our approach. To get a better hold on the effect of migration background on precarity which we could partially confirm, it would be necessary to construct a multilevel model with random effects for different immigration groups. This would make it possible to isolate different effects of dependent variables and understand the idiosyncratic effect of migration background.

Another limitation is our data source. We used the German Microcensus which is a household survey and therefore our data are not likely to cover migrant workers in temporary makeshift shelters, for example, on construction sites and in agriculture. A look at the nationality, the inflow as well as the outflow in the German business registration statistics allows for the assumption that bogus (or pseudo) self-employment is a relevant factor. Thus, it is reasonable to assume that our data do not cover the most vulnerable forms of precarious self-employment. However, a quantitative estimate of the extent of pseudo self-employment in general and in comparison between migrants and natives remains an area of further research.

It is also potentially problematic to compare net incomes, since we do not know how biased income data of self-employed are. There are strong indications that self-employed do not pay sufficiently into pension schemes and social security, which is not adequately controlled for in surveys. Therefore, it can be assumed that the information about net incomes is often biased. Furthermore, we also did not compare self-employed with paid-employed. When doing this, further research has to take the employer's contribution to health insurance, social security payments and pension payments into account. In total, these contributions raise the gross income of paid-employed by about 20 per cent compared to self-employed. Data provided by Seifert et al. (2015, p. 10), indicate that the lower half of the self-employed income earners earn less than the paid employed, whereas the upper half of the self-employed earn better than their paid-employed counterparts. This raises the question of under which conditions self-employment becomes a viable path to social advancement and under which conditions it raises the risk of working precariously. To find answers to these questions, panel data are essential. Regarding the self-employment of migrants, we have to keep in mind, that for many unemployment would be the alternative.

SUMMARY

In this study, we examine the extent of precarious migrant self-employment vis-à-vis natives using data from the German Microcensus. We find that migrants are more affected by precariousness overall, confirming the common narrative about migrant entrepreneurship in public discourse. Every fourth migrant self-employed works under precarious conditions, while this is the case only for every fifth German native. This means however, that the distance to native Germans is not very large (6 per cent). Taking post-Fordism into account we cannot prove that migrants are especially prone to be the subject of post-Fordist work arrangements. This could be an effect of the dataset used, which does not cover pseudo self-employment. However, our data provide firm evidence for the assumption of many scholars that cultural professions often lead to precarious working conditions. Regarding the drivers for the higher risk of precarity of migrant self-employment our results are ambiguous. On the one hand there is evidence of a strong influence of endowment effects (e.g. over-representation in hospitality and retail trade), on the other hand there are also indications for various group effects. For example, we observe that the risk of precarious work in hospitality is much lower for migrants than for natives. Another example is the missing positive effect of high levels of education in the case of migrants, which could be a result of the German practice of recognizing foreign certificates. In sum, the study cannot confirm a direct relationship between migration background and precarious self-employment. We thus have to assume that the higher risk of precarity in migrant self-employment is the result of a complex combination of different influences, which remain to be analyzed in further depth in future research. Future studies along these lines should also take a European comparative perspective that addresses different economic and institutional contexts of European countries as well as their heterogeneous immigration histories. Our results are more likely to replicate those European countries with comparable socio-economic context and immigration history, for example Austria or Switzerland, but are less likely to apply to France and Belgium or the (Anglo-Saxon) Great Britain. In general, a comparative approach seems to be a promising path for further research to gain deeper insights into the mechanisms that lead to precarious self-employment.

REFERENCES

Apitzsch, U. (2006). Die Chancen der Zweiten Generation in selbständigen Migrantenfamilien: Intergenerationelle Aspekte. In: Kongress Der Deutschen Gesellschaft Für Soziologie *Soziale Ungleichheit-Kulturelle Unterschiede.* Campus Verl, pp. 737–51.

Arum, R. and Müller, W. (2004). The Reemergence of Self-Employment: Comparative Findings and Empirical Propositions. In: Arum, R. and Muller, W. (eds), *The Reemergence of Self-Employment. A Comparative Study of Self-Employment Dynamics and Social Inequality.* Princeton: Princeton University Press, pp. 426–54.

Beck, U. (2000). *The Brave New World of Work.* Cambridge and Malden, MA: Polity Press.

Becker, G. (1985). Human Capital, Effort, and the Sexual Division of Labor. *Journal of Labor Economics,* 3(1), 33–58.

Betzelt, S. and Fachinger, U. (2004). Selbständige-arm im Alter? Für eine Absicherung Selbständiger in der GRV. *Wirtschaftsdienst*, 84, 379–86.

Block, J., Sander, P. and Wagner, M. (2011). Selbständigkeit von Ausländern in Deutschland. Einkommenseffekte und Implikationen für die Gründungsförderung. *Soziale Welt*, 62(1), 7–23.

Blossfeld, H.-P. (1985). *Bildungsexpansion und Berufschancen: empirische Analysen zur Lage der Berufsanfänger in der Bundesrepublik*. Frankfurt and New York: Campus.

Bögenhold, D. and Fachinger, U. (2007). Micro-Firms and the Margins of Entrepreneurship: The Restructuring of the Labour Market. *The International Journal of Entrepreneurship and Innovation*, 8, 281–92.

Bögenhold, D. and Fachinger, U. (2016). *Berufliche Selbstständigkeit: theoretische und empirische Vermessungen*, Essentials. Wiesbaden: Springer VS.

Bögenhold, D. and Leicht, R. (2000). Neue Selbständigkeit und Entrepreneurship: Moderne Vokabeln und damit verbundene Irrtümer. *WSI Mitteilungen*, 53, 779–87.

Bonacich, E. and Modell, J. (1980). The Economic Basis of Ethnic Solidarity. *Pacific Affairs*, 55.

Bosch, G. (2013). Normalarbeitsverhältnis. In: Hirsch-Kreinsen, H. and Minssen, H. (eds), *Lexikon Der Arbeits- Und Industriesoziologie*. Berlin: Edition Sigma, pp. 376–82.

Brenke, K. and Beznoska, M. (2016). *Solo-Selbständige in Deutschland – Strukturen und Erwerbsverläufe. Kurzexpertise für das BMAS*. Forschungsbericht. Berlin: BMAS.

Brinkmann, U., Dörre, K. and Röbenack, S. (2006). *Prekäre Arbeit: Ursachen, Ausmaß, soziale Folgen und subjektive Verarbeitungsformen unsicherer Beschäftigungsverhältnisse*. Bonn: Friedrich-Ebert-Stiftung.

Brüderl, J., Preisendörfer, P. and Ziegler, R. (1996). *Der Erfolg neugegründeter Betriebe: eine empirische Studie zu den Chancen und Risiken von Unternehmensgründungen*. Betriebswirtschaftliche Schriften. Berlin: Duncker & Humblot.

Bührmann, A.D. and Pongratz, H.J. (2010). *Prekäres Unternehmertum: Unsicherheiten von selbständiger Erwerbstätigkeit und Unternehmensgründungen*. Wiesbaden: VS Verlag.

Conen, W., Schippers, J. and Schulze-Buschoff, K. (2016). Solo-Selbstständigkeit – zwischen Freiheit und Unsicherheit. *WSI Working Paper*. Düsseldorf.

Destatis (2017). *Persons with a Migration Background*. Destatis. https://www.destatis.de/EN/FactsFigures/SocietyState/Population/MigrationIntegration/Methods/MigrationBackground.html (accessed 30 October 2017).

Federal Statistical Office of Germany (2011). Mikrozensus. https://www.forschungsdatenzentrum.de/de/haushalte/mikrozensus (accessed 13 March 2019).

Fritsch, M., Kritikos, S. and Sorgner, A. (2015). Why did Self-employment Increase so Strongly in Germany? *Entrepreneurship & Regional Development*, 27, 307–33.

Gill, R. and Pratt, A. (2008). In the Social Factory?: Immaterial Labour, Precariousness and Cultural Work. *Theory, Culture & Society*, 25, 1–30.

Gottschall, K. and Betzelt, S. (2001). Alleindienstleister im Berufsfeld Kultur: Versuch einer erwerbssoziologischen Konzeptualisierung. *ZeS-Arbeitspapier*, 18, 1–25.

Henrekson, M. and Sanandaji, T. (2014). Small Business Activity Does Not Measure Entrepreneurship. *Proceedings of the National Academy of Sciences*, 111, 1760–5.

Kautonen, T., Hatak, I., Kibler, E. and Wainwright, T. (2015). Emergence of Entrepreneurial Behaviour: The Role of Age-based Self-image. *Journal of Economic Psychology*, 50, 41–51.

Keller, B. and Seifert, H. (2011). Atypische Beschäftigungsverhältnisse. Stand und Lücken der aktuellen Diskussion. *WSI Mitteilungen*, WISO Diskurs 3.

Kloosterman, R. (2010). Matching Opportunities With Resources: A Framework for Analysing (Migrant) Entrepreneurship from a Mixed Embeddedness Perspective. *Entrepreneurship & Regional Development*, 22(1), 25–45.

Kloosterman, R. and Rath, J. (2001). Immigrant Entrepreneurs in Advanced Economies: Mixed Embeddedness Further Explored. *Journal of Ethnic and Migration Studies*, 27, 189–201.

Koch, A., Rosemann, M. and Späth, J. (2011). *Solo-Selbstständige in Deutschland. Strukturen, Entwicklungen und soziale Sicherung bei Arbeitslosigkeit*. WISO-Diskurs, February.

Lehmann, D., Dörre, K. and Scherschel, K. (2009). *Prekarität und Migration: ausgewählte Daten und Trends* (Working Papers: Economic Sociology Jena, 7/2009). Jena: Universität Jena, Fak. für Sozial- und Verhaltenswissenschaften, Institut für Soziologie Lehrstuhl für Arbeits-, Industrie- und Wirtschaftssoziologie.

Leicht, R. and Berwing, S. (2017). *Gründungspotenziale von Menschen mit ausländischen Wurzeln: Entwicklungen, Erfolgsfaktoren, Hemmnisse (Kurzfassung)*. Berlin: Bundesministerium für Wirtschaft und Energie.

Leicht, R. and Langhauser, M. (2014). *Ökonomische Bedeutung und Leistungspotenziale von Migrantenunternehmen in Deutschland*: Studie im Auftrag der Abteilung Wirtschafts- und Sozialpolitik, Arbeitskreis Mittelstand und Gesprächskreis Migration und Integration der Friedrich-Ebert-Stiftung, WISO-Diskurs. Abteilung Wirtschafts- und Sozialpolitik der Friedrich-Ebert-Stiftung, Bonn.

Leicht, R., Humpert, A., Zimmer-Müller, U., Lauxen-Ulbirch, M. and Fehrenback, S. (2004). *Die Bedeutung der ethnischen Ökonomie in Deutschland. Push- und Pull-Faktoren für Unternehmensgründungen ausländischer und ausländischstämmiger Mitbürger*. Berlin: Bundesministerium für Wirtschaft und Energie.

Leicht, R., Berwing, S. and Langhauser, M. (2015). Heterogenität und soziale Position migrantischer Selbständigkeit in Deutschland. *Sozialer Fortschritt*, 64, 233–41.

Leicht, R., Berwing, S., Philipp, R., Block, N., Rüfer, N., Ahrens, J.-P., Förster, N., Sänger, R. and Siebert, J. (2017). *Gründungspotenziale von Menschen mit ausländischen Wurzeln: Entwicklungen, Erfolgsfaktoren, Hemmnisse (Langfassung)*. Berlin: Bundesministerium für Wirtschaft und Energie.

Light, I. (2005). The Ethnic Economy. In: Smelser, N.J. and Swedberg, R. (eds), *The Handbook of Economic Sociology*. Princeton, NJ: Princeton University Press; New York: Russell Sage Foundation, pp. 650–77.

Light, I.H. and Gold, S.J. (2000). *Ethnic Economies*. San Diego: Academic Press.

Luber, S. and Leicht, R. (2000). Growing Self-employment in Western Europe: An Effect of Modernization? *International Review of Sociology*, 10, 101–23. doi:10.1080/713673991.

Manske, A. and Merkel, J. (2009). Prekäre Freiheit – Die Arbeit von Kreativen. *WSI Mitteilungen*, 295–301.

Marcuse, P. (1997). The Enclave, the Citadel, and the Ghetto: What has Changed in the Post-Fordist U.S. City. *Urban Affairs Review*, 33(2), 228–64.

McManus, P. (2000). Market, State, and the Quality of New Self-Employment Jobs among Men in the U.S. and Western Germany. *Social Forces*, 78, 865–905.

Mincer, J. and Polachek, S. (1974). Family Investments in Human Capital: Earnings of Women. *The Journal of Political Economy*, 82(2), 76–108.

OECD (2000). *Employment Outlook*. Paris: Organisation for Economic Co-operation and Development.

Pongratz, H. and Simon, S. (2010). Prekaritätsrisiken unternehmerischen Handelns. In: Bührmann, A.D. and Pongratz, H. (eds), *Prekäres Unternehmertum: Unsicherheiten von Selbständiger Erwerbstätigkeit Und Unternehmensgründungen*. VS Verlag, Wiesbaden, pp. 27–61.

Ram, M., Jones, T. and Villares-Varela, M. (2017). Migrant Entrepreneurship: Reflections on Research and Practice. *International Small Business Journal*, 35(1), 3–18.

Sassen, S. (1990). Economic Restructuring and The American City. *Annual Review of Sociology*, 16, 465–90.

Schimpl-Neimanns, B. (2003). *Mikrodaten-Tools: Umsetzung der Berufsklassifika tion von Blossfeld auf die Mikrozensen 1973–1998*. Mannheim: Zentrum für Umfragen, Methoden und Analysen – ZUMA.

Schmiz, A. (2013). Migrant self-employment between precariousness and self-exploitation. *Ephemera*, 13, 53–74.

Schulze Buschoff, K. (2007). *Self-employment and social risk management: comparing Germany and the United Kingdom*. Berlin: Wissenschaftszentrum Berlin für Sozialforschung gGmbH.

Seifert, H., Amlinger, M. and Keller, B. (2015). *Selbstständige als Werkvertragsnehmer Ausmaß, Strukturen und soziale Lage*. WSI Dikussionspapier, 201. Düsseldorf: WSI.

Suprinovič, O., Kranzusch, P. and Haunschild, L. (2011). *Einbeziehung freiberuflicher Gründungen in die Gründungsstatistik des IfM Bonn – Analyse möglicher Datenquellen, IfM-Materialien*. Bonn: IfM Bonn.

Vosko, L.F., Zukewich, N. and Cranford, C. (2003). Precarious jobs: a new typology of employment. *Perspectives*, 16–26.

Waldinger, R., Aldrich, H. and Ward, R. (1990). *Ethnic Entrepreneurs: Immigrant Business in Industrial Societies*, 1st ed, Sage Series on Race and Ethnic Relations. Newbury Park, London and New Delhi: Sage Publications.

Wilpert, C. (2000). Migranten als Existenzgründer. In: *Zukunft Der Arbeit IV: Arbeit Und Migration. Dokumentation Der Vierten Tagung Der Heinrich-Böll-Stiftung in Der Reihe 'Zukunft Der Arbeit' am 10./11. November 2000 in Berlin*. Berlin: Heinrich-Böll-Stiftung, pp. 45–54.

Wingerter, C. (2009). Der Wandel der Erwerbsformen und seine Bedeutung für die Einkommenssituation Erwerbstätiger. *Wirtschaft und Statistik*, 35, 1080.

Yildiz, Ö. (2017). *Migrantisch, weiblich, prekär? Über prekäre Selbständigkeiten in der Berliner Friseurbranche*. Transcript. Bielefeld.

PART III

Implications and future research agenda

12. The matter of representation: precarious self-employment and interest organizations

Giedo Jansen and Roderick Sluiter

INTRODUCTION

As shown in previous chapters, self-employed workers do not constitute a homogenous group, but are (increasingly) diverse in terms of their resources, opportunities and vulnerabilities (see also Arum and Müller, 2004; Conen et al., 2016; Jansen, 2016). Given this heterogeneity, the issue of interest representation has become more pressing. Typically, businesses or business-owners are organized into business' and employers' associations (Eurofound, 2010; Brandl and Lehr, 2016). In the Netherlands – the empirical setting of this study – approximately 90 per cent of all businesses are affiliated with a business or employer association (SER, 2017). Our understanding of their interest representation is predominantly based on the notion that the self-employed are typically entrepreneurs and (potential) employers. As employers, they would depend on hiring (cheap and flexible) labour and thus prefer free markets and a low level of social protection (Iversen and Soskice, 2001). In this perspective self-employment is linked to autonomy, self-reliance and 'entrepreneurialism', that is, to a deliberate choice in creating one's own business, and taking both the risks and returns of undertaking an entrepreneurial activity and developing one's own business (Eurofound, 2017). By implication, self-employed workers are assumed to be organized into business and employers' associations promoting business freedom, market deregulation and employment flexibility.

However, an alternative approach has emerged. In this perspective – also developed elsewhere in this book – self-employment may also take the form of precarious work. The focus is often on the so-called 'new self-employed' who are believed to work on the borderline of self-employment and dependent wage-employment – and potentially unemployment. From this perspective, instead of autonomous, stable and voluntary, self-employment is increasingly dependent, precarious and involuntary. As other chapters have also shown, this type of self-employment tends to be 'solo' (i.e. without employees) and does not necessarily fit the archetypal employer-model of entrepreneurship. Consequently, falling in-between the category of employers and employees, this type of solo self-employment is argued to be poorly accommodated by traditional systems of interest representation through which employers are represented in employers' associations, and employees are represented by trade unions (Schulze Buschoff and Schmidt, 2009). Indeed, unlike other businesses, the organization rate among solo self-employed is much lower, that is, only 10–20 per cent are affiliated with an employer or business association (Van der Berg et al., 2009). Yet, as in other countries trade unions in the Netherlands have set up new branches for self-employed workers, and also a variety of new (independent) solo self-employment organizations were established over the last decade (Eurofound, 2017; Jansen, 2017a). Approximately 40 per cent of solo self-employed in the Netherlands are affiliated with other types of organization, including professional organizations (19 per cent), trade unions (11 per cent), or independent solo self-employed worker organizations (12 per cent) (cf. Jansen, 2017a).

In this chapter, we investigate membership of interest organizations through the lens of precarious self-employment. First, we aim to identity different 'types' of self-employment based on their degree of precariousness. To identify different forms of self-employment we build upon the theoretical framework by Vosko (2006) and explore four dimensions of precariousness in self-employment, that is, (a) the degree of uncertainty of work, (b) the degree and autonomy or control over the work process, (c) the degree of protection and insurance against risks, and (d) the degree of financial vulnerability. Second, we study whether different types of self-employed workers have diverging expectations of interest organizations, and/or diverging membership patterns. After establishing a typology of self-employment, we use insider–outsider theory (Rueda, 2007; Emmenegger, 2014) to formulate hypotheses on whether precarious self-employed workers relative to secure self-employed are organized differently – if they are organized at all. The hypotheses are tested using survey data from the Netherlands, a country where self-employment rapidly increased over the last decade (see also Chapter 7), and with a diverse supply of interest organizations, ranging from employer organizations, to trade union and independent self-employed worker organizations (see also Jansen, 2017a). The data for this chapter are from the second wave of the 2014 *Solo Self-employment Panel* (abbreviated in Dutch as 'ZZP Panel'). This survey (N=851) was specifically designed to disentangle the organizational patterns of self-employed workers in various socio-economic positions.

Perceptions of Interest Organizations

To illustrate that solo self-employed do not adhere to stereotypical patterns of interest representation, we begin by mapping their perceptions of interest organizations – starting with traditional employers' organizations. Using the Solo Self-Employment Panel 2014-2, Figure 12.1 confirms that the solo self-employed hold rather negative instead of positive views towards employer organizations. Only a few (13 per cent) respondents (fully) agree that 'employer organizations pay attention to the needs of small business-owners' (Figure 12.1A). Instead, respondents more often (48 per cent) tend to (fully) agree with the statement that 'employer organizations are only there for big companies' (Figure 12.1B). It should be noted, however, that non-trivial portions of respondents use the 'don't know' response category, which may indicate that sizeable shares of the solo self-employed are relatively unfamiliar with the system of interest representation.

Regarding representation by trade unions, Figure 12.1 shows that the attitudes towards trade unions are mixed. Both the positive statement 'It is good that unions also focus on the needs of solo self-employed' (Figure 12.1C) as well as the negative statement 'trade unions are employee organizations, where self-employed people do not belong' (Figure 12.1D) are more often supported than rejected. Support for these statements indicates that there is disagreement among self-employed workers regarding the perceptions of trade union representation. A similar pattern depicting diverging perceptions can also be observed with respect to independent solo self-employment organizations. While the positive statement that 'the interest of the self-employed are represented best by specific solo self-employment organizations' is more often supported than rejected (Figure 12.1E), another substantial share (29 per cent) (fully) agrees with the negative statement that 'the solo self-employed do not need a separate organization, they belong with other small and medium-sized enterprises'. To further explore such discrepancies this chapter continues in the next section by deriving hypotheses about which groups of self-employed workers are attracted to interest organizations, and in particular whether different types of organizations attract different segments of self-employed workers.

THEORY

Self-employment Heterogeneity and Precarious Self-employment

Conventional approaches to defining self-employment treat the self-employed as a relatively unified group, one that is very distinct from

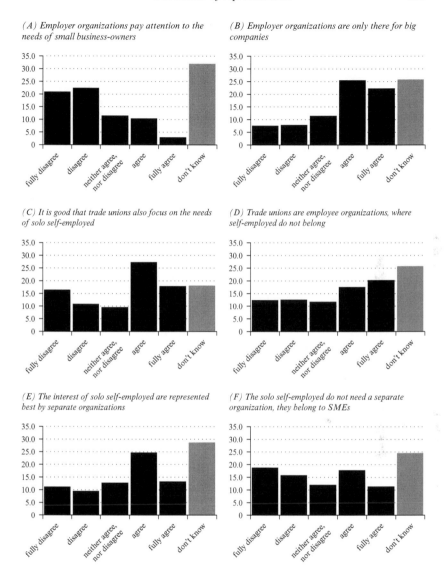

(A) Employer organizations pay attention to the needs of small business-owners

(B) Employer organizations are only there for big companies

(C) It is good that trade unions also focus on the needs of solo self-employed

(D) Trade unions are employee organizations, where self-employed do not belong

(E) The interest of solo self-employed are represented best by separate organizations

(F) The solo self-employed do not need a separate organization, they belong to SMEs

Note: All items asked on a 10-point scale. Fully disagree (0,1); disagree (2,3,4); neither agree, nor disagree (5); agree (6,7,8); fully agree (9,10).

Figure 12.1 Perceptions of interest organizations (in %)

wage-employment. People in such 'traditional' forms of self-employment usually produce or sell goods, and hold occupations that require capital intensive investments such as craftsmen, shopkeepers or farmers (cf. Arum and Müller, 2004). Recently, a growing body of research stresses the (increasingly) diverse nature of self-employment (Arum and Müller, 2004; Vosko, 2006; Jansen, 2016). The most popular notions of self-employment heterogeneity often use binary distinctions between different segments of self-employment, that is, voluntary versus involuntary self-employment (Kautonen et al., 2010), 'atypical' versus autonomous self-employment (Stanworth and Stanworth, 1995), independent versus dependent self-employment (Muehlberger, 2007), 'entrepreneurial' versus precarious self-employment (Dekker, 2012), or insider versus outsider self-employment (Muffels, 2013). The rationale for making distinctions is often based on the idea that some forms of self-employment have 'employee-like' features. Instead of producing or selling goods, self-employed workers in 'new' occupational types more often provide services against wage-like tariffs, and hold occupations requiring little or only small-scale capital investments, such as both low-skilled manual jobs and high-skilled professional jobs (cf. Arum and Müller, 2004; Jansen, 2016).

The question addressed here is whether these new forms of self-employment are also the most difficult to organize. People in more 'traditional' forms of self-employment (e.g. craftsmen, shopkeepers and farmers), are typically represented by specific trade and employer organizations (Eurofound, 2010, p. 2). In this study, we test whether, and to what extent their organizational alignments are different from those in new and/ or precarious forms of self-employment. To study the heterogeneity and precarity in self-employment in a systematic way, we build on the theoretical approach by Vosko (2006). Following Rodgers (1989, p. 35), Vosko identified four dimensions central to defining whether (self-)employment is 'precarious'. In Rodgers' original conceptualization, these dimensions assumed the situation of a wage-worker. Vosko adapted these dimensions to fit self-employment. The first dimension is the degree of *certainty of continuing employment*. Here, the emphasis is on time horizons and the risk of job loss. Despite the absence of an employment contract, uncertainty in self-employment is characterized by insecure and unstable work – most likely reflected by irregular orders and volatile income (cf. Jansen, 2017b). The second dimension relates to the *control over the labour process*. Here, control over working conditions, wages and pace of work are emphasized. Modified to the situation of self-employment, the (lack of) job autonomy is reflected by a hierarchical and/or dependent work relationship. It is assumed that, although formally owning their own business, some self-employed work in hierarchical subordination to a single client, on which they are economically dependent (Muehlberger, 2007). The third dimension is the degree of *regulatory protection*. Here, the degree of legal protection and access to social benefits is emphasized. In this study, we assume that the degree of precariousness is lower if self-employed workers are more strongly insured against risks such as illness, disability and professional liability. The fourth dimension is the *level of income*. Regardless of whether a given job is secure in the sense that it is stable and long-term, Vosko emphasizes the importance of the extent to which income is sufficient to maintain a decent standard of living. In this study, we do not only take the level of income into account, but also the availability of financial back-up (De Vries and Dekker, 2015; Jansen, 2017b).

Solo Self-employment: Between Insiders and Outsiders

Based on the aforementioned dimensions, the empirical part of this chapter starts by establishing a typology of self-employment. We will use this typology to investigate whether precarious self-employment has implications for individual attitudes and behaviour towards interest organizations. Before doing so, we therefore first formulate expectations regarding the impact of precarious self-employment on two outcomes, that is, the *support for services* provided by interest organizations, and the *propensity to be(come) a member* of interest organizations. For both types of outcomes, the main theoretical argument departs from the assumption that precarious self-employed workers, more than other types of solo self-employed, are outsiders not just on the labour market, but also to the system of interest representation.

Insider–outsider theories have been used to explain differences in partisanship and labour market policy preferences (Rueda, 2007; Sluiter and Akkerman, 2018) as well as trade union membership (Sánchez, 2007; Emmenegger, 2014) between people with secure and stable jobs (insiders) versus those without secure jobs (outsiders). Based on insider–outsider theory, outsiders would not be accommodated by left-wing parties or trade unions that primarily protect the job security of insiders (i.e. standard wage employees). Neither would they be represented by right-wing parties or employer organizations that primarily promote business freedom, market deregulation and employment flexibility. Typically, studies dealing with the insider–outsider divide include people in self-employment either with the insiders, or with a third category of economically privileged 'upscale' groups (i.e. a composite category consisting of "self-employed professionals (lawyers, architects, etc.), owners of shops, business proprietors, farmers, fishermen and general and middle management" (Rueda, 2007, p. 39).

In Rueda's conceptualization, 'outsiderness' is defined not only by insecurity, but also by the *involuntary* nature of insecure employment relationships: That is, people with insecure jobs are assumed to aspire to more secure jobs. Hence, self-employment should be 'involuntary' when someone prefers to have a job in wage-employment. Following this line of reasoning, Jansen (2017b) refined the insider–outsider divide by accounting for precarity within self-employment. His study shows that self-employed workers who worked in self-employment on an involuntary basis are more likely to deviate from traditional right-wing voting patterns. This finding may be adapted with regard to interest organizations.

We expect that there are at least three reasons why precarious self-employed workers may deviate more strongly from traditional (employer/unionist) interest representation. For one, for this group the costs of membership may be too high: even though we expect individual services (e.g. practical help involving legal advice and tax assistance, and networking or training activities) to be useful, cost-benefit calculations might prevent precarious self-employed workers from joining as membership fees may be too expensive to maintain given their low and irregular income. Second, the time horizons may be too short for precarious self-employed, and the risk of exiting out of self-employment too high. Especially those who are in self-employment on an involuntary basis would have fewer incentives to invest in long-term representation. The less stable the self-employment, the higher the short-term costs of membership, in particular because those who are self-employed on a temporary basis may not use certain (long-term) services, neither individual nor collective services. Third, the collective services (e.g. lobbying activities and collective bargaining), provided by interest groups may not be beneficial to precarious self-employed workers. This argument would particularly hold for traditional corporatist interest organizations, such as trade unions (lobbying and bargaining on behalf of wage-employees) and business associations (lobbying and bargaining of behalf of employers). Precarious self-employed would not be interested in employment protection policies advocated by trade unions, and mainly benefitting paid-employees in protected 'insider' jobs (Gumbrell-McCormick, 2011). Nor would they be interested in the collective services provided by trade and business associations that are biased towards the interests of large firms (Battisti and Perry, 2015). Hence, we formulate the following hypotheses:

Hypothesis 1:   *The more precarious a self-employed worker*
   (a)   *the less likely (s)he is to support collective services by interest organizations.*
   (b)   *the more likely (s)he is to support individual services by interest organizations.*

Hypothesis 2: The more precarious a self-employed worker
  (a)   the less likely (s)he is to be a member of any interest organization.
  (b)   the less likely (s)he to be a member of trade associations/business associations.
  (c)   the less likely (s)he is to be a member of trade union/solo self-employment organizations.

DATA AND MEASURES

The Solo Self-employment Panel (2014 Wave 2)[1]

We use the Solo Self-employment Panel (2014 wave 2) data to test our hypotheses. The panel was initiated by the Dutch Ministry of Social Affairs and conducted by the research company Panteia in order to map characteristics and developments of solo self-employment in the Netherlands. The panel was a repeated survey among 3,000 solo self-employed persons and was held between 2009 and 2015. Selection criteria for participants in the panel were (1) having a self-employed job, (2) employing no other people, and (3) working at least 15 hours per week on their business. Respondents are recruited using the DM-CD address file of *MarktSelect*, which is derived from the trade registers of the Dutch Chamber of Commerce, using stratified sampling by 10 areas of economic activity. To deal with panel attrition new panel members were recruited once per year to ensure at least 3,000 panel members. Surveys were held twice a year: a first wave, where a fixed set of questions were asked to the respondents using a telephone survey, and a second wave, with rotating question modules using internet-based questionnaires. Hoevenagel et al. (2015) provide more (technical) information on the ZZP Panel.

Fieldwork for the second wave of the 2014 ZZP Panel was conducted between mid-December 2014 and mid-January 2015. All participants in the first wave of 2014 were invited to take part in the second wave. Eventually, 851 respondents participated in the second wave of the 2014 ZZP Panel, resulting in a response rate of 34 per cent. This response rate is similar to the response rates of the second waves in earlier years of the ZZP Panel (Hoevenagel et al., 2015). By and large, the sample corresponds to demographic figures by Statistics Netherlands, showing that the solo self-employed are often higher educated, predominantly male and that the majority is between 35 and 55 years old (CBS, 2015).

This wave's questionnaire includes a one-time module on interest representation that was tailor-made for a research project by Jansen. Questions on interest representation (i.e. items about perceptions towards interest organizations and membership propensity) were designed and included in the questionnaire for this purpose. Details on measurements of the key variables can be found below.

ANALYSES AND RESULTS

The statistical analyses in the chapter consist of two parts. In the first part, latent class analyses (LCAs) are used to identify types or 'classes' of solo self-employment (henceforth, SSE). Latent class analysis (LCA) is a data-reduction technique that makes it possible to identify different (latent) classes based on a number of observed variables. In doing so, we use detailed indicators on, inter alia, the degree of (a) uncertainty, (b) autonomy, (c) risk insurance, and (d) financial vulnerability. After mapping the varieties in self-employment and precariousness, regression analyses techniques are used to study differences in the support for collective and individual services, and to establish whether different types diverge regarding their propensity to join professional associations, trade unions, '*zzp*'-organizations, and trade/business associations.

Latent Class Analysis: a Self-employment Typology

First, we selected variables to account for the four dimensions of precariousness of SSE (Rodgers, 1989; Vosko, 2006). (1) We included a three-category variable measuring the *uncertainty of continuing employment*.[2] (2) We added a three-category autonomy index and the dependence on one customer to measure *control over the labour process*. (3) We include variables measuring whether or not respondents have illness, disability and liability insurances and pension savings to account for the *regulatory protection*. (4) The *level of income* is measured by a three-category income variable and a variable accounting for the financial buffer of respondents. We further include whether or not respondents are involuntary SSE, and whether or not they have been working as SSE for more than five years. We also include variables to account for the type of occupation,[3] educational level and working hours per week.

After selecting the variables for the LCA, the next step is to determine the number of classes. This selection is based on both a model fit evaluation (by studying BIC values and the changes in these values) and the interpretation of the class responses. Based on these criteria, we selected a four-class solution. Table 12.1 presents the outcomes of the four-class solution LCA. The estimated class population shares are indicators of the relative class size. Of the sample, 23 per cent are in Class I, 17 per cent

Table 12.1 *LCA outcomes: class response percentages and overall statistics (N=747)*

		Class I Prec. Prone Trad. SSE	Class II Secure Trad. SSE	Class III Prec. Prone Prof.	Class IV Secure Prof.	Overall M	Overall SD
Estimated class population shares		23%	17%	27%	33%		
Uncertainty of	Low	20%	13%	14%	34%	22%	0.41
employment	Middle	41%	57%	34%	51%	45%	0.50
	High	39%	29%	52%	15%	33%	0.47
Autonomy	Low	18%	18%	15%	7%	14%	0.34
	Middle	42%	42%	23%	28%	32%	0.47
	High	40%	40%	62%	64%	54%	0.50
Dependent on one customer		12%	17%	12%	16%	14%	0.35
Insurance	Illness	3%	59%	0%	23%	18%	0.39
	Disability	1%	100%	7%	59%	38%	0.49
	Liability	80%	95%	64%	78%	77%	0.42
Pension savings		41%	65%	26%	79%	54%	0.50
Income	Low	43%	13%	70%	2%	32%	0.47
	Middle	50%	60%	26%	45%	43%	0.50
	High	7%	27%	5%	52%	25%	0.43
Buffer	< 6 months	45%	44%	28%	15%	30%	0.46
	6–12 months	15%	24%	15%	23%	19%	0.39
	> 1 year	41%	32%	57%	63%	51%	0.50

Table 12.1 (continued)

		Class I Prec. Prone Trad. SSE	Class II Secure Trad. SSE	Class III Prec. Prone Prof.	Class IV Secure Prof.	Overall M	Overall SD
Involuntary SSE		13%	12%	12%	1%	9%	0.28
Working as SSE	> 5 years	87%	90%	75%	83%	83%	0.38
Occupational type	Technocratic	11%	8%	23%	58%	30%	0.46
	Social-cultural spec.	0%	6%	63%	39%	31%	0.46
	Agric. & sole prop.	36%	21%	11%	2%	15%	0.36
	Manual	53%	66%	3%	2%	24%	0.43
Educational level	Lower	18%	25%	0%	0%	8%	0.27
	Middle	63%	56%	11%	6%	29%	0.45
	Higher	19%	19%	89%	94%	63%	0.48
Working hours	< 12 hours	1%	1%	4%	0%	2%	0.13
	12–34 hours	30%	3%	48%	17%	26%	0.44
	35–40 hours	15%	7%	25%	31%	22%	0.41
	> 40 hours	54%	90%	22%	52%	50%	0.50

are in Class II, 27 per cent are in Class III and 33 per cent are in Class IV. Further, we present the conditional probabilities (as percentages). These figures show that, for instance, 20 per cent of the people in Class I score 'Low' on the uncertainty of continuing employment, 41 per cent score 'Middle' and 39 per cent score 'High'.

Looking at the conditional probabilities of Class I, we find that this Class does not deviate much from the entire sample in terms of the dimension of *uncertainty of continuing employment*. However, people in Class I score low on the autonomy index, and they are somewhat less dependent on one customer,[4] indicating less *control over the labour process*. In terms of *regulatory protection*, this class also scores low. Although individuals in Class I have a liability insurance slightly more often than average, illness and disability insurances are almost completely absent, and the percentage of people with pension savings is below average. Further, with respect to *level of income*, we see that this group does not stand out in terms of income, but, compared to the other classes, relatively many of them have little buffers. However, in absolute terms, over 40 per cent of the people in this class have buffers lasting for more than a year. Next, compared to other classes, individuals in Class I are most often involuntary SSE. Most of the people in Class I work in manual or agricultural occupations and as small proprietors. People in this class are less often higher educated and about half of them work more than 40 hours per week. Given these responses, we label this class the **precarity-prone traditional SSE**. Note that we deliberately use the term 'precarity-prone' rather than 'precarious', since this class of traditional SSE scores low on some, but not all dimensions of precariousness.

In Class II, most people score on the Middle-category on the *uncertainty of continuing employment*. Hence, this class does not stand out in terms of employment security. This class has little *control over the labour process,* relatively few of them score high on the autonomy index and, compared to other classes, has most individuals that are dependent on one customer. Class II stands out in terms of *regulatory protection*: this class has the most people who have illness, disability and liability insurances. A majority of them also have pension savings. Looking at their *level of income*, they score moderately low: most people fall in the 'Middle' income category, but relatively few of them have large buffers. Further, we see that most people have been working as a SSE for more than five years, and relatively many individuals in Class II are involuntary SSE. Most of the people in this class work in manual occupations. They are less often higher educated. A large majority of the people in Class II work more than 40 hours per week. All in all, we label this class the **secure traditional SSE**.

If we look at the class response percentages of Class III, we see that people in this class score (relatively) high on the *uncertainty of continuing employment*. This class has much *control over the labour process*, as shown by the high scores on the autonomy index, and the somewhat below-average score on dependence on one customer. The class scores low on *regulatory protection*, since individuals in this class have no illness insurance and relatively few of them have disability and liability insurances or pension savings. With respect to their *level of income*, we see a mixed pattern: they often have buffers to last for longer than a year, but their income is most often low. Further, we see that in Class III, compared to other classes, fewer people work as solo self-employed for more than five years. Further, we see that the majority of people in Class III are working as social-cultural specialist, and they are often higher educated. They make, compared to other classes, relatively few working hours. Hence, we label this class the **precarity-prone SSE professionals**.

Table 12.1 shows that Class IV consists of people who generally score lower regarding *uncertainty of continuing employment*. People in Class IV score high on the autonomy index, and they are somewhat more often dependent on one customer. This indicates a somewhat mixed pattern when it comes to *control over the labour process*. Further, relatively many of the individuals in this class have illness, disability and liability insurances, and, compared to the other classes, the people in this class are most likely to have pension savings. This indicates strong *regulatory protection*. The income of the people in this class is often high and they often have large buffers. Further, hardly any of the people in Class IV are involuntary SSE. Most of the people in this class work in technocratic or social-cultural specialist occupations. Almost all individuals in Class IV are higher educated. About half of the people in Class IV work more than 40 hours per week. Based on this pattern, we label this class the **secure SSE professionals**.

Patterns of Representation

The latent class analysis calculates four estimated class proportions for each respondent: the likelihood that someone belongs to each class. These proportions are included as predictors in regression models on support for collective and individual services, and propensity to join (a) a professional organization, (b) a branch organization, (c) a union, (d) a solo self-employment interest organization, and (e) an employer organization. We did not include any other variables in these models.

For each respondent, the sum of the estimated class proportions adds up to one. The class proportions thus have perfect collinearity, and we therefore need to exclude one of the class proportions in a regression analyses to avoid singularity. This excluded class can then be interpreted as the reference category. In our regression analyses, we excluded each class once to establish the differences and significance thereof between each class combination.

Hypothesis 1 read that the more precarious a self-employed worker is, (a) the less likely (s)he is to support collective services by interest organizations, and (b) the more likely (s)he is to support individual services by interest organizations. To account for the support for collective and individual services by interest organizations, we first applied a principal component analysis on ten items related to such services. Using an oblimin rotation, the analyses distinguished two components. The first component is measured by six items related to collective services. These items measure (0=little attention, 10=very much attention) the extent to which respondents think that interest groups should pay attention to (1) lowering taxes for entrepreneurs, (2) strive for fewer rules for entrepreneurs, (3) providing access to social security, (4) strive for fair tariffs, (5) prevent false self-employment, and (6) provide discounts for services. The second component is measured by four items related to individual services. These items measure (0=little attention, 10=very much attention) the extent to which respondents think that interest groups should pay attention to (1) provide training and workshops, (2) organize network meetings, (3) provide assistance with filing taxes, and (4) stimulate entrepreneurship.[5] We used the factor scores for each component as dependent variables in the models explaining support for collective and individual services.

Table 12.2 shows the results of these models. Here, we see that secure SSE professionals are less likely to support collective services from organizations than all other SSE classes (Model A1 to A4). The other classes do not significantly differ from each other in terms of support for collective services. This finding thus refutes our hypotheses that more precarious self-employed workers show less support for collective services, in fact, the (most) secure SSE professionals show the least support for such services. Next, we see that support for individual services (Model B1 to B4) is highest among precarity-prone SSE professionals. This class shows significantly stronger support for such services than any of the other classes of SSE. The other classes do not significantly differ from each other. This finding is partly in line with the expectation that more precarious self-employed workers are more likely to support individual services from organizations. While this holds true for precarity-prone professionals, we find no evidence for such support from precarity-prone traditional workers.

Model C1 to C4 in Table 12.3 show the regressions of the willingness to join a professional organization, with the classes of SSEs as independent variables. Here, we see that precarity-prone and secure SSE professionals are more willing to join a professional organization than both secure and precarity-prone traditional SSE are. These differences are relatively large:

Table 12.2 *Results of OLS regression analyses explaining the support for collective and individual services from organizations*

| | Support for collective services (R²=0.03; N=544) | | | | | | | |
| | Model A1 | | Model A2 | | Model A3 | | Model A4 | |
	b	s.e.	b	s.e.	b	s.e.	b	s.e.
Precarity-Prone Traditional SSE	ref. cat.		0.15	0.14	0.20	0.13	0.47***	0.12
Secure Traditional SSE	−0.15	0.14	ref. cat.		0.05	0.14	0.33*	0.13
Precarity-Prone SSE Professionals	−0.20	0.13	−0.05	0.14	ref. cat.		0.28*	0.12
Secure SSE Professionals	−0.47***	0.12	−0.33*	0.13	−0.28*	0.12	ref. cat.	
Intercept	0.19*	0.09	0.04	0.11	0.00	0.09	−0.28***	0.07

| | Support for individual services (R²=0.02; N=544) | | | | | | | |
| | Model B1 | | Model B2 | | Model B3 | | Model B4 | |
	b	s.e.	b	s.e.	b	s.e.	b	s.e.
Precarity-Prone Traditional SSE	ref. cat.		0.05	0.15	−0.39**	0.14	−0.13	0.12
Secure Traditional SSE	−0.05	0.15	ref. cat.		−0.45**	0.14	−0.19	0.14
Precarity-Prone SSE Professionals	0.39**	0.14	0.45**	0.14	ref. cat.		0.26*	0.12
Secure SSE Professionals	0.13	0.12	0.19	0.14	−0.26*	0.12	ref. cat.	
Intercept	−0.11	0.10	−0.17	0.11	0.28**	0.09	0.02	0.08

Note: *** $p<0.001$; ** $p<0.01$; * $p<0.05$.

Table 12.3   Results of OLS regression analyses explaining the willingness to join organizations

Willingness to join a professional organization (R^2=0.08; N=627)

	Model C1		Model C2		Model C3		Model C4	
	b	s.e.	b	s.e.	b	s.e.	b	s.e.
Precarity-Prone Traditional SSE	ref. cat.		−0.93	0.52	−3.00***	0.31	−2.65***	0.44
Secure Traditional SSE	0.93	0.52	ref. cat.		−2.06***	0.50	−1.72***	0.48
Precarity-Prone SSE Professionals	3.00**	0.49	2.06***	0.50	ref. cat.		0.34	0.43
Secure SSE Professionals	2.65**	0.44	1.72***	0.48	−0.34	0.43	ref. cat.	
Intercept	1.54***	0.35	2.47***	0.39	4.53***	0.31	4.19***	0.27

Willingness to join a branch organization (R^2=0.01; N=622)

	Model D1		Model D2		Model D3		Model D4	
	b	s.e.	b	s.e.	b	s.e.	b	s.e.
Precarity-Prone Traditional SSE	ref. cat.		−0.56	0.47	0.59	0.45	0.36	0.41
Secure Traditional SSE	0.56	0.47	ref. cat.		1.15*	0.46	0.92*	0.44
Precarity-Prone SSE Professionals	−0.59	0.45	−1.15*	0.46	ref. cat.		−0.23	0.40
Secure SSE Professionals	−0.36	0.41	−0.92*	0.44	0.23	0.40	ref. cat.	
Intercept	2.83***	0.32	3.39***	0.35	2.24***	0.29	2.47***	0.25

Willingness to join a union (R^2=0.01; N=641)

	Model E1		Model E2		Model E3		Model E4	
	b	s.e.	b	s.e.	b	s.e.	b	s.e.
Precarity-Prone Traditional SSE	ref. cat.		−0.49	0.38	−0.72*	0.36	0.06	0.32
Secure Traditional SSE	0.49	0.38	ref. cat.		−0.23	0.36	0.55	0.35
Precarity-Prone SSE Professionals	0.72*	0.36	0.23	0.36	ref. cat.		0.78*	0.32
Secure SSE Professionals	−0.06	0.32	−0.55	0.35	−0.78*	0.32	ref. cat.	
Intercept	1.09***	0.25	1.58***	0.28	1.80***	0.23	1.03***	0.20

Table 12.3 (continued)

	Willingness to join a solo self-employment interest organization (R²=0.00; N=631)							
	Model F1		Model F2		Model F3		Model F4	
	b	s.e.	b	s.e.	b	s.e.	b	s.e.
Precarity-Prone Traditional SSE	ref. cat.		−0.19	0.45	−0.31	0.43	−0.26	0.38
Secure Traditional SSE	0.19	0.45	ref. cat.		−0.12	0.43	−0.07	0.42
Precarity-Prone SSE Professionals	0.31	0.43	0.12	0.43	ref. cat.		0.05	0.38
Secure SSE Professionals	0.26	0.38	0.07	0.42	−0.05	0.38	ref. cat.	
Intercept	2.79***	0.30	2.98***	0.33	3.10***	0.27	3.05***	0.24

	Willingness to join an employer organization (R²=0.01; N=622)							
	Model G1		Model G2		Model G3		Model G4	
	b	s.e.	b	s.e.	b	s.e.	b	s.e.
Precarity-Prone Traditional SSE	ref. cat.		−0.45	0.28	0.18	0.26	−0.11	0.24
Secure Traditional SSE	0.45	0.28	ref. cat.		0.63*	0.26	0.34	0.26
Precarity-Prone SSE Professionals	−0.18	0.26	−0.63*	0.26	ref. cat.		−0.29	0.23
Secure SSE Professionals	0.11	0.24	−0.34	0.26	0.29	0.23	ref. cat.	
Intercept	0.83***	0.18	1.28***	0.20	0.65***	0.17	0.94***	0.15

Note: *** $p<0.001$; ** $p<0.01$; * $p<0.05$.

for instance, precarity-prone SSE professionals score, in general, three points higher on the 0 to 10 scale of willingness to join a professional organization than precarity-prone traditional SSE (see Model C1), and secure professionals, on average, 2.65 points higher than precarity-prone traditional SSE. Neither the differences between precarity-prone and secure traditional SSE (see Model C1 and C2), nor those between precarity-prone and secure SSE professionals (see Model C3 and C4), are significant.

Model D1 to D4 show that secure traditional SSE are more willing to join a branch organization than precarity-prone and secure professionals are. In line with our expectation, precarity-prone professionals deviate from traditional SSEs the most. That is, relative to secure traditional SSE, precarity-prone professionals are the least willing to join a branch organization. We find no other significant differences in the willingness to join such organization.

In Model E1 to E4, we look at the willingness to join a union. Here, we see that precarity-prone SSE professionals are, compared to secure SSE professionals and precarity-prone traditional SSE, most willing to join a union. This refutes our expectation based on the assumption that precarious self-employed workers would be outsiders. We find no other significant differences between the four classes of SSE.

In Model F1 to F4, we see that there are no significant differences between the four groups of SSE in their willingness to join a solo self-employment interest organization: none of the coefficients are statistically significant. When we turn to the willingness to join an employer organization (Model G1 to G4), we see that secure traditional SSE are more willing to join an employer organization than precarity-prone SSE professionals. The differences between other classes are not significant.

CONCLUSION AND DISCUSSION

The main goal of the current chapter was to establish the relationship between precarious self-employment and attitudes towards interest organizations. In doing so, we first set out to conceptualize and measure precariousness among solo self-employed workers. Using a series of Latent Class Analyses this study has identified four types of self-employment relating to differences in resources, opportunities and vulnerabilities. In the policy debate, the increased attention for precarity among self-employed workers is often closely tied to the rise of so-called 'new' self-employment (Schulze Buschoff and Schmidt, 2009). Our typology, however, shows that precarity proneness cuts across the line between traditional and newer self-employment occupations. Also for more traditional modes of self-employment (e.g. in shop keeping, retailing or farming) we find a precarity-prone type in addition to a secure type. This finding brings more nuance to standard reasoning in which especially new self-employment would be synonymous with precariousness. Similarly, our results show that risks and returns cut across professional occupations. Also higher educated professionals – especially those in social-cultural jobs – sometimes work under precarious conditions, while others (and mainly those in techno-cratic occupations) are far more secure.

As a second step, the four-category typology of solo self-employment (i.e. secure traditional / precarity-prone traditional / secure professional / precarity-prone professional) was linked to expectations about the tasks of interest organizations. Our data confirmed previous research showing that the services offered by interest organizations are a mix of collective and individual services (cf. Bennett and Ramsden, 2007). On the basis of insider–outsider theory we expected that precarious self-employed workers would be less inclined to support the collective services, as these services would be less instrumental to their needs. Yet, the results show that instead of the precarity-prone self-employed, the secure self-employed professionals are less likely to support collective services from organizations relative to other self-employed workers. The interpretation of this effect is not straight-forward. On the one hand, this finding may indicate that professionals do not require the collective services offered by organizations, because their secure and stable positions allow them to be self-reliant. But it may also indicate that this security allows professionals to take a more individualistic approach. Collective services do not yield immediate personal benefits, and especially secure professionals might be inclined to 'free-ride' on non-excludable, col-lective services. That is, the fruits of lobbying activities may also be harvested by non-members. Regardless of potential 'free-rider' effects, we find little to no support for outsider effects. With respect to individual services, we even find the highest support rates among precarity-prone professionals. More than any other type of self-employment, precarity-prone professionals have a stronger demand for individual services from interest organizations. Also, more than precarity-prone traditional self-employed, precarity-prone pro-fessionals have a stronger demand for individual services such as legal advice and tax assistance or networking and training activities.

Finally, we aimed to establish whether different types of self-employed workers have different (potential) membership patterns. Regarding the willingness to join various organizations, the most notable group of self-employed, again, are the precarity-prone professionals. Supporting the insider–outsider theories, we find that self-employed professionals who worked in self-employment on a more precarious basis are more likely to deviate from traditional patterns of interest representations. That is, relative to the employer/business organization's traditional membership base (i.e. secure SSE professionals and traditional SSE), precarity-prone professionals are least willing to join these types of organizations. We also find that precarity-prone professionals, more than other types of self-employed, are most willing to join a trade union. This finding resonates with Jansen (2017a), who showed that trade unions in the Netherlands are able to mobilize self-employed workers on social security issues. Taken together, the results provide evidence for new alignments between professional but precarious self-employed workers and trade unions. Of course, the precise working of the insider–outsider division remains to be elucidated as the most relevant comparison group – wage employees – are not included in this study. A future study needs to carry out comparisons of organization membership not only with wage-employees, but also between self-employed workers with and without employees.

NOTES

1. For this chapter, the same dataset is used as in Jansen (2017a). The data description is derived from that study.
2. The indicator for continuing employment is based on four items. Respondents were asked to rate on an 11-point scale whether (a) their income is stable (regular [0] versus irregular [10]); (b) their clients/orders are stable (very fixed [0] versus very volatile [10]) and whether (c) their income and (d) clients/orders are predictable (foreseeable in advance [0] versus not foreseeable [10]). With a Cronbach's alpha of 0.83, a reliability analysis confirmed that these items comprise a reliable scale. Instead of a scale, we here use a three-category version to allow comparison with other categorical variables in the Latent Class model. A similar procedure is followed regarding the indicator for control over the labour process. Job autonomy is based on two items: Respondents were asked to rate on an 11-point scale whether (0) they themselves or (10) their client decided on (a) which tasks are carried out, and (b) how tasks are conducted. Again, an index (range 0–1, Cronbach's alpha of 0.65).
3. Occupation is initially measured in an open question by asking respondents to describe their business (i.e. what kind of goods they sell or what kind of services/labour they provide). On the basis of this information each respondent was assigned an occupational code, using the International Standard Classification of Occupations 2008. Applying the classification of Arum and Müller (2004), these occupations are first classified into traditional self-employment, manual self-employment, and professional-managerial self-employment. Next, applying the same sub-division as Jansen (2017a) professionals are further classified into sub-groups for technocratic occupations and social-cultural specialists.
4. Counter-intuitively, dependence on one customer is associated with greater employment security. Following Muehlberger (2007) this finding may be interpreted by assuming that dependent self-employed sometimes have long-lasting and stable relationships with a single client. Muehlberger illustrates this argument with the example of insurance agents who have tied and long-lasting business relationships with insurance companies. Using the same data as this chapter, Jansen (2017b) showed that 'dependent' self-employment is most common among technocratic professionals, who are economically relatively well-off. In the analyses presented in this chapter we also see that the discriminating power of this variable is low. Additional analyses (available upon request) excluding this variable

resulted in substantially similar outcomes of both the LCAs (Table 12.1) and subsequent regression analyses (Table 12.2).
5. We find this item to load on one dimension (i.e. individual services). Theoretically, one could argue that stimulating entrepreneurship can also tap into collective services. We therefore ran the analyses that we present in Table 12.2 also using factor scores excluding this item. These analyses (not reported) yield similar results.

REFERENCES

Arum, R. and Müller, W. (eds) (2004). *The Reemergence of Self-Employment: A Comparative Study of Self-Employment Dynamics and Social Inequality.* Princeton: Princeton University Press.

Battisti, M. and Perry, M. (2015). Small enterprise affiliations to business associations and the collective action problem revisited. *Small Business Economics*, 44(3), 559–76.

Bennett, R.J. and Ramsden, M. (2007). The contribution of business associations to SMEs: strategy, bundling or reassurance? *International Small Business Journal*, 25(1), 49–76.

Brandl, B. and Lehr, A. (2016). The strange non-death of employer and business associations: an analysis of their representativeness and activities in Western European countries. *Economic and Industrial Democracy* (Published ahead of Print). doi.org/10.1177/0143831X16669842.

CBS (2015). Achtergrondkenmerken en ontwikkelingen van zzp'ers in Nederland. [Background characteristics and developments of solo self-employed in the Netherlands]. www.cbs.nl (accessed 25 May 2015).

Conen, W., Schippers, J. and Schulze Buschoff, K. (2016). *Self-employed Without Personnel: Between Freedom and Insecurity.* Düsseldorf: WSI. Institute of Economic and Social Research.

De Vries, N. and Dekker, F. (2015). Determinants of a precarious financial position of solo self-employed. Paper Presented at the CRSE Global Workshop on Freelancing and Self-employment Research, London.

Dekker, F. (2012). Zzp'ers als werkzekere ondernemer of precaire werknemer [Solo self-employed as job-secure or precarious employee]. *Economische Statistische Berichten*, 97(4647), 30–33.

Emmenegger, P. (2014). *The Power to Dismiss: Trade Unions and the Regulation of Job Security in Western Europe.* Oxford: Oxford University Press.

Eurofound (2010). *Self-employed Workers: Industrial Relations and Working Conditions.* Dublin: European Foundation for the Improvement of Living and Working Conditions.

Eurofound (2017). *Exploring Self-employment in the European Union.* Dublin: European Foundation for the Improvement of Living and Working Conditions.

Gumbrell-McCormick, R. (2011). European trade unions and 'atypical' workers. *Industrial Relations Journal*, 42(3), 293–310.

Hoevenagel, R., De Vries, N. and Vroonhof, P. (2015). Arbeidsmarktpositie van zzp'ers. Zzp Panel: Resultaten eerste meting 2014. Rapportnummer A201435. [Labour market position of solo self-employed. ZZP Panel: Results first meeting 2014]. Zoetermeer: Panteia.

Iversen, T. and Soskice, D. (2001). An asset theory of social policy preferences. *American Political Science Review*, 95(4), 875–93.

Jansen, G. (2016). Self-employment as atypical or autonomous work: diverging effects on political orientations. *Socio-Economic Review* (Published ahead of print). doi: 10.1093/ser/mww017.

Jansen, G. (2017a). Solo self-employment and membership of interest organizations in the Netherlands: economic, social and political determinants. *Economic and Industrial Democracy* (Published ahead of print). doi.org/10.1177/0143831X 17723712.

Jansen, G. (2017b). Farewell to the rightist self-employed? 'New self-employment' and political alignments. *Acta Politica*, 52(3), 306–38.

Kautonen, T., Down, S., Welter, F., Vainio, P., Palmroos, J., Althoff, K. and Kolb, S. (2010). 'Involuntary self-employment' as a public policy issue: a cross-country European review. *International Journal of Entrepreneurial Behavior & Research*, 16(2), 112–29.

Muehlberger, U. (2007). *Dependent Self-employment: Workers on the Border between Employment and Self-employment*. New York: Palgrave Macmillan.

Muffels, R. (2013). ZZP'ers: Insiders of outsiders? [Solo self-employed: Insiders or outsiders?]. In: Dekker, F. (ed.), *En toen waren er ZZP'ers [And then there were solo-self-employed]*. Den Haag: Boom Lemma Uitgevers.

Rodgers, G. (1989). Precarious work in Western Europe: the state of the debate. In: Rodgers, G. and Rodgers, J. (eds), *Precarious Jobs in Labour Market Regulation: The Growth of Atypical Employment in Western Europe*. Geneva: International Institute for Labour Studies, 1–16.

Rueda, D. (2007). *Social Democracy Inside Out: Partisanship and Labor Market Policy in Advanced Industrialized Democracies*. Oxford: Oxford University Press.

Sánchez, D.L. (2007). Explaining union membership of temporary workers in Spain: the role of local representatives and workers' participative potential. *Industrial Relations Journal*, 38(1), 51–69.

Schulze Buschoff, K.S. and Schmidt, C. (2009). Adapting labour law and social security to the needs of the 'new self-employed': comparing the UK, Germany and the Netherlands. *Journal of European Social Policy*, 19(2), 147–59.

SER (2017). *Veel gestelde vragen – Over de overlegeconomie. [Frequently asked questions – About the consultative economy]*. www.ser.nl/nl/secretariaat/faq/over legeconomie/organisatiegraad-nederland-werkgevers-werknemers.aspx (accessed 3 November 2017).

Sluiter, R. and Akkerman, A. (2018). Tijdelijk werk en het stemmen op rechtspopulistische partijen. [Temporary work and voting for right-wing populist parties]. *Tijdschrift voor Arbeidsvraagstukken*, 34(2), 238–56.

Stanworth, C. and Stanworth, J. (1995). The self-employed without employees. Autonomous or atypical? *Industrial Relations Journal*, 26(3), 221–9.

Van der Berg, N., Mevissen, J.W.M. and Tijsmans, N. (2009). *Zzp'ers en hun marktpositie. Onderzoek naar de mate waarin zzp'ers investeren in en ondersteuning (kunnen) krijgen bij het behouden en vergroten van hun marktpositie. [Solo self-employed and their labor market position. Research about the extent to which solo self-employed invest in and (can) get support in remaining and improving their labor market position]*. Den Haag: RWI.

Vosko, L.F. (ed.) (2006). *Precarious Employment: Understanding Labour Market Insecurity in Canada*. Kingston: McGill-Queen's University Press.

13. The 'new' self-employed and hybrid forms of employment: challenges for social policies in Europe

Karin Schulze Buschoff

INTRODUCTION[1]

Many European countries have witnessed a rise in self-employment in the last few decades (Eurofound, 2017, p. 7). Among these is a growing number of people who do not fit the traditional profiles of the self-employed (for example, small-scale tradespersons or small and mid-sized business owners). Self-employment is increasingly becoming a heterogeneous employment category covering a wide range of sectors and professional fields (Conen et al., 2016, p. 4). The 'new' self-employed are not only IT experts, business consultants and click workers but also brick layers, carpenters, lorry drivers or home-care workers. The new self-employment often concerns employment activities that are based on personal know-how and personal job profiles and that require relatively little financial and human resources to set them up. Many small enterprises, microenterprises or sole proprietorships are started without any or with very little capital. The various causes for the growing numbers of microenterprises in many countries include the increased outsourcing of corporate divisions and functional areas, organizational decentralization, more flexible employment policies, the rising significance of the service sector and such new business models as the digital platform economy (Schulze Buschoff, 2018, p. 2). On average, more than two-thirds of all self-employed workers in the EU are solo self-employed (Conen et al., 2016, p. 29). 'Solo self-employed' refers to people who run their own businesses or who exercise their professions on a self-employed basis without employing other people on a regular basis.

The digitization of the working world and the increasing use of online platforms will presumably give further rise to new forms of self-employment. The use of digital technologies allows employers and customers to reduce transaction costs. Highly transparent online platforms with their high-speed interactions enable the flexible awarding of business contracts to external contractors, while the commercial risks are being shifted to the providers and the purchasers. Characteristic of this industry is that platform operators generally regard themselves as mere facilitators of the activities and treat everyone working for them as self-employed workers (without any employee rights such as minimum wages, protection against (wrongful) dismissal or social insurance (Klebe, 2017, p. 1)). The platform economy is flourishing, particularly in those business fields largely involved in the provision of services and where investment needs are low. The types of activities range anywhere from highly skilled development services to simple and once-only services. It is estimated for 2025 that the global platform economy in the five key sectors will generate around 335 billion dollars (see Peterson, 2015). A large number of people are also already working in this area, often as second, additional jobs.

In addition to the 'new self-employment', the hybridization of employment is also becoming characteristic of the working world in the Member States of the EU. 'Hybridization' may refer to either a parallel existence of several dependent employment relationships or a combination of dependent employment and self-employment activities at the same time, as well as multiple switching from dependent employment to self-employment. People's work histories are characterized not only by various successive periods of dependent employment and self-employment. But more and more people are also holding down multiple jobs or are working in combinations of self-employment and/or dependent employment. Periods of marginal part-time employment or marginal self-employment as sole forms of paid employment are also gaining significance in people's employment histories.

From the point of view of working people, the reasons for choosing solo self-employment or hybrid forms could be the absence or the unsatisfactory nature of dependent employment opportunities (Kautonen et al., 2010). But in many cases, solo self-employment or hybrid forms of employment are voluntarily chosen over standard employment. Many of the solo self-employed regard the high degree of independence and the freedom of 'being one's own boss' as definite advantages over dependent employment (Taylor, 1996; Dawson et al., 2009). Disadvantages include various forms of insecurity, for instance from fluctuating order volumes, economic pressures associated with it and by exclusion from social security systems. The new dynamics in the labour market have special implications for social security systems. Historically, social protection systems in European countries have primarily been developed to protect people in standard employment and existing forms of social security are considered to be in need of new parameters for accommodating these insecurities (Eurofound, 2017, p. 3).

All of these developments create special challenges for social policy making. This chapter focuses on the following questions: how and to what extent do social security systems prevent poverty among the 'new' self-employed and hybrid workers? To what extent does EU law support social security of the self-employed and of hybrid workers? With respect to social security of the self-employed and of multiple-job holders, are there approaches taken by social security systems and the underlying institutional structures of the European countries that could serve as suitable models for other countries?

Social security systems largely differ between European countries and encompass many dimensions. The following will highlight and compare the situations in Germany, the Netherlands and Austria in terms of how the social security systems deal with poverty in old age. As described in Chapter 3 this is an area with the largest expenses for social security and with high impact when inadequately designed. The countries chosen may be thought of as all belonging to the conservative welfare states (Esping-Andersen, 1990), but nevertheless largely differ in how they have organized their pension system and their minimum floors in order to ensure that citizens have a decent standard of living. The systems largely differ in how they are able to deal with labour market developments as described before.

With the country selection, three examples of a fundamentally different treatment of self-employed and hybrid employees are chosen. The Dutch system is based on a basic pension, which is granted regardless of previous gainful employment. On the other hand, in Austria and Germany, the benefits of the pension system depend on the contributions made on the basis of gainful employment. Although both countries have a strong insurance-centred system, they differ significantly in terms of the involvement of the self-employed and hybrid employees. That makes it interesting to zoom on the three countries.

CURRENT SITUATION

As in many other Member States of the EU, self-employment is also on the rise in the Netherlands, Austria and Germany. The share of self-employed workers in relation to paid workers in total rose in the Netherlands in 1992 from barely 10 per cent to over 15 per cent by 2015. In the same period, the share of self-employed workers in relation to all paid workers rose in Austria only minimally from 10.5 per cent to 11 per cent and in Germany from 8.3 per cent to 9.6 per cent (Eurostat, 2016).

The increasing share of self-employment is primarily attributable to the increased significance of solo self-employment. In the period 1992 to 2015, the share of solo self-employed workers in relation to the total number of paid workers rose in Germany and in the Netherlands and Austria: In 1992 only 3.7 per cent of paid workers in Germany were solo self-employed, whereas by 2015 it had increased to 5.3 per cent. In the Netherlands, the same share increased in this time period from 6.3 per cent to 11.5 per cent. This means that more than every tenth paid worker in the Netherlands is now solo self-employed. The share of solo self-employed workers in Austria in relation to paid workers in total rose in the same period from 5.6 per cent to 6.6 per cent (Conen et al., 2016, p. 134).

An increasing number of people in Europe also have more than one job. Around 8.8 million people, or 4 per cent of all paid workers, in the EU in 2014 had at least one secondary job in addition to their main jobs. The number of these was therefore around 13 per cent higher than in 2005 (Crößmann and Mischke, 2016, p. 58). This increase is clearly recognizable in Germany. The number of persons with paid secondary jobs has more than doubled from barely one million in 2005 to over two million in 2015 (Eurostat, 2016). Thus around 5 per cent of all paid workers in Germany over 15 years of age had a second job. And 38 per cent of these secondary jobs takes the form of self-employment. Therefore self-employment in Germany is far more frequently a form of second, additional employment rather than a person's main (or only) employment. While the number of persons whose main employment is self-employment has declined in Germany in the last years, the number of those whose secondary employment is self-employment has increased (Suprinovič and Norkina, 2015, p. 19).

In line with the favourable developments on the labour markets and rising employment rates, the share of persons holding secondary jobs in Germany has risen in the last decade from 3.4 per cent (2005) to 5.1 per cent (2015) in relation to paid workers in total. The share of persons in Austria holding secondary jobs rose in the same period from 4 per cent to 4.5 per cent. Particularly interesting is the trend in the Netherlands: In 2005, 6.1 per cent of all paid workers already had more than one job – a share that has risen to 8.7 per cent in 2015. This means that nearly every tenth paid worker in the Netherlands holds down at least two jobs. And not only did the share of multiple-job holders increase in the Netherlands, but the number of (solo) self-employed rose very significantly and steadily as well.

The erosion of the standard contract will presumably lead to a significant amount of switching between various forms of employment, including marginal part-time jobs and secondary jobs. The working histories of a growing share of the population already contain one or several periods of self-employment and/or independent or dependent secondary employment. The studies conducted by Suprinovič et al. (2016) show that hybrid self-employment – meaning the parallel exercising of self-employment and dependent employment – as well as multiple switching from dependent employment to self-employment are continuously rising in Germany in the last decades.

These dynamics – that is, multiple switches from one form of employment to another and frequent periods of parallel or multiple employment – have special implications for social security, such as for old-age security. In light of this trend towards more flexible employment models: How and to what extent are these periods to be incorporated in the various social security systems, especially in the statutory old-age pension schemes? How are labour market transitions taken into account?[2]

Using three European countries as examples, the following discussion focuses on the question of the extent to which self-employed workers and multiple-job holders are exposed to higher risks of existential insecurity or precariousness, especially in their old age. Highlighted are the (compulsory) statutory old-age pension schemes, the goal of which is to provide examples of 'good practices'. Which statutory old-age pension schemes are particularly good at meeting the social security needs of the respective groups of working persons – especially the need for protection from old-age poverty?

In addition to making a comparative analysis of the countries, social and labour policies at the EU level will also be discussed. What procedures and programmes are being employed by the EU to adequately tackle the structural changes to the labour markets and especially the increasing hybridization of employment?

SOCIO-POLITICAL PARAMETERS AT THE NATIONAL LEVEL

The following highlights and compares the statutory old-age security situations in Germany, the Netherlands and Austria for self-employed workers and multiple-job holders. Austria's statutory old-age system is based on principles similar to those of the German system, namely on strong insurance and equivalence principles. On the other hand, the Dutch statutory old-age security system is regarded as being based on a systemic logic completely different than the German system, namely on the principle of a basic old-age pension independent of income. Minimum floors ensuring that various types of workers/citizens have at least a decent standard of living are typically organized within the first pillar. Second and third pillar savings tend to function as additional incomes, in order to maintain one's living standard during retirement and have a 'nice evening of life' rather than a 'poverty-avoiding' function. So how and to what extent do these social security systems prevent poverty in old age among the 'new' self-employed and hybrid workers?

Germany

The German statutory old-age pension scheme (abbreviated in German as the 'GRV') is strongly based on income and on the principle of equivalence. It clearly adheres to the principle that the pension mirrors the person's work history. The factor that determines the amount of pension benefits is primarily the amount of wages that were insured through contributions made during the entire insurance period. The contribution payments are split equally between employers and employees. The calculation of the contributions is based on a person's insured wages up to the contribution-assessment wage limit, on periods of childcare in the first three years after the child's birth (these periods are credited as contribution periods based on average wages) and periods of caring for family members (Paragraph 55 ff. of the [German] Social Code VI (SGB VI)).

Government policy since the beginning of the twenty-first century has primarily focused on stabilizing the contribution rates to the detriment of benefit amounts. The implementation at that time of 'pension-reduction reforms', for example, reforms that weakened rights under pension law to have apprenticeship periods or periods when unemployment benefits II were collected taken into account, in conjunction with the rise in hybrid employment, the growth of the low-wage sector, and the increasing number of discontinuous work histories will in the long run lead to an increased risk of old-age poverty for future old-age pensioners (Hinrichs, 2012; Blank and Schulze Buschoff, 2013, p. 318). It is evident today already that the pension amounts actually paid out ('Rentenzahlbeträge') to 'entry' pension recipients (i.e. recipients after 1 January 2005, so-called 'Zugangsrentner') are sinking considerably in comparison to the amounts paid to the 'existing' pension recipients (i.e. recipients before 1 January 2005, so-called 'Bestandsrentner') (Trischler, 2012, p. 254).

With respect to the social security of self-employed workers, Germany is unique among the European countries. While in the majority of European countries self-employed workers are systematically included in the compulsory statutory insurance systems, access to the compulsory statutory insurance system in Germany is limited to a few special groups of self-employed persons. The reasons for this are rooted in the traditional social welfare system introduced by Bismarck. The underlying idea is that the self-employed can take care of themselves and that they do not need the collective protection provided by the solidarity of the community of insured persons. This idea persists to the present day with the exception of special laws that include certain individual groups of self-employed persons in the statutory social security system. Since it was assumed that the perceived lack of a need for protection does not apply to these groups, they were integrated incrementally in the statutory old-age pension scheme. Special compulsory systems therefore exist today for around one-quarter of self-employed persons, although the conditions vary greatly depending on the professional group. Compulsory old-age pension schemes apply to persons performing paid work for others in their own self-chosen work places ('Hausgewerbetreibende'), teachers, childcare workers, nursing care workers, midwives, marine/harbour pilots, coastal sailors and coastal fishers, crafts/tradespersons registered in the so-called 'Handwerksrolle', district master chimney sweeps, artists, published authors, farmers, and members of the 'free professions' such as lawyers, notary publics or medical doctors, and the so-called employee-like workers pursuant to Paragraph 2 no. 9 SGB VI (a detailed discussion of this is found in Fachinger, 2016 and Schulze Buschoff, 2016a).

For self-employed artists and published authors there is the compulsory statutory health insurance and old-age pension scheme called the 'Künstlersozialkasse' (KSK), an insurance scheme for artists that was created in 1983. The amount of the contributions to the KSK is calculated on the basis of estimated annual income, which is calculated in advance and converted into monthly amounts. Like dependent employees, the insured persons must pay half of the contribution amounts to the social insurance. The other half is paid through a federal government subsidy and through the social insurance contributions for self-employed artists that must be paid by the clients.

It is obvious that other groups of self-employed persons, especially among the 'new self-employed' (Schulze Buschoff and Schmidt, 2007, p. 71; Bögenhold and Fachinger, 2012, p. 7), are as dependent on the sale of their labours as those groups of self-employed persons and dependent employees already participating in the compulsory statutory insurance scheme. They too are equally exposed to the risks of aging, illness and periods of little or no work. Therefore the extension of the statutory compulsory old-age pension scheme to include self-employed workers of all occupations has been the subject of many a demand (see Fachinger et al., 2004; Fachinger and Frankus, 2011; Fachinger, 2016; Schulze Buschoff, 2016a).

The present old-age security regulations for self-employed persons are particular and selective. Because the different forms of work and professions are protected in very different ways under German social law, status changes and changes of professions can be seriously detrimental to these persons. The absence of a form of minimum social security means a danger of old-age poverty, particularly in the case of:

1. Self-employed persons who are not compulsorily insured,
2. Compulsorily insured self-employed persons with low incomes, and
3. Persons with flexible work histories, especially when these contain periods of non-compulsorily insured self-employment or periods of limited-income employment (so-called 'geringfügige Beschäftigung').

Whereas low-income earners in other EU countries are better protected from old-age poverty by granting them replacement rates higher than those of average income earners, the replacement rate in Germany is identical (at 42.0 per cent) for average income earners and for persons that only earn half as much (OECD, 2014, p. 147). With this low gross replacement rate, Germany is at the lower end of the scale in comparison to other EU pension models.[3] Compared to other countries, the risk of old-age poverty is particularly high in Germany for low-income earners on account of the insufficient securing of them in the statutory social security scheme.

Austria

Like Germany, the statutory old-age security scheme in Austria is principally designed as an insurance system financed equally [by employers and employees] and based on the principle of equivalence. But unlike Germany, Austria has chosen a rigorous path of strengthening the first pillar, that is, strengthening the statutory old-age security scheme, the aim of which was to create social insurance for all paid workers. In the wake of the reforms of the statutory old-age pension scheme in 1998, all paid workers without exception were included in the statutory scheme, even self-employed workers who were not included up to that time. From a socio-political point of view, the distinct advantages of the Austrian system are the consistently effected structural revisions and closing of gaps during the course of the reforms. This has resulted in clear, transparent and universal rules without exceptions for all paid workers. The closing of gaps and the structural revisions made in the course of the reforms to the statutory old-age pension scheme in Austria in 1998 included not only the introduction of the category of the new self-employed but also a concrete definition of 'employee', clear rules for multiple insurance and a defined order for reviewing entitlements. In cases of doubt, the category 'new self-employed' is chosen (a kind of 'catch-all' category).

The first pillar was strengthened in Austria in order to further secure the living standard basically for all paid workers. But in Germany the first pillar has been systematically weakened. And as compensation for this weakening, the options of (voluntary) private insurance and company pension schemes are pointed to. Although both the Austrian and the German systems are based on strong contribution equivalence with its resulting negative consequences for low-income earners and for persons with discontinuous employment and insurance histories, this situation is markedly defused in Austria through the paying of higher benefits and the provision of a minimum level of social security. The difference between the levels of social security in the two countries is enormous. One reason for the higher benefits in Austria is the higher contribution rate for old-age security, which for dependent employees was 22.8 per cent in 2016. The Austrian example shows that a higher contribution rate for old-age security based on a social consensus is sensible and implementable without prejudice to the competitiveness of the economy (Blank et al., 2016, p. 23 ff.).

The basis for calculating the contributions of self-employed workers in Austria is their income as per their (formal) tax assessment notices. The contribution rate for self-employed workers was 18.5 per cent in 2016. By comparison, the contribution rate for dependent employees is 22.8 per cent. The difference between the contribution rate for self-employed workers and the 22.8 per cent for dependent employees is paid out of federal resources as a so-called 'partner benefit of the federal government'.

The Netherlands

The old-age pension scheme in the Netherlands rests on two main pillars. One is the basic statutory social security scheme (AOW) and the other is a quasi-compulsory supplemental company pension scheme based on income. With the introduction of the AOW (Algemene Ouderdomswet = statutory old-age pension) in the Netherlands in 1957, a comprehensive basic statutory security system was created. The AOW is based on compulsory old-age security pursuant to an allocation procedure for everyone residing in the Netherlands. The AOW basic social security is a fixed benefit independent of contributions paid during a person's working life.

The government of the Netherlands provides every citizen from the age of 65 with basic statutory social security. Entitlement to it is contingent on residency only, that is, residency in the Netherlands, and it is completely independent of employment. Even residents who have never worked at a job subject to compulsory social insurance or who worked at limited-income jobs are entitled to a statutory pension. No assessment of need is made.

The maximum amount of this basic pension is the same for every recipient and is geared to the statutory net minimum wage. For every AOW insurance year, two per cent of the full amount of the AOW basic pension is being amassed. Persons between the ages of 15 and 65 who have not been insured uninterruptedly pursuant to the AOW, that is, were not residing in the Netherlands, are not entitled to a full AOW basic pension. The full amount of the AOW basic pension is reduced by 2 per cent per missing insurance year. The basic statutory pension is financed through tax-like contributions, which are obligatorily levied on employment income and paid solely by the employees. The gross monthly amount of the benefits paid out of the statutory old-age pension scheme are currently around 1,100 euros for a single person after 50 years of uninterrupted participation (Thalen, 2016).

The old-age basic pension is a secure form of old-age income. It prevents old-age poverty, including those who were atypically employed. Switching from dependent employment to self-employment also has no impact on the amount of the old-age benefits from the statutory core system. All that matters is the length of residency in the Netherlands. Very important to the Dutch system, however, is the major role played by the second pillar of old-age security, namely company pensions and sector funds. Around 90 per cent of all paid workers in the Netherlands are covered by such old-age security contracts.

Compared to other European countries, atypical- and hybrid-job holders with discontinuous work histories, and especially the solo self-employed, have a relatively low risk of old-age poverty in the Netherlands. Like all residents, they too are entitled to a basic old-age pension, which prevents old-age poverty (Table 13.1).

SOCIAL POLICIES FOR THE SELF-EMPLOYED AND HYBRID WORKERS AT THE EU LEVEL?

This section will discuss whether there are socio-political imperatives and instruments at the supranational level, and particularly at the EU level, to counteract the potential old-age poverty of the self-employed and of hybrid workers.

Instruments that guarantee social rights in the multi-level European system are found basically at the level of international law in the form of treaties ratified by the Member States of the EU. Examples of these include the European Social Charter, the European Convention on Human Rights and the conventions of the International Labour Organization (ILO).[4] Because Union law has precedence over the laws of the individual states, it will have precedence over any social rights granted by the laws of the Member States or by international law. The guaranteeing of these

*Table 13.1   Comparison of the old-age security systems in Austria,
Germany and the Netherlands*

	Germany	Austria	The Netherlands
First pillar	Statutory old-age pension scheme (GRV) as compulsory insurance for dependent employees; compulsory insurance schemes for only around one-quarter of self-employed workers; benefits are contingent on income (equivalence-based), i.e. dependent on work history	Insurance for all paid workers, i.e. compulsory insurance for all paid workers, including the self-employed and limited-income workers; benefits are contingent on income (equivalence-based), i.e. dependent on work history	Basic old-age pension scheme with universal coverage for all residents, including for all self-employed, uniform benefits independent of the contributions paid or of the work history
Second pillar	A good half of dependent employees are included in a company pension scheme;* the solo self-employed have no entitlement due to their lack of employment with a company	Company old-age pensions play a subordinate role; 34 per cent of dependent employees are covered; solo self-employed workers are not entitled but they do receive statutory severance (so-called 'Abfertigung') since 2008	Company pension or sector funds play a major role (more than 90 per cent of dependent employees are covered); solo self-employed workers are not (yet) entitled
Third pillar	Private voluntary products; 'Riester' pensions (accessible to dependent employees and few groups of self-employed workers) are tax incentives; the solo self-employed can collect the 'Rürup' pensions (also tax incentives)	Private voluntary pension products	Private voluntary pension products, often with tax benefits

Note: *Because vested pension entitlements are subject to forfeiture depending on the length of employment with a company, the number of employees who actually collect an old-age company pension when they reach the retirement age is lower (same in Austria and the Netherlands).

Source: Own compilation (see Zeibig, 2011; Blank et al., 2016; Conen et al., 2016; Schulze Buschoff, 2016b).

rights in the multi-level European system, especially when Union law is included as a supranational legal system, is in no way without its tensions (Schlachter, 2016, p.478).

Not to be forgotten in the European political context is the imbalance that still exists between economic and socio-political goals: socio-political goals play a subordinate role in relation to economic policies. The rules of the internal market and the monetary union restrict the Member States in their national labour and socio-political policies.

While the 1980s and 1990s witnessed an expansion of the European Commission's socio-political competences, what can be seen today is a regression behind the achievements of that time. In the 1980s and 1990s, the social dialogue was strengthened, for example through the systematic inclusion of the social partners. A key role was played by the social partner agreements, which in the form of a directive proposal are introduced by the European Commission to the Council of the European Union. Regarding atypical employment forms, there are the following legally binding directives based on social-partner agreements initiated by the Commission: a directive regulating working conditions for part-time employment,[5] another regulating fixed-term employment contracts[6] and a directive regulating hired-out temporary employment.[7] These directives – which are principally aimed at setting minimum standards and at preventing discrimination of groups of atypical-job holders and which must be implemented in national law – have led to perceptible legal advancements in many countries. But since the beginning of the 2000s, the importance of the social dialogue has been dwindling. And particularly since the crisis in the European monetary union, this dialogue now seems to have more of a legitimating function, it gets very little support from the European Commission and it has been seriously weakened by the crisis policies. The fact that no binding agreements are being created through the social dialogue at the moment means a fundamental weakening of the social dimension of the European Union (Schellinger, 2015, p.13 ff.).

Although the legislating of binding labour-market and socio-political policies has lost importance at the EU level since the end of the 1990s, the nonbinding coordination of national policies is still being pursued. The Union or the EU Member States use what is referred to in the Lisbon Treaty as the 'open method of coordination' (OMC) as a nonbinding procedure for coordinating the European employment strategy (EES) in the form of an annual programme on planning, assisting, reviewing and adapting the policies of the Member States. Since the introduction of the so-called six pack[8] in 2011, the OMC is a formal part of the European Semester. It is an annual procedure participated in by the European Council and the European Commission in which national political fields are coordinated through annual growth reports, national reform programmes and country-specific proposals.

The Lisbon Strategy underlying the OMC and scheduled for 2010 has been succeeded by the Europe 2020 strategy. This strategy was a response to the severe impact of the economic crisis on national labour markets. Like the Lisbon Strategy, its primary focus is still on economic and employment growth. The new goal is a general employment rate of 75 per cent for men and women between the ages of 20 and 64 by 2020. What is surprising is that there is now an integrated guideline explicitly targeted at combating poverty and fostering social inclusion. There is also a quantitative target, namely that at least 20 million less people from 2010 to 2020 should be affected or threatened by poverty and social exclusion EU-wide. However, since 2008/2009, the number of people threatened or affected by poverty has risen EU-28-wide from 114 million to 124 million, which means that the discrepancy to the targeted goal has risen by 10 million and is now 30 million (Hacker, 2014, p. 5).

Whether such socio-political goals as the reduction of poverty will be attained or not will seriously depend on labour and income conditions or on transforming employment relationships and social security, especially old-age security. According to the coordinating old-age pension policies at the European level, which were introduced in 2001 at the Laeken Summit, or the OMC on pensions, the prevention of old-age poverty is one of the main goals. The list of goals in the area of pension coordination are currently dominated by two major projects. The first is a socio-political goal aimed at guaranteeing adequate pension levels in the long-term as well, especially with an eye to preventing old-age poverty. The second goal is to ensure the financial sustainability of the pension systems particularly in light of demographic challenges (European Commission, 2012, pp. 28 and 43). The dominant targets at the EU level are closely tied to the proposal to consolidate financing in the form of low benefit levels in public systems combined with minimum social security elements. The European Commission is – with a view to demographic changes – still preferring longer working hours or a raising of the statutory retirement age and more saving or – despite the financial crisis – more investment in private forms of capital-market products (Schmähl, 2012, p. 21; Hacker, 2013, p. 15).

For reasons of fiscal consolidation, low benefit levels in the national statutory old-age pension schemes (meaning the first pillar) combined with minimum social security elements and the expansion of the second and third pillars are still the dominating aims at the EU level. This means that people are not only working longer but also that the material securing of old age should be done privately or at the company level. These aims are of no help to people with hybrid work models. Their often low income levels and the inability to save that goes along with this leaves very little room for them to save anything. The solo self-employed and other (often discontinuous) hybrid workers are excluded from access to company pensions due to the absence of (permanent) employment with a company. Furthermore, the social balancing that takes place primarily in the public systems will be much harder to realize in the company or private old-age pension schemes due to their general market dependency.

Economic policy decisions at the EU level have a much more direct impact on labour and living conditions than do labour, social or pension policies. In the countries of the troika programme, especially in Greece, Portugal and Spain, some of the measures that were introduced – such as the legal relaxation of atypical employment, the lowering of minimum wages, the weakening of collective bargaining agreements, and the dilution of (wrongful) dismissal protection – have led to social instabilities. They also counteract such socio-political goals as the reduction of poverty. And although some of these measures are limited in time, they are generally expected to have long-term consequences for the working and living conditions of the people living there (Schellinger, 2015, p. 3 ff.).

The living and working conditions of atypical- and multiple-job holders are also affected by so-called 'judge-made law', especially by decisions of the Court of Justice of the European Union. One example of these is a decision of the Court of Justice from 4 December 2014. The Court held that Union law is to be interpreted such that collective bargaining agreements that prescribe minimum wages for self-employed service providers may only apply if it is a matter of 'false self-employment'.[9] This decision would severely restrict the applicability of collective bargaining agreements[10] and would counteract the goal of combating the working poverty of the self-employed. It would also be incompatible with the European Parliament resolution of 14 January 2014 on 'social protection for all, including self-employed workers', which appeals to the social partners and asks them to review '. . . if and how self-employed workers should be included in collective bargaining . . .' (Haake, 2016, p. 318).

A current initiative aimed at strengthening the social dimension of the European Union is the so-called 'European Pillar of Social Rights' (EPSR) (see European Parliament, 2017). This initiative is being pushed particularly by Jean-Claude Juncker since he took office as President of the European Commission. The EPSR comprises three areas: Equal opportunities and access to the labour market, fair working conditions and adequate and sustainable social protection. The initiative is also meant to help overcome the socio-political crisis in Europe and to reinstate convergence in the eurozone. These are no doubt ambitious goals, but the EPSR is not a supplement to the laws that already exist. It does not amend any laws, it merely compiles the social standards that already exist in European law or in other international laws (Seikel, 2016b).

CONCLUSION

Social protection systems in Europe face challenges to provide effective coverage for workers in all forms of employment, including self-employed and 'hybrid' workers. It is necessary to strengthen and adapt social protection systems to enable them to fulfil their key role in preventing and reducing poverty, enhancing income security and limiting inequality (Behrendt and Anh Nguyen, 2018, p. 1). Ensuring universal social protection requires closing coverage gaps and adapting to new contexts related to the emergence of new forms of employment, so as to realize the human right to social security for all (Behrendt and Anh Nguyen, 2018, p. 30). All types of employment should be protected not only in the case of unemployment and old age, but also during critical transitions throughout life-course, such as the transition from dependent employment to self-employment (Schmid, 2011). Building comprehensive social protection systems with strong, nationally appropriate social protection floors is fundamental to promoting sustainable and solid social security (Behrendt and Anh Nguyen, 2018, p. 31).

In order to adequately include the 'new' forms of self-employment and the growing number of hybrid work forms in the national statutory old-age security systems, an employment paradigm that takes such things as status changes, dynamics, periods of irregular income and work interruptions into account is necessary. A central concern of this must be the prevention of old-age poverty in the most comprehensive and universal way possible.

In the Netherlands, access to the basic old-age pension (and basic health insurance) is, as a right of residence, a relatively comprehensive form of social security. This basic statutory old-age pension, which is based on a needs-oriented notion, grants all residents a poverty-preventing, uniform basic pension independent of employment history or previous work achievements. With respect to overcoming the risks caused by increasingly flexible labour markets, this system is more persuasive than systems that are clearly performance oriented. Such universal security, that is, the equal treatment under social security law of dependent employment and self-employment, also prevents dependent forms of employment from being converted into self-employed forms so that social security contributions can be 'saved', a practice that also fosters social security gaps. A universal security also prevents the occurrence of social security gaps, which can occur on account of 'alternating' or hybrid employment histories. It also takes into account the growing grey zone in which it is becoming increasingly difficult to draw a clear line between dependent employment and self-employment. However, pension gaps in terms of maintaining one's living standard during retirement do also exist in the Netherlands.

The statutory old-age pension system in Germany is clearly insurance-based and strongly aligned to the principle of equivalence. Gaps in employment histories and low levels of income are mirrored in the pension levels. It seems inevitable that the negligible reallocation function of this employment-based pension system will lead to a perceptible increase in old-age poverty in the coming years – the result of a sacrificing of pension levels on the altar of contribution stability.

Self-employed workers are an especially problematic group here. Special compulsory old-age security schemes are available to only around one-quarter of self-employed workers, although the conditions vary greatly depending on the particular professional group. And because other groups of self-employed workers – just like self-employed workers who already have compulsory insurance – are equally exposed to social risks and particularly to the risk of old-age poverty due to their generally low income levels and the resulting inability to save, continual demands are being made for a more comprehensive and compulsory old-age security for self-employed workers in all professions (Schulze Buschoff, 2016b, p. 42). There are basically two options for compulsory insurance for self-employed workers in all professional fields. The first would be compulsory insurance in the sense of an obligation to be insured with an insurer of one's free choice (which also includes private insurers). The second would be obligatory insurance in the statutory old-age pension scheme (GRV).

The advantages of obligatory insurance in the GRV include the wide range of benefits prescribed by law for this form of social security. In addition to the paying of old-age pensions, this form of social security also includes pensions for reduced earning capacity, pensions for widow(er)s and orphans and the provision of rehabilitation services. GRV benefits contain elements of solidarity (social) balancing, something that is very difficult to realize in private and usually market-based systems. And when insurers can be freely chosen, there is also the problem of reviewing whether the insurance obligation is actually being fulfilled and the problem of coordinating entitlements from different insurers, something which would entail a great deal of administrative work. For self-employed workers with discontinuous work histories, compulsory insurance in the GRV would also mean that they would not have to change insurers when switching between self-employment and dependent employment. This would support the continuity of the payment of contributions, which would be of benefit especially to persons with discontinuous insurance histories.

Although Austria, like Germany, has a social insurance system financed basically by employees and employers equally, Austria already included (solo) self-employed workers without exception in the statutory system several years ago. Austria has therefore chosen a rigorous path of strengthening the first pillar, the aim of which is insurance for all paid workers.

The Austrian example shows that clear, transparent and universal rules – without exception for all working people, including the self-employed and limited-income workers – can work even in a system where contributions are paid equally by the participating parties. The distinct advantages of the Austrian system are the structural corrections and the closing of gaps that were consistently implemented in the course of the 1998 reforms.

The broadening of the severance provision in Austria in 2008 to include the self-employed also shows that it was possible to create effective rules for self-employed workers not only in the first but in the second pillar of old-age security as well (Zeibig, 2011, p. 242 ff.).

The new forms of employment in the platform economy present a special challenge with respect to regulating employment and social security. Questions of regulation must take into account the numerous platforms with their various possibilities and the limits of regulation. Particularly in need of regulation is the outsourcing of services or the offshoring of functions/processes to the detriment of local labour markets, including beyond national borders. For these forms of employment in particular an EU-wide framework for regulation is necessary.

What is decisive at both the national and at the EU levels is the way in which the different forms of workers in the platform economy are being classified from a legal policy point of view: as dependent employees or as self-employed workers. If they are classified as self-employed workers, then they are subject to tight restrictions under EU competition law: Price-fixing agreements between self-employed workers are regarded as cartels and are not permitted unless such self-employment is found to be 'false self-employment' (decision of the Court of Justice, C-413/13). Legal policy demands that the employment relationship also be defined based on a 'functional' definition of employers or by taking the different entrepreneurial possibilities of structuring the relationship into account (Klebe, 2017). This would make it easier to classify platform workers as dependent employees who would then enjoy the protective rights associated with this status. Court decisions, especially those of the national courts, on whether platform workers are to be regarded as dependent employees or self-employed workers are currently defining the scope within which their wages and their working conditions are being regulated via collective bargaining agreements.

Policies at the EU level regarding the social securing of atypical-job holders and self-employed workers appear contradictory at the moment. While the European Parliament for example is in favour of including self-employed workers in collective bargaining negotiations, the Court of Justice has decided that collective bargaining agreements may not apply to self-employed workers but only to 'false self-employed workers', thereby making it more difficult to (socially) secure hybrid work histories through collective bargaining agreements. The decisions of the Court of Justice in particular are clearly at odds with such social rights as the freedom of collective bargaining. In light of the foregoing, and in light of the priority that economic policy is being given over socio-political goals, it appears necessary that the achievements made in the area of social welfare, such as national social security systems and collective bargaining regulations, be protected from attacks from Brussels and Luxembourg (Seikel, 2016a, p. 8).

In 2006 the European Commission presented a Green Paper on employment law, which contained concrete proposals particularly on the securing of paid workers under employment law in borderline cases between dependent employment and self-employment. This chapter theoretically favours the idea of extending employment rights beyond the employee status and of creating fundamental protection for all persons who perform personal services in situations of economic dependency (European Commission, 2006, p. 12). In light of the increasing polarization of the labour markets, the rise in atypical and often precarious forms of employment in the EU countries and the increase in hybrid forms of employment, it appears urgently necessary to rekindle this debate and to define minimum standards as the foundation for a modern form of employment law at the European level (Casale and Perulli, 2014).

The defining of minimum standards could be a good basic starting point for strengthening the social dimension of Europe. Minimum standards for welfare statism in the form of regulatory 'ratchets' aimed at preventing the underbidding of each other could secure and further economic and social development in the Member States (Seikel, 2016a, p. 11). In the area of labour-market and social policy, the idea is not to introduce EU-wide uniform standards. The idea is rather the creation of regulatory standards for implementation by the Member States in the context of their country-specific circumstances, for example in relation to minimum social security elements or minimum wage rates in the case of transfer payments (Busch, 2005, p. 44; Seikel, 2016a, p. 10). Not to be forgotten, however, is the fact that the European Union is completely devoid of procedural or legislative powers in such areas as the right to strike, freedom of association and the setting of wages.[11] Therefore without an amendment of the TFEU, there can be no enactment of European minimum wage regulations, for example.

On 19 January 2017, a large majority of the European Parliament adopted a report on a European Pillar of Social Rights (2016/2095 (INI)) in which compliance with the social aims of the treaties and the combating of poverty are demanded. The MEPs are calling for a

> proposal for a framework directive on decent working conditions in all forms of employment ... extending existing minimum standards to new kinds of employment relationships. (European Parliament, 2017, p. 13)

The European Parliament is thereby calling on 'the social partners and the Commission to work together to present a proposal for a framework directive on decent working conditions in all forms of employment'. As to what impact this report will have is not yet clear. Whether the social partners and the Commission will act on the request and create such a framework directive remains to be seen. If the request is acted on and a framework directive drafted, it is uncertain as to whether it will go beyond the existing norms or will merely demand compliance with the existing norms. What this report can certainly not be seen as is a major step towards the strengthening of the social dimension and the social security of hybrid-job holders. At the current time, the increasing hybridization of employment is a development that is not receiving the attention it deserves from the political stakeholders at the EU level. And the initiatives that exist regarding the social securing of hybrid forms of employment appear to be contradictory and inadequate.

The extension of social security protection to all paid workers – including to self-employed workers and atypical-, flexible- and hybrid-job holders – is a fundamental prerequisite for strengthening Europe's social dimension and for resolving the imbalance between economic and social goals. Strengthening Europe's social dimension must first and foremost be aimed at eliminating inequalities and income disparities in the EU and preventing poverty. To continue to pursue economic policies that foster atypical and flexible employment relationships with low wages and little social protection is not constructive (Dauderstädt and Keltek, 2015, p. 4).

NOTES

1. I would like to thank the anonymous reviewers of this chapter for the very helpful feedback. I would also like to thank Nadine Absenger for her valuable ideas.
2. The consideration and securing of transitions is a central element of the concept of transitional labour markets, developed by Günther Schmid (2002, 2011).
3. Not to be overlooked here, however, is the criticism of the indicator used by the OECD. See for example Fachinger and Künemund (2009).
4. Plus Regulation (EC) No 883/2004 on the coordination of social security systems.

5. Council Directive 97/81/EC.
6. Council Directive 1999/70/EC.
7. Directive 2008/104/EC.
8. The six pack refers to a legislation package containing five regulations and one directive. Its aim is the reform of the Stability and Growth Pact (SGP). A more detailed discussion of this is found in Bieling (2013).
9. Decision of the Court of Justice of 4 December 2014–C-413/13, NZA 2015, 55–57. In Germany, Paragraph 12a of the German Act on Collective Bargaining Agreements (TVG) allows for the negotiation of collective bargaining regulations on behalf of 'employee-like workers'. This provision is most frequently made use of in the media and cultural sectors.
10. Although the Court of Justice speaks of 'false self-employment' in this decision, the Court's reasoning implies that 'employee-like workers' is what is actually meant. If this is correct, then collective bargaining agreements could at least continue to apply to and be concluded on behalf of employee-like workers (= economically dependent solo self-employed workers).
11. Article 153(5) of the Treaty on the Functioning of the European Union.

REFERENCES

Behrendt, C. and Anh Nguyen, Q. (2018). *Innovative Approaches for Ensuring Universal Social Protection for the Future of Work*. International Labour Office. Geneva: ILO.

Bieling, H.-J. (2013). Sixpack. In: Große Hüttmann, M. and Wehling, H.-G. (eds), *Das Europalexikon. Begriffe, Namen, Institutionen*. Bonn: Dietz Verlag.

Blank, F. and Schulze Buschoff, K. (2013). Arbeit, Leistungsgerechtigkeit und Alterssicherung im deutschen Wohlfahrtsstaat. *WSI Mitteilungen*, 05/2013, 313–20.

Blank, F., Logeay, C., Türk, E., Wöss, J. and Zwiener, R. (2016). *Alterssicherung in Deutschland und Österreich – Vom Nachbarn lernen?* WSI Report, 27, Düsseldorf.

Bögenhold, D. and Fachinger, U. (2012). *Neue Selbstständigkeit. Wandel und Differenzierung der Erwerbstätigkeit*. Expert report at the request of the Department for Economic and Social Policies at the Friedrich-Ebert-Stiftung (Bonn), WISO Diskurs, October 2012.

Busch, K. (2005). *Die Perspektiven des Europäischen Sozialmodells*. Expert report at the request of the Hans-Böckler-Stiftung, Arbeitspapier 92.

Casale, G. and Perulli, A. (2014). *Towards the Single Employment Contract: Comparative Reflections*. Geneva: International Labour Organization Publications.

Conen, W., Schippers, J. and Schulze Buschoff, K. (2016). *Self-employed Without Personnel Between Freedom and Insecurity*. WSI Study, 5, Düsseldorf.

Crößmann, A. and Mischke, J. (2016). *Arbeitsmarkt auf einen Blick – Deutschland und Europa*. Wiesbaden: Federal Statistical Office.

Dauderstädt, M. and Keltek, C. (2015). Das soziale Europa in der Krise. *WiSo direkt – Analsysen und Konzepte zur Wirtschafts- und Sozialpolitik*, May 2015, Bonn: Friedrich-Ebert-Stiftung.

Dawson, C., Henley, A. and Latreille, P.L. (2009). Why do individuals choose self-employment? *IZA Discussion Paper*, No. 3974.

Esping-Andersen, G. (1990). *The Three Worlds of Welfare Capitalism*. Princeton, NJ: Princeton University Press

Eurofound (2017). *Exploring Self-employment in the European Union*. Luxembourg: Publications Office of the European Union.

European Commission (2006). *Modernising Labour Law to meet the Challenges of the 21st Century*. European Commission Green Paper. Brussels: Commission of the European Communities.

European Commission (2012). *An Agenda for Adequate, Safe and Sustainable Pensions*. White Paper, Brussels: European Commission.

European Parliament (2017). *A European Pillar of Social Rights*. European Parliament report of 19 January 2017 on a European Pillar of Social Rights (2016/2095(INI)). http://www.europarl.europa.eu/sides/getDoc.do?pubRef=-//E P//NONSGML+TA+P8-TA-2017-0010+0+DOC+PDF+V0//EN (accessed 30 September 2017).

Eurostat (2016). *Database Employment and unemployment*. https://ec.europa.eu/euro stat/statistics-explained/index.php/Employment_statistics (accessed 30 October 2017).

Fachinger, U. (2016). *Alterssicherung von Selbstständigen. Eine Bestandsanalyse auf Basis des Mikrozensus 2013*. Discussion Paper 28/2016, Vechta: Research Group Economics and Demographic Change.

Fachinger, U. and Frankus, A. (2011). Sozialpolitische Probleme bei der Eingliederung von Selbstständigen in die gesetzliche Rentenversicherung. *WISO Diskurs: Expertisen und Dokumentationen zur Wirtschafts- und Sozialpolitik*. February 2011, Bonn: Friedrich-Ebert-Stiftung.

Fachinger, U. and Künemund, H. (2009). Die Auswirkungen alternativer Berechnung smethoden auf die Höhe der Lohnersatzquote. *Deutsche Rentenversicherung*, 64, 414–31.

Fachinger, U., Oelschläger, A. and Schmähl, W. (2004). *Alterssicherung von Selbständigen. Bestandsaufnahme und Reformoptionen*. Münster: Lit-Verlag.

Haake, G. (2016). Digitalisierung und Gewerkschaften: Solo-Selbstständige integrieren. In: Schröder, L. and Urban, H.-J. (eds), *Gute Arbeit. Digitale Arbeitswelt – Trends und Anforderungen*. Frankfurt am Main: Bund-Verlag, pp. 310–25.

Hacker, B. (2013). *Sollbruchstelle Krisenkurs. Auswirkungen des neuen Wirtschafts governance auf das Europäische Sozialmodell*. Berlin: Friedrich-Ebert-Stiftung.

Hacker, B. (2014). *Konfliktfeld Soziales Europa. Vier Herausforderungen und Chancen zur Gestaltung des Europäischen Sozialmodells*. Berlin: Friedrich-Ebert-Stiftung.

Hinrichs, K. (2012). Germany: A flexible labour market plus pension reforms means poverty in old age. In: Hinrichs, K. and Jessoula, M. (eds), *Labour Market Flexibility and Pension Reforms. Flexible Today. Secure Tomorrow?*, Basingstoke: Palgrave Macmillan, pp. 29–61.

Kautonen, T., Down, S., Welter, F., Vainio, P., Palmroos, J., Althoff, K. and Kolb, S. (2010). 'Involuntary self-employment' as a public policy issue: a cross-country European review. *International Journal of Entrepreneurial Behaviour & Research*, 16(2), 112–29.

Klebe, T. (2017). Arbeitsrecht 4.0: Faire Bedingungen für Plattformarbeit. WISO DIREKT, 22/2017.

OECD (2014). *Pensions at a Glance 2013. OECD and G20 Indicators*. Paris: OECD Publishing.

Peterson, A. (2015). The FTC wants to talk about the 'sharing economy'. *Washington Post*, 17 April.

Schellinger, A. (2015). *Wie sozial ist die EU? Eine Perspektive für die soziale Dimension*. Berlin: Friedrich-Ebert-Stiftung.

Schlachter, M. (2016). Stärkung sozialer Rechte durch Grundrechtsschutz im europäischen Mehr-Ebenen-System? *Europarecht*, 5/2016, 478–89.

Schmähl, W. (2012). Finanzmarktkrise, Europa und die deutsche Alterssicherung. Einige Anmerkungen zu bisherigen Erfahrungen und künftigen Entwicklungen. *ZeS-Arbeitspapier*, 08/2012.

Schmid, G. (2002). *Wege in eine neue Vollbeschäftigung – Übergangsarbeitsmärkte und eine aktivierende Arbeitsmarktpolitik*. Berlin.

Schmid, G. (2011). *Übergänge am Arbeitsmarkt*. Baden-Baden: Nomos Verlags gesellschaft.

Schulze Buschoff, K. (2016a). Alterssicherung für Selbstständige. Reformvorschläge. *WSI Policy Brief*, 05/2016, Düsseldorf: Hans-Böckler-Stiftung.

Schulze Buschoff, K. (2016b). *Atypische Beschäftigung in Europa – Herausforderungen für die Alterssicherung und die gewerkschaftliche Interessenvertretung*. WSI Study, Düsseldorf: Hans-Böckler-Stiftung.

Schulze Buschoff, K. (2018). Selbstständigkeit und hybride Erwerbsformen. *WSI Policy Brief*, 03/2018, Düsseldorf: Hans-Böckler-Stiftung.

Schulze Buschoff, K. and Schmidt, C. (2007). *Neue Selbstständige im europäischen Vergleich. Struktur, Dynamik und soziale Sicherheit*. Edition der Hans-Böckler-Stiftung 201, Europa und Globalisierung, Düsseldorf: Hans-Böckler-Stiftung.

Seikel, D. (2016a). Ein soziales und demokratisches Europa? Hindernisse und Handlungsoptionen. *WSI Mitteilungen*, 1/2016, 5–13.

Seikel, D. (2016b). The european pillar of social rights – no 'social triple a' for Europe. *Social Europe*, 24 March.

Suprinovič, O. and Norkina, A. (2015). *Selbstständigen-Monitor 2014: Selbstständige in Deutschland 2011 bis 2014*. Bonn: Institut für Mittelstandsforschung, Federal Statistical Office.

Suprinovič, O., Schneck, S. and Kay, R. (2016). *Einmal Unternehmer, immer Unternehmer? Selbstständigkeit im Erwerbsverlauf*, in IfM Bonn: IfM Materialien Nr. 248, Bonn.

Taylor, M.P. (1996). Earnings, independence or unemployment: why become self-employed? *Oxford Bulletin of Economics and Statistics*, 58(2), 253–66.

Thalen, W. (2016). *Grundzüge des niederländischen Alterssicherungssystems und die Entwicklung des Fondssystems*. Contribution to the workshop on 19 December 2016 in Berlin on the basic principles of the old-age pension system in the Netherlands.

Trischler, F. (2012). Auswirkungen diskontinuierlicher Erwerbsbiografien auf die Rentenanwartschaften. *WSI Mitteilungen*, 04/2012, 253–61.

Zeibig, N. (2011). *Allgemeiner Kündigungsschutz und Abfertigungszahlungen bei der Beendigung von Arbeitsverhältnissen in Österreich*. Baden-Baden: Nomos Verlag.

14. Between freedom and insecurity: future challenges

Joop Schippers and Wieteke Conen

INTRODUCTION

> Self-employment attracted virtually no interest among labour market research-
> ers until the first half of the 1980s . . . Until recently most labour market analysis
> focused on the employee workforce, and especially on the male employee work-
> force working full-time hours. Self-employment is one of the Cinderella's of
> labour market research, only recently invited to the ball. (Hakim, 1988, p. 421)

As on many other occasions Hakim was right when she wrote these lines.
However, over thirty years much has changed. The once Cinderella is now
a regular guest at the research ball. But still many of us do not know what
to make of her. Is she the dancing queen of the ball, "having the time
of (her) life",[1] or is she more of "a lonely wallflower waiting by the wall
without the willpower to face the music at all"?[2]

If one picture emerges from the previous chapters in this book it is a
picture of diversity. Among various authors the conclusion prevails that
the majority of the self-employed do rather well and that most of them
follow the career path they set out for themselves. Some authors come to
the conclusion that the self-employed constitute a group of workers at
risk from the perspective of precariousness, although the scale and nature
seems to differ between countries and demographic groups. The picture is
further complicated by the different voices sounding from the community
of self-employed. The group of the 'new' self-employed – especially young
people from the laptop generation – know how to make themselves heard
on social media and do not hesitate to do so frequently. In such discussion
groups, many of the traditional self-employed as depicted in Chapter 2 are
hardly ever heard.

While in many research areas statistics can help to provide a rather
complete image of a specific group in the labour market, different chapters
in this volume show that our information on the self-employed is still far
from complete. On the one hand, this may reflect a bias in labour market
researchers' and policy makers' focus of attention, as the self-employed

were not considered to constitute a problem for a long time. On the other hand, it may reflect that traditional research and data collection strategies have difficulties reaching self-employed who are not included in all kinds of regular data collection procedures – as most employed workers are. Moreover, researchers will almost always exclusively monitor 'survivors', as only those who succeed in continuing their status as self-employed end up in datasets as 'self-employed'. This selection effect is likely to affect findings, especially when studying dimensions of precariousness.

While the image may be mixed and incomplete, some general conclusions can be drawn from the previous chapters on self-employment as precarious work in Europe. In addition, we will point to future policy challenges and present suggestions for future research.

THREE DIMENSIONS OF PRECARIOUSNESS

As a starting point we defined precarious work as an employment situation in which individuals or households are unable to fulfil fundamental physiological and security needs while working. Throughout the book we emphasized three dimensions of precariousness which seem particularly relevant in the context of self-employment:

1. Income inadequacy while working (related to concepts such as in-work poverty, low-income households and financial resilience);
2. A lack of adequate social benefits and regulatory protection (related to concepts such as false or bogus self-employment and social security provisions);
3. Work with a high uncertainty of continuing work (related to concepts such as work insecurity, lack of employability and financial unrest).

In Chapter 2, Schippers pointed out that in order to understand the position and conditions of working in self-employment, it is essential to realize that self-employment is to be regarded the ultimate expression of labour market flexibility. This puts self-employment in a well-developed theoretical framework and helps us to ask the right questions. As Bögenhold et al. point out in Chapter 6 there is also an alternative theoretical framework; in this framework (solo) self-employment is primarily considered a special case of entrepreneurship. Using different parts of both theoretical frameworks the authors of the subsequent chapters studied several European countries focusing on one or more of the three dimensions mentioned above.

The Country Perspective

The Netherlands is among the European countries with the largest increase in solo self-employment. Comparing the Netherlands and Germany, Conen and Debets (Chapter 7) find indications that financial resilience, social protection and (perceived) work uncertainty are often largely influenced by extant other sources of income (such as financial back-up) or expected sources of income (e.g. inheritance), which the self-employed take into account in their decision-making. Although some groups have adequately and 'traditionally' taken care of social risks and some have 'alternative' ways to deal with social risks, for a seemingly substantial group of solo self-employed social protection is a genuine sore point.

In Chapter 6, Bögenhold et al. find for Austria that one-person entrepreneurs are mainly driven by motives like self-realization or working without hierarchies. However, there are also one-person entrepreneurs who have been crowded out from the (dependent) labour market and are therefore driven by economic reasons (e.g. self-employment as an alternative to unemployment). This economically driven group of one-person enterprises is comparatively dissatisfied with their professional situation, is less optimistic regarding their entrepreneurial future, and generates lower incomes.

For Italy, Borghi and Murgia (Chapter 8) highlight four relevant characteristics of independent professionals: the growing difficulty in defining successful professional careers; the ambivalence of autonomy that can lead to self-exploitation; the social protection gap in comparison with employees; and the new interest of traditional and emerging organizations dealing with their collective representation. They conclude that the risks connected to the ambivalent condition of being 'precariously free' are a challenge both for the new generation of independent professionals and for the organizational and institutional actors aimed at regulating and protecting this category of workers.

For the United Kingdom, Meager (Chapter 5) concludes that recent evidence suggests that on many indicators, after controlling for other factors, the self-employed report higher quality of work than their employee counterparts in similar jobs (this is also consistent with their higher levels of reported job satisfaction, which could previously be explained only by some kind of 'selection effect' and preference for independence and autonomy among the self-employed). However, there is also evidence that this quality advantage may have been reduced in the recent period following the financial crisis, with survey evidence suggesting that the quality of self-employed jobs has fallen in recent years, and fallen faster than among employees. Alongside this latter evidence, this period saw not only the changes in composition of self-employment (more short-hours working, different occupations etc.), but also emerging findings that the median earnings of the self-employed fell rapidly (and to a greater extent than employee earnings).

Drawing on the last wave of the European Working Conditions Survey and using standard econometric techniques Anxo and Ericson (Chapter 9) analyse the prevalence of bogus self-employed in the EU-28 and Nordic countries and examine the main differences between self-employment and bogus self-employment. They find that Sweden displays a lower incidence of bogus self-employment compared to other EU member states. Bogus self-employment appears to be more prevalent in certain segments of the labour market, in particular in industries such as construction, transport and personal household services. The specificity of the industrial relations system in Sweden, with strong social partners, high union density and coverage rate of collective agreements in all sectors of the economy, may explain the limited development of bogus self-employment and relatively low incidence compared to other member states.

The Group Perspective

Other chapters did not take one specific country as their focal point, but social groups like women, older workers and migrants. In Chapter 2, Schippers reports that women are underrepresented in self-employment. This result contradicts the argument that self-employment would be especially attractive for women from the perspective of a better work-life balance and escaping from employer discrimination. Still, Bögenhold et al. (Chapter 6) find the improved reconciliation of work and family life, as well as more flexible working time, play a greater role for women to engage in self-employment than for men, while higher income opportunities are a major incentive for male entrepreneurs. So, the work–family argument may not pull women massively into self-employment, but for those women who opt for this labour market position it does appear to be a major argument. For the United Kingdom, Meager (Chapter 5) reports a shift towards female self-employment and short-hours working in the post-financial crisis period, from 2008 onwards. According to Anxo and Ericson (Chapter 9) women living in the Nordic countries are ceteris paribus less likely to be bogus self-employed as compared to their male counterparts.

The risk of poverty in old age entails the problems of financing and receiving an adequate pension. According to Fachinger (Chapter 4) some of the risks are determined by factors which may be influenced by individuals, and which have to be seen in the context of ability and willingness to save part of their earnings of self-employed people. The other group of factors, which determine the risk of old age poverty, cannot be influenced by individual action or behaviour. These factors include the institutional and legal framework and developments in capital markets. Here the stability and security of the entitlements, the replacement rate, and the adjustment of pensions during retirement to maintain one's living standard pose special problems to avoid poverty in old age. In Chapter 10, Conen's conclusions support earlier findings that relatively privileged workers tend to work beyond state pension age. However, her findings also indicate that some self-employed may be precarity-driven in their decision to work beyond state pension age. Necessity-based motives do not only seem to play a role in the transition into self-employment, but also in the prolongation of working life beyond state pension age. Also for Austria, Bögenhold et al. (Chapter 6) find that the age group of 45+ is overrepresented among precarious workers in self-employment.

With respect to migrant workers, Berwing et al. (Chapter 11) find that quantitative analyses for Germany reveal that while migrants are more frequently engaged in precarious self-employment in absolute terms, this difference does not reach statistical significance. However, they do find clear differences for the sectors of economic activity and profession, which can be interpreted as endowment effects. Overall, they conclude that their results tend towards debunking the assumption that equates migrant self-employment in Germany to precarious work. For the United Kingdom, Meager (Chapter 5) refers to Clark et al. (2017) who find much higher rates of self-employment among specific traditional immigrant groups (e.g. Pakistani men) than among other immigrant groups and the native population. However, the study also reports high rates among migrants from the newer member states of the EU, and highlights significant differences in the factors driving these rates: among traditional migrants from 'New Commonwealth' countries (former British colonies), high self-employment largely reflects poor opportunities for waged work and discrimination in the labour market; while among the more recent EU migrants it is more influenced by policy changes which allowed or encouraged migrant entrepreneurs. In Sweden, however, foreign born workers are less likely working in self-employment than the native population (Chapter 9).

Summarizing Remarks

The general picture that emerges from comparing the situation of the self-employed in different countries and from different groups underlines the outcomes of several earlier studies referred to in different chapters in this volume, that is, the picture of the self-employed in Europe is diverse and far from uniform. Many of the self-employed do well, some do not; men are overrepresented in self-employment, while women are underrepresented; a majority of the self-employed takes this labour market position on their own accord, but a substantial group reports motives that point in the direction of necessity-driven self-employment. Returning to the three dimensions mentioned earlier, one may conclude – though with a degree of caution – that:

1. For a majority of the self-employed, current income is not an immediate or pressing problem, although for some this is mostly because their income from self-employment is not the only source of income (i.e. they have other sources of income at either the individual or household level). Still, many self-employed lack the opportunity to put something aside for a rainy day.
2. Social benefits and regulatory protection are often relatively poor, though very much depending on specific national conditions. In various countries, the current form of organizing social benefits and regulatory protection is in line with the interpretation of self-employment as the most far reaching form of labour market flexibility. The self-employed do not always bother much about social benefits and regulatory protection issues; considering it part of the deal and implicitly supporting the view of self-employment as a special case of entrepreneurship.

    In various countries, the limited access and entitlements to pension provisions may be particularly problematic. Older self-employed have to continue working beyond the official retirement age to make ends meet and younger generations of self-employed seem to have limited possibilities for private savings. In combination with the general myopic view of young and middle aged individuals one may wonder whether future problems regarding pensions for the self-employed are currently underestimated (both by themselves and by policy makers).
3. Uncertainty for the self-employed is often high, as the continuity of their work is not always guaranteed, although for many self-employed this is regarded as part of the job. A lack of maintenance or improvement of employability among the self-employed seems of concern in the prospects of continuing work and career enhancement.

From these conclusions – interim and tentative as they may be – it is easy to switch over to the policy challenges that lie ahead for both national governments and the European Union.

POLICY CHALLENGES

The most important and probably also most complicated challenge for policy makers with respect to self-employment lies at a relatively high level of abstraction and concerns the question of whether to approach the self-employed and self-employment primarily from the perspective of *entrepreneurship* (as has been the dominant perspective in past policy making) or from the perspective of *labour market flexibility*. The first perspective calls primarily for market regulation (fair competition, transparency, equal access); well-regulated markets within this framework entail that the self-employed negotiate with their clients and customers and agree on tasks and tariffs. The tradition of the social welfare state, looking at self-employment from the perspective of labour market flexibility, rather brings to mind concepts like social protection and guarantees for a decent living. From this perspective there is much more logic to setting restrictions to the behaviour of both clients and the self-employed than from the perspective of self-employment as a form of entrepreneurship. On a more practical level, the two approaches need not be lightyears away from each other. Market regulation can go together very well with some form of price regulation in order to avoid destructive competition or with quality requirements to protect the public interest. Still, the overall approach may colour the implementation or even the outcome of legal procedures in case of violation of the rules and regulation.

When it comes to concrete protective measures – like for instance minimum tariffs for the services of the self-employed or a rise on their tariffs to enable pension savings – policy makers sometimes seem to overlook the fact that the labour market is a very special market to which not automatically all 'normal' market relations apply. While capital, stocks or real estate have no feelings whatsoever, the involvement of human beings in the labour market brings along personal feelings, (dis)likes, needs and so on. Even if the government has issued minimum tariffs, a self-employed person may be in such high need of a commission, for example because (s)he has not had any commissions for the past few months and all savings have gone up in smoke, that both the self-employed and the client may make common cause and agree to negotiate a lower price than the minimum tariff set by the government. Of course, the government can invest in extensive control systems, but still it is likely that part of the measures designed to protect the self-employed may not be effective in the end. The effectiveness is even more to be doubted given that so many self-employed – sometimes despite their own insecure position – oppose a high degree of government intervention in their activities.

This broad variety and often bi-modal division of opinions among the self-employed constitutes a complication for any public regulation. One of the natural characteristics of public regulation is that, by definition, it applies to everyone who is in the same situation. When the government issues some form of regulation, it cannot limit the application to those who are in favour and except those who oppose regulation. Only the actual labour market position counts.

In the meantime, several issues related to self-employment and the position of the self-employed are on the policy agenda of national member states or the European Union as a whole. This holds for instance for bogus self-employment, that is, workers who register as self-employed but de facto qualify as employees, carrying out work under authority or subordination. If self-employment is only a veil under which someone actually works as an employee, while in the meantime benefitting from any tax deduction, the result is a distortion of the market. So, it is clear that member states will want to take action against this kind of bogus self-employment.

Another issue that is regularly debated in different member states is the representation of the self-employed and their role in the (national) social dialogue. Both at the level of the member states and at the EU-level there are the traditional partners involved in the social dialogue. Unions represent workers and employers' organizations represent employers; no matter what their exact role is and what their specific competences are it is clear who sits around the table and whom they represent within the national social dialogue. Usually, this representation does not include the self-employed, who do not identify themselves with employees and consequently do not feel represented by the *unions* around the table, except – as Jansen and Sluiter show in Chapter 12 – precariousness prone professionals, who are most willing to join a trade union. However, the interests of the self-employed often do not match with those of the *employers' organizations* either, especially if these organizations are dominated by a few multinational companies. In many cases, organizations representing SMEs are likely to be their best allies. Yet, SMEs may also be their clients or customers, creating some natural distance between SMEs and the self-employed. The chapter by Jansen and Sluiter on representation does not only show that the self-employed do not feel represented by existing organizations like unions and employers' organizations, many of them also reject the idea of an independent organization for the self-employed. And once again the opinions are rather diverging. This lack of representation and (organizational) power to speak with one voice makes it difficult for public authorities to include the self-employed in the preparation or implementation of policies regarding self-employment. The big discord and lack of unity among the self-employed deprives them of the opportunity to influence policies in a similar way as organizations and lobby groups of farmers, medical specialists or even consumers have done so successfully over the years.

Meager (Chapter 5) and Schulze Buschoff (Chapter 13) signal that recently the policy debate has been given further impetus by the emergence of hybrid forms of work in the 'gig' economy, which share some characteristics with self-employment and others with employees. Here the discussion will be probably even more complicated, because services like Uber or Airbnb do not only mix up the role of entrepreneurs and employees, but those who are (temporarily) involved in providing these services are also often consumers. So, here the question for the lawgiver is not only whether to approach the self-employed as an entrepreneur or as an employee, but also whether someone who is involved with this kind of economic activity should primarily be considered a producer or a consumer. The latter distinction may be even more important as the difference between rules and regulations regarding producers and consumers is way larger than between the rules guiding entrepreneurs and employees.

FUTURE RESEARCH

Throughout the book various authors have pointed to the absence of specific information and analyses on certain topics concerning self-employment and the self-employed. To conclude this final chapter we will make an effort to translate the various questions and suggestions into a future research agenda.

A first and major point on this research agenda concerns changes within employment biographies over time. Just like employees have some sort of career – some with a lot of transitions and strong upward mobility, while others remain in one single job with one single employer throughout their career – the life course of the business of self-employed workers may show different developments over time too. Do the self-employed show similar patterns as compared to larger companies in terms of start, development, take-off, stagnation and decline? What are the determinants of these patterns? And are there critical moments during the various phases in a self-employment career in terms of who is going to succeed and who will not? Related – and important from the life course perspective – is how much precariousness the self-employed can stand before they call it quits. Earlier, we already addressed the issue that cross-sectional survey studies only include 'survivors', that is, those who remain in self-employment. 'Losing' the non-survivors deprives us of the opportunity to find out what precariousness in self-employment does for the rest of a person's life course. Can he or she regain employment as an employee or is quitting self-employment the start of a downward spiral that does not only affect working life, but also one's private situation? From a policy perspective one may want to know what could have helped them – in terms of rules and regulations or financial or other forms of support – and what could have prevented them from giving up self-employment. Moreover, it would be interesting to see how those self-employed who have/had to quit look back on their experiences in self-employment. Is there anything they take with them for the rest of their working career?

The perspective of what could have helped touches upon the issue addressed earlier that precariousness holds different dimensions. Once again returning to the three dimensions of precariousness discussed above we concluded that it can very well be that the self-employed must be considered precarious on one of these dimensions, but not necessarily also on (one of) the other two; in several cases the available empirical evidence supported this conclusion. However, our image of which of the self-employed are vulnerable on what dimension and to what extent is still sketchy, blurred and incomplete. The more so is our understanding of who (or what) is 'responsible' for this vulnerability. Of course, answering such questions requires much more in-depth research than the analysis of some statistics collected by a national or a European agency, how useful such statistics in themselves may be.

Applied to the context of the self-employed, it would be useful to develop measures that capture employment insecurity (e.g. how easy or hard it will be to find new, generally comparable, work). Insecurity in terms of work and income may lead to individuals becoming more fearful of long-term plans and commitments in other life domains; couples, for instance, often find economic stability a crucial condition for taking a long-term decision such as having children. Especially the involuntary solo self-employed often seem to experience their uncertainty as troublesome (Scherer, 2009; Conen et al., 2016; Kremer et al., 2017). As part of the research agenda on self-employment it would be interesting to get a sharper look at this issue.

After having established to what extent different groups of self-employed are at risk in terms of different dimensions of precariousness, to what extent and which factors contribute to these risks is a major policy question about how member states or Europe can organize social protection. Here especially comparative research may be useful. Different countries have organized the social protection of the self-employed in different ways and the open method of coordination within the European Union may help countries to design and implement the optimal social protection system for their own country. This is, of course, not only or not even primarily a 'technical' problem, but essentially a political question for the answering of which researchers can provide a lot of analyses and information. The final answer regarding the question of a decent and suitable system of proper social protection for the self-employed remains, however, in the hands of political decision makers. With the rapid developments in and around the world of self-employment one can be sure that it will be on the research agenda for a long time.

NOTES

1. Benny Andersson, Bjoern K. Ulvaeus, Stig Anderson (1976). *Dancing Queen* lyrics. London: Sony/ATV Music Publishing LLC, Universal Music Publishing Group.
2. Lynsey De Paul (1973). *Won't Somebody Dance With Me* lyrics. London: ATV Music and Music Sales Ltd.

REFERENCES

Clark, K., Drinkwater, S. and Robinson, C. (2017). Self-Employment amongst Migrant Groups: New Evidence from England and Wales. *Small Business Economics*, 48(4), 1047–69.

Conen, W.S., Schippers, J.J. and Schulze Buschoff, K. (2016). *Self-Employed without Personnel – Between Freedom and Insecurity*. Düsseldorf: Hans Böckler Foundation.

Hakim, C. (1988). Self-Employment in Britain. Recent Trends and Current Issues. *Work, Employment and Society*, 2(4), S. 421–50.

Kremer, M., Went, R. and Knottnerus, A. (2017). *Voor de zekerheid: De toekomst van flexibel werkenden en de moderne organisatie van arbeid [For the Sake of Security. The Future of Flexible Workers and the Modern Organisation of Labour]*. The Hague: The Netherlands Scientific Council for Government Policy.

Scherer, S. (2009). The Social Consequences of Insecure Jobs. *Social Indicators Research*, 93(3), 469–88.

Index

age of the self-employed 97, 99–100, 102, 114, 163, 165, 166, 170, 173, 177–83, 190, 202, 205, 208, 264, 265

ageing workforce 171–2

alternative work arrangements *see* nonstandard work

atypical employment *see* nonstandard work

Austria 10, 16, 30, 32, 34, 86–103, 175, 181, 211, 240–42, 245–6, 248, 254, 262, 264

bogus self-employment *see* false self-employment

bridge employment 170, 173

collective bargaining 33, 135, 145–6, 161, 222, 251, 254–5

collective representation 4, 16, 17, 145–6, 148, 216–35, 262, 267

competition 33, 117, 119, 124, 129, 135–6, 141, 156, 157, 160, 161, 187, 192, 266

law 13, 43, 47, 254

continental corporatist countries 10, 15, 29, 35, 129, 192, 222 *see also* Austria; Germany; Netherlands

contingent work 3–4

country differences 9–10, 15–17, 23–38, 44, 88–89, 108, 127–9, 181, 240, 242, 252–4, 262–3 *see also* Austria; Denmark; Finland; Germany; Italy; Netherlands; Nordic countries; Norway; Sweden; UK

Denmark 10, 29–30, 32, 34, 161–2, 165, 166, 175, 181

demographics 15, 55, 171–2, 189–90, 250

dependent self-employment 41, 43, 47, 132, 138, 220

disability insurance *see* social protection/risk/security

earnings 4, 6–8, 33, 54–5, 68, 80, 159, 263

related contribution rate 58

education

level of 158, 181, 186, 190–91, 198, 200, 201, 204, 206, 208, 211, 226

sector 75, 77, 81, 163–6, 194

training and 14, 35–7, 68, 79, 82, 222, 229

employability 4, 6, 13, 14, 35–7, 261, 265

employers organisations 218, 267

employment relations 3, 41–3, 145, 193, 222

entrepreneurship 1–2, 11, 16, 28, 40, 46, 48, 65, 69, 71, 77–8, 82, 86–7, 90–92, 102, 103, 109, 122, 129, 132, 153–5, 174, 187, 188, 200, 216, 266, 268

European Quality of Life Survey 8–10

European Working Conditions Survey (EWCS) 36, 132, 154, 161, 162, 163, 165, 166

false self-employment 6, 13, 16–17, 41, 43, 64–5, 67, 132, 135–8, 153–67, 210, 251, 254–5, 261, 263, 267

family and self-employment *see* work, and family life

female self-employment 31–3, 42, 45, 73–5, 89, 93, 97, 144, 157, 164, 181, 201, 204, 263 *see also* gender differences

financial

crisis 67, 70–82, 139, 262–3

resilience 6, 10, 115, 116, 118, 120, 121, 122, 262

Finland 10, 30, 32, 34, 161, 162, 163,
     164, 165, 166
flexibility 15, 23–38, 65, 69, 98, 136–8,
     147, 155, 159, 170, 186, 188,
     190–91, 221, 256, 261, 265
  forms of 24–5, 153, 156

gender differences 31–3, 42, 45, 73–5,
     89, 93, 97, 144, 157, 164, 166, 181,
     200, 201, 204, 206, 263
Germany 9–10, 15, 16, 17, 30, 32, 34,
     55–7, 88–9, 108–29, 171–2, 174–5,
     181, 186–211, 240–45, 248, 253,
     262, 264
governmental policies/debate regarding
     self-employment 2, 24, 38, 109,
     260–61, 266–8
  in the Netherlands 109
  in Sweden 153–5, 167
  in the UK 65, 66, 70–71

health 170, 174, 175
  index on activity limitations (GALI)
     176, 179–80, 182–3
  insurance 110, 112, 155, 210, 244,
     252
  safety and 43, 44–5
  sector 77, 94, 136, 163, 165, 166
  self-perceived 176, 179–83
heterogeneity of the self-employed 2,
     69, 79, 80, 81, 86, 91, 102, 132,
     158, 190, 200, 216, 218–20, 264–5
households 5, 7, 8, 9–10, 115, 120, 128,
     265
  characteristics of 50, 122–3, 173
  income 50, 116, 117–18, 180–81
  low-income 6, 8, 95, 175–6, 178,
     180–82
  resources 7, 9–10, 176, 179, 180–82
human capital 14, 35–8, 82, 170, 174,
     182, 200
hybrid employment 17–18, 64, 92, 102,
     145, 239, 242, 247, 252, 255–6, 268
  contract 136

immigrants and self-employment *see*
     migrant self-employment
income 2, 5, 6–10, 37, 49–51, 54, 58–9,
     68, 95, 100–102, 110, 115, 116,
     118, 120, 128, 159, 175–82, 187,

191, 195–8, 200–204, 206, 221,
     224–5, 262, 265, 269
  disposable 7, 52–5, 58, 175
  inadequacy 4, 6–10, 261
  household 5, 25, 50, 116, 117–18,
     128, 176, 180–81, 262
independent professionals 16, 88, 102,
     133, 139–48, 262
industry *see* sector of industry
insecurity 6, 13–14, 53, 54, 57, 82, 147,
     193, 222, 239, 242, 261, 269
insider-outsider theory 217, 220,
     221–3, 234, 235
insurance *see* social protection
interest organisations 17, 217–19,
     221–3, 228, 232–4
in-work poverty *see* poverty
Italy 10, 15, 16, 29, 30–34, 88–9,
     133–48, 171–2, 175, 181, 203,
     262

jobs
  conditions 1, 3, 17, 36–7, 43, 46, 47,
     69, 138, 148, 155, 160, 187, 189,
     192–3, 195, 210–11, 251, 256
  contracts 4, 25, 36–7, 43, 46, 137,
     153, 249
  quality 2–4, 69, 71, 78–82, 262

labour
  force survey 30, 32, 66, 70, 72, 74,
     76, 77, 89, 138–9, 158, 160
  market flexibility *see* flexibility
  process, control over 4, 109, 115,
     220, 224, 227–8
legislation 11, 13, 15, 41–4, 51, 55, 65,
     112, 133–8, 143, 144, 154–7, 208,
     254
life-long-learning 36, 37, 68, 82

migrant self-employment 15, 17, 76,
     78, 156, 161, 167, 186–211,
     263–4
motives 17, 31, 90, 94, 96, 98–102,
     173–4, 177–8, 180, 182, 189, 262,
     264

necessity-driven 27, 69–71, 79, 102,
     103, 170, 173–4, 176–80, 182, 183,
     264–5

Netherlands 10, 15, 16, 30, 32–4, 88–9,
 108–29, 172, 175, 181, 216, 217,
 240–42, 246–8, 252–3, 262
nonstandard work 3–4, 137, 142, 144
Nordic countries 16, 154, 161–6, 263
 see also Denmark; Finland;
 Norway; Sweden
Norway 30, 32, 161, 162, 163, 165, 166

occupational
 pension *see* pensions
 position 31, 64, 67, 68, 75–6, 80–82,
 108, 114, 159–61, 198–201,
 203–4, 207, 209, 220, 226, 234
Office for National Statistics (ONS) 66,
 70, 72, 74, 76, 77
older workers 17, 170–83, 263–4

part-time self-employment 73, 80, 81,
 87, 92, 93, 163–6, 195, 239, 249
pensions 11, 15, 48–60, 110–12, 118,
 126–8, 136–7, 144, 155, 170–83,
 224–5, 240, 242–8, 250, 252–3,
 263–4
 occupational 111, 126
 savings 11–12, 111–12, 115, 116,
 122–3, 126, 224–5
poverty
 in-work 6–8, 33–5, 175
 in old age 10–11, 15–16, 48–60, 110,
 125, 128, 263–4
precariousness/precarious work 2–6,
 11–13
 definition 5
 dimensions 4–6, 11–13, 109, 115,
 120–25, 178–80, 193–4, 196,
 217, 220–21, 261
 measurement 5, 6, 13, 116, 119

qualitative research 16, 112–14, 117,
 120, 122–9, 140, 144, 145, 147,
 187, 189
quality
 of life in older age (CASP-12) 176,
 179–80, 182–3
 of life survey *see* European Quality
 of Life Survey
 of work 2, 4, 80, 81, 262 *see also*
 jobs, quality

replacement rate 15, 49, 59, 110, 245,
 264
representation *see* collective
 representation
retirement 170–83
 saving adequacy 123

sector of industry 17, 23, 28, 31, 40, 64,
 66, 75, 77, 80–82, 94, 97, 108, 114,
 141, 153, 156–7, 163, 181, 186,
 189, 198–9, 201, 203, 204, 207,
 238, 264
social-democratic state 10, 15, 29, 129,
 263
social protection/risk/security 10–12,
 15–16, 18, 33, 35, 40–47, 59–60,
 112, 115–29, 136–8, 143–5, 147,
 154–7, 239, 251–6, 262, 266,
 269
Survey of Health, Ageing and
 Retirement in Europe (SHARE)
 175, 179, 181
Sweden 10, 15, 17, 29, 30, 32, 34,
 153–67, 172, 175, 181, 263, 264

trade unions 3, 4, 5, 17, 33, 72, 108,
 109, 145–6, 148, 156, 157, 167,
 217–19, 221–4, 228, 231, 233, 235,
 263, 267
training 2, 14, 35–7, 68, 79, 82, 193,
 222, 229, 234

unemployment 3, 11, 14–16, 24, 25, 47,
 69–72, 80, 82, 95, 99, 101, 144,
 173, 187, 189, 210, 252
unions *see* trade unions
UK 10, 15, 24, 30, 32, 34, 64–82, 88–9,
 171–2, 262, 263, 264

welfare states 9, 11, 13, 15, 24, 29, 35,
 109, 129, 171, 240, 243, 266
women *see* gender differences
work
 characteristics 1, 3, 17, 36–7, 43, 46,
 47, 69, 138, 148, 155, 160, 187,
 189, 192–3, 195, 210–11, 251,
 256
 and family life 31, 50, 94, 98, 173,
 174, 263